P9-CKL-012

Praise for

TAKE PRIDE

"Sometimes a major component of human experience falls through the cracks and is overlooked by psychology, and that has been true of the emotion of pride and its associated phenomena like accomplishment, ambition, and arrogance. No longer! With scientific and personal insight, and with a gift for vividly presenting both technical research and real-life personalities, Jessica Tracy enlightens us about how this emotion permeates our waking lives and shapes our social worlds."
— Steven Pinker, best-selling author of *How the Mind Works* and *The Blank Slate*

"Pride gets a bad rap, says Jessica Tracy. Instead of being an unalloyed vice, it can become something closer to a virtue. In this fascinating book, Tracy uses original research to show that pride is a major part of what it means to be human and can be harnessed as a force for good."
— Daniel H. Pink, best-selling author of *Drive* and *To Sell Is Human*

"An insightful and engaging exploration of a noble joy, a deadly sin, and an essential piece of the human experience."
— Daniel Gilbert, best-selling author of *Stumbling on Happiness*

"This book stopped me in my tracks and left me questioning my beliefs about what motivates us. Jessica Tracy is the world's leading expert on pride, and reading this book is like having a coveted front-row seat in her classroom."
— Adam Grant, best-selling author of *Originals* and *Give and Take*

"Jessica Tracy has flipped the script on pride, showing that it's not just a deadly sin to be avoided, but also a vitalizing virtue to be nurtured. She does it so convincingly and engagingly that she ought to be proud."
— Robert Cialdini, best-selling author of *Influence*

"*Take Pride* is a revelation. A renowned psychologist, Jessica Tracy explains that seeking our best self is nothing to be ashamed of, but that seeking praise at all costs gets us into the worst kind of trouble."
— Angela Duckworth, best-selling author of *Grit*

"Pride drives us to success and achievement, but also arrogance and hubris. Tracing its roots to primate social dominance, Jessica Tracy found that humans everywhere express this emotion the same way. Here she offers an eye-opening discussion of both its indispensability and its pitfalls."
— Frans de Waal, best-selling author of
Are We Smart Enough to Know How Smart Animals Are?

"From a remote village in Burkina Faso to the East Room of the White House to the victorious grins of blind judo masters, Jessica Tracy tells the story of our most double-edged emotion. Tracy is the world's foremost scientific expert on pride, having shown that pride is more distinctive, universal, and psychologically pivotal than anyone had thought. This brilliant book distills her insights and brings them to life."
— Joshua Greene, author of *Moral Tribes*

"A new and fascinating suggestion for attaining success . . . A must-read for anyone pursuing noteworthy goals."
— *Publishers Weekly*

TAKE PRIDE

Why the Deadliest Sin
Holds the Secret
to Human Success

Jessica Tracy

Houghton Mifflin Harcourt

BOSTON   NEW YORK

2016

Library of Congress Cataloging-in-Publication Data
Names: Tracy, Jessica L., author.
Title: Take pride: why the deadliest sin holds the secret to human success /
Jessica Tracy.
Description: Boston : Houghton Mifflin Harcourt, 2016
Identifiers: LCCN 2016004635 (print) | LCCN 2016014096 (ebook) | ISBN
9780544273177 (hardback) | ISBN 9780544273085 (ebook)
Subjects: LCSH: Emotions. | Pride and vanity. | Social psychology. | BISAC:
PSYCHOLOGY / General. | PSYCHOLOGY / Social psychology. | PSYCHOLOGY /
Emotions. | SCIENCE / General.
Classification: LCC BF511 .T73 2016 (print) | LCC BF511 (ebook) | DDC
152.4 — dc23
LC record available at http://lccn.loc.gov/2016004635

Printed in the United States of America
DOC 10 9 8 7 6 5 4 3 2 1

Illustration credits appear on page 218.

For Harper, who gives me pride every day
And, also, for Kristin

Contents

Preface: The Most Human Emotion   ix

1. The Nature of Pride   1
2. A Virtuous Sin   33
3. Me, Myself, and I   62
4. Like a Boss   84
5. The Carrot and the Stick   113
6. The Highest Form   145
7. Take Pride   169

Acknowledgments   199
Notes   203
Illustration Credits   218
Index   219

Preface:
The Most Human Emotion

IN 1885, the painter Paul Gauguin suffered what might be considered the fin-de-siècle version of a midlife crisis.

It had been a long time coming. For eleven years, Paul's wife, Mette, had tolerated her husband's blatant lack of interest in the high-society life she thought she'd married into. When they got engaged, he was a French stockbroker with solid family connections and a promising future; she was a Danish tutor, eager for something better. With Paul, she'd thought, she could raise a family and join the ranks of the bourgeoisie. And, by all appearances, she had done exactly that. After the birth of their first child, the couple moved from their cramped apartment in central Paris to a larger home in the sixteenth *arrondissement* — at the time an up-and-coming neighborhood on the outer edge of the city. Seemingly happy, they lived a life of apparent suburban bliss, eventually having four more children.

But for Paul — a salesman who had always been far more interested in the world of art than the world of business — something was missing. Almost immediately after moving to the outskirts of Paris, he began taking every opportunity he could find to sneak off to the gallery openings and impressionist art shows that were regular occurrences in the more bohemian corners of the city. Eventually, his craving for this other kind of life completely consumed him.

In 1885, Paul Gauguin took the plunge; he quit his day job and became a full-time artist. He left his wife and children to fend for themselves while he lived in poverty on the streets of Paris — and, later, in Panama and Martinique. Over the subsequent years, he suffered a range of ills: malaria, dysentery, depression, chronic pain from a never-healed ankle injury, and syphilis. Life as a starving artist was not easy or pain-free — not for Paul or for the people who had previously depended on him. But in choosing that life, Paul Gauguin became the person he had always wanted to be — a person whose paintings now hang in museums all over the world.

Many of us have experienced this same sense of dissatisfaction that Gauguin felt in his married life with Mette. Like him, we may have already achieved certain successes; maybe a job that pays well, a comfortable home, or a supportive and loving family. But despite it all, we know that something is missing. We might be craving greater respect from our peers or others we admire. Or perhaps we hunger for a way to feel like we're accomplishing something that has some impact on the world. Whatever it is we are missing, in order to find it, we need to change our lives. We need to sacrifice the ease and stability we've managed to secure for the potential of something better: the chance to create, or become, something meaningful.

Almost two decades ago, I experienced this same feeling, a sense that something was missing from my life. It was 1997, and I had recently graduated from a small liberal arts college in New England and moved across the country to San Francisco with five friends. My aim had been to explore the West Coast and take a break from the constant stress of exams and paper deadlines before embarking on my *real,* adult life. I found a job as a barista in a local café, where I learned to make lattes and a mean tuna bagel. I had become friends with the regulars — mostly artists and writers — and with the café's owner, who would come upstairs from his basement printmaking studio each day around three to split a chocolate chip cookie. The tips were generous, the job couldn't have been more anxiety-free, and the conversations I had with my coworkers and the café clientele — along with the abundant reading time I found between the lunch and happy-hour rushes — provided just enough intellectual stimulation to prevent my brain from atrophying.

By many measures, life was good. But about a year in, I felt something stirring — something like what Gauguin must have felt during all those years of forcing himself to try to succeed in business. People from across the neighborhood would come to the café requesting *my* soy lattes, but my life was lacking.

I missed something that I'd had in college. It wasn't the beer-soaked dance parties, or the ready availability of any number of close friends, or the peacefulness of life on a rural and secluded Massachusetts campus. It definitely wasn't the snow. What I was missing during those long, quiet San Francisco afternoons were the late nights spent in my college's mid-1990s computer room as three friends and I madly rushed around trying to pull together the political newsmagazine we'd founded. I was missing the *feeling* I had those nights as I anxiously triple-checked that the right kind of paper was loaded into the dot-matrix printer, drove to the twenty-four-hour Kinko's, and scrambled to copyedit.

I missed working hard with other people who cared about something that felt larger than ourselves. During those long days of perfected soy lattes, I was missing the feeling of *pride* I experienced from creating that magazine — the feeling of building something that seemed important.

I'm not talking about the feeling I had when I saw our first completed issue of the magazine dispersed all over campus. I wasn't missing the feeling of pride in a job well done or of basking in others' (remarkably restrained) appreciation of the magazine. What I was missing was that late-night, hard-working, *knowing-we-were-doing-something-we-cared-about* pride, which had no equivalent in my San Francisco barista life.

The absence of that pride made me realize that my break was over, and it was time to begin my real life. The desire to feel pride again prompted me to apply to graduate school, where, sure enough, I came to experience that feeling of working hard toward something I cared about on a daily basis.

Pride kick-started my career, and it's what kick-starts the career of all people who find a way to do something they care about or that fills their lives with meaning. This desire for pride is the motivation that underpins ambition. In her memoir *Not That Kind of Girl*, writer/actor/director Lena Dunham reports experiencing the very same feeling in *her* early twenties in the midst of an easy and pleasurable life filled with friends and parties and freedom. "Ambition is a funny thing," she writes. "It creeps in when you least expect it and keeps you moving, even when you think you want to stay put. I missed making things, the meaning it gave this long march we call life."

The desire for pride creeps in and manifests itself in different ways. For Dunham and me, it meant abandoning our bohemian lives and hourly-pay jobs to pursue paths that felt bigger and better; for Gauguin, it meant abandoning a bourgeois life to seek out something more bohemian. For others, the desire for pride might mean starting a family, taking a dance class, applying for a promotion, or training for a marathon. And for still others, it might mean reckless, even self-destructive behaviors, like cheating on an exam, doping before a race, or taking credit for someone else's accomplishment.

I have spent much of the past fifteen years studying the emotions that shape human behavior, and the emotion I've focused on most closely is pride. One conclusion I've reached is that the desire to feel pride is one of *the most important motivational forces* propelling human achievement, creation, and innovation, and, as a result, all cultural inventions, from art and architecture to science, math, and philosophy. Yes, pride is at least partly responsible for many of our species' greatest successes, including artistic masterpieces, groundbreaking scientific discoveries, and world-changing technological inventions.

This might surprise you. Many of us like to think that creators, discoverers, and inventors are, quite simply, geniuses — people with some innate brilliance who work tirelessly out of a pure desire for truth or understanding. In fact, the mythical genius is precisely that: a myth. The discoverer does not want merely to find the truth — she wants to be the *one* who finds it. Innovation takes more than a desire to seek or know; *pride* is the reason we bother to try to learn, discover, and achieve.

Of course, this is not what we typically tell ourselves about why we do the most important things we do. That's because most of us buy into the myth. We don't want to believe that we work hard at our jobs or strive to be morally upright people who care for our partners and are loyal to our friends solely because we want to feel good about ourselves. We prefer to believe that we do these good things because we are good people. But *pride* is the reason we so urgently need to believe that we are good.

Yet pride does not always make us into good, or even happy, people. Gauguin's decision to abandon his family and, later, take on multiple underage Tahitian wives can hardly be considered good. Indeed, for every Bill Gates and Warren Buffett out there — extreme achievers driven by pride to work their hardest and then to use the fruits of their labors to help others — there's a Lance Armstrong. He's also an extreme achiever but one motivated by pride to go beyond hard work, to lie, cheat, and bully his way to the kind of success he wanted to attain.

This is because the pride that motivates human achievement and the innovations that led to the development of complex culture in every human society *is not the only pride there is.* There's another pride that influences us too. It's the pride we feel when we sit back and egotistically bask in our successes, when we arrogantly glow in others' appreciation of our talents and see them as the best and most important parts of ourselves. This other, more conceited and hubristic pride can be found in Donald Trump's regular reminders to everyone of his wealth, intelligence, and business acumen, and sprinter Usain Bolt's claim to be the greatest athlete who ever lived. This pride can be disturbing or unseemly, and while it can motivate a desire for greatness — or at least *greater*-ness — it can also bring otherwise promising careers to a premature end.

Both prides — the creativity-boosting, achievement-motivating kind and the arrogant and self-aggrandizing kind—are the result of the same evolutionary forces that shaped much of our human psychology, yet their consequences could not be more antithetical. The hubristic, gloating pride *is* part of our human nature, but rather than generating hard work and a desire to be good, it evokes a desire to control others and to use aggression, manipulation, and deception to attain power and dominance—and maintain it once we're there.

Because of this two-sided nature, pride can explain acts of genius as well as acts of apparent insanity. Why would Lance Armstrong seek not only to enhance his own already stupendous cycling performance by cheating with illegal EPOs but also to manipulate and intimidate his teammates to do the same, thereby exponentially increasing his risk of getting caught? Why would rising-star social psychologist Diederik Stapel fabricate data out of thin air instead of actually conducting research when the level of deception required to get away with faked data makes cheating a good deal more difficult than actually doing the work? Why would talented science writer Jonah Lehrer risk having his book removed from the shelves (as it was) by embellishing the details of an already compelling story? What makes these extraordinarily competent and successful individuals so unsatisfied with what they already have that they are willing to risk everything for just a little bit more?

The hubristic form of pride can explain these seemingly inexplicable acts, and it may be the only thing that can. Yes, pride *is* a source of human greatness, but it's also a source of the greatest human downfalls. For this reason, pride—perhaps more than any other emotion—lies at the heart of human nature.

The understanding that pride is a natural part of our species' evolved emotional architecture is a relatively new scientific discovery. Research conducted by myself and other psychological scientists has only recently revealed that pride is not something we *learn* to feel; it's something we feel *because we are human,* and we evolved to feel it. This means that pride is functional. It serves a purpose, and that purpose is the reason that the potential for pride exists in all humans.

So what is the purpose of pride?

Pride makes us care about how others see us and — just as important — how we see ourselves. It makes us want to feel good about ourselves and make sure others look up to us, admire us, and see us as competent and powerful. It prods us to figure out who we want to be and then to do whatever is needed to become that person. The desire to feel pride can consequently push us to work hard and strive for excellence but also to cheat, lie, and take advantage of others. In the end, if our pride gets what it wants out of us, we will have climbed the ranks that make up our society's intricately structured hierarchy.

Pride's ultimate evolved function, in other words, is to help us raise our social status. Pride gets us power, influence, and an ability to wield control over others. These outcomes are adaptive, because those who exist at the top of the hierarchy are more likely to survive and reproduce than those at the bottom.

But in getting us up that social ladder, pride also gets us much more. It motivates us to strive to become a certain kind of person, to learn from others, to create, and to innovate. It allows us to take what our culture has to offer and make it our own, and then make it even better.

In short, pride has, in many ways, made us the incredible species we are, and it continues to shape humans' cultural evolution. But pride is not a pure force for progress and innovation; it also has a dark side, which influences our behaviors, our hierarchies, and the way we treat one another just as much as its lighter side does. The hubristic side of pride is every bit as powerful as the more authentic and achievement-oriented side. As a result, pride can make us want to help people but it can also push us to seek domination over them.

Pride can feel like a sin, and a very serious one; in ancient Christianity, pride was considered not only the deadliest of the seven mortal sins but also the root of all the others, from sloth, greed, and gluttony to lust, envy, and wrath. But as we will see, we don't need to reject our pride to be good people. In fact, without pride, we wouldn't be motivated to become good people — or even to get off the couch. We need our pride. And we have a choice about which pride we experience. We can force our pride to serve us, rather than the other way around.

The human drive for pride also explains why so many of us have, at some point, felt that same sense of emptiness that Gauguin felt — and that I felt working at that San Francisco café — and not quite known how to fill it. If we understand how pride works and accept the importance of this emotion to human life, we can harness this motivation and use it to become the kind of person we've always wanted to be. If, however, we fail to control our pride, its more arrogant variety may take over, and this very same emotion can wreck our lives, making us behave in ways we know are wrong and turning us into people we no longer recognize. The science of pride allows us not only to understand the difference between these two feelings and recognize both within ourselves but also to choose between them.

Rather than pushing your pride aside or trying to stifle it, you can intentionally seek out the more desirable form of this vital human emotion. Listening to your pride is one of the best ways to figure out who you are, what you want out of life, and how you can get there. That inner voice that tells you something is missing is also telling you how to find yourself — how to find the identity that feels most right to you. It's the voice that makes you want to achieve, get more out of your world, and do things that mean something. That voice — your desire for pride — will guide you and push you toward what you need to do to become the person you want to be.

But again, this is not the only way to feel pride. Following your pride when it's arrogant and hubristic can lead you down a path that makes you *less* — rather than more — like the person you truly are. One of my ultimate aims in this book is to demonstrate that you can choose to control those darker impulses and follow your more authentic prideful voice. I believe that understanding the science of pride — both sides of pride — will allow you to fully appreciate and benefit from this natural capacity all members of our species share. It's an ability not only to feel good about ourselves but also to use those feelings toward our own ends, to change our lives.

1

The Nature of Pride

DEAN KARNAZES, also known as the Ultramarathon Man, has run more consecutive miles than just about anyone else in the world. His longest race ever was three hundred and fifty miles, and to complete it he ran continuously for three days and nights, without sleep. He's run a two-hundred-mile relay race *solo* — not just once, but ten times. At the age of forty-four, Karnazes ran fifty marathons in fifty days.

As these feats demonstrate, Karnazes is clearly off the charts in endurance, but he's also very, very fast. He's won many of the long-distance races he's run — races most people wouldn't believe exist, including the Badwater Ultramarathon, a 135-mile run across Death Valley, where temperatures soar to 120 degrees. Karnazes is without question one of the most impressive long-distance runners in the world today.

Karnazes began his professional running career relatively late in life — shortly after midnight on his thirtieth birthday. As a teenager, he'd been a top runner on his school's cross-country team, but he quit the team when a beloved coach retired, and he soon stopped running altogether. For more than a decade, life took over. Karnazes went to college, got a graduate degree, got married, and began a promising business career. He was a hard worker who had done well in school, and he quickly rose in the ranks of his sales job. But eventually, something began to change. In his memoir *Ultramarathon Man*, Karnazes explains, "I became aware of an inner hollowness. Something was missing in my life." Closing one big deal after another no longer felt like much of an accomplishment. He was at the peak of his career, but he was bored and felt that his life lacked purpose.

On the morning he turned thirty, Karnazes awoke with a shock. "At that moment," he writes, "I realized that my life was being wasted." He felt confused and trapped, and told his wife, "I'm not sure what's important anymore. My fear is that I'll wake up thirty years from now and be in the same place, only wrinkled and bald . . . and really fat. And bitter." That night, Karnazes went out drinking with friends at a swanky San Francisco nightclub. His wife headed home early, and Karnazes found himself flirting with an attractive stranger — a woman who clearly wanted to make his birthday special.

Within inches of cheating on his wife, Karnazes had an epiphany. He knew that the proudest moments of his life were the couple of times he'd done something physically punishing entirely on his own. At the age of twelve, he'd ridden his bicycle for ten hours, pedaling all the way from his parents' home in Los Angeles to his grandparents' house in Pasadena, forty miles away — without any clear idea of how to get there. Later, as a high-school teenager, Karnazes had led his cross-country team to a league championship by pushing himself to run harder and faster than any other kid on the track — even after taking an elbow to the nose that resulted in a bloody finish. Now, at thirty, Karnazes was desperate to feel something like that once again. He escaped the bar he was in and started running.

He ran all night, from his home in San Francisco to Half Moon Bay, thirty miles down the coast. Somewhere along the way he reached the top of a mountain and found himself gazing above the fog at a sky full of stars. "For the first time in years," he writes, "I felt like this spot was precisely where I belonged." Karnazes hadn't run in fifteen years, and after that night, he couldn't walk — let alone run — for days. But at the age of thirty years and one day, he felt more alive than he had in over a decade. He had found a sense of purpose that he'd been missing, and he wasn't going to let it go.

Since that day, Karnazes has become the world's most famous ultramarathoner (an ultramarathon is any race longer than a marathon's twenty-six miles). He's earned major sponsorships and brought ultramarathoning — previously a fringe event — into the mainstream. His 2005 memoir became a bestseller that not only introduced the sport to millions but also inspired many thousands to have their own metaphorical thirtieth birthdays — to realize the ways in which their lives lacked meaning and figure out how to change that.

Before he published his book, Karnazes had a hard time explaining his favorite pastime. He notes, "Whenever I tell people that I've run 100 miles at a clip, they inevitably ask two questions. The first is, 'How can you do that?' The second, and much harder to answer, is . . . '*Why?*'"

Karnazes's extreme running has brought him fame and fortune and made him a hero to runners and nonrunners alike. In 2007, *Time* magazine named him one of the one hundred most influential people in the world. But these outcomes — Karnazes's success and the many people who've benefited from it — don't resolve that fundamental question: *Why?* What makes Karnazes *want* to run so tirelessly? What pushes him to get up early every morning and start running, and often spend all day and all night running too?

This is a question of motivation. We humans, like all animals, do not do things that are good for us just because we know they are good for us. This might sound counterintuitive — after all, when you brushed your teeth this morning, you *knew* it was good for you — but the fact is, we are not motivated solely by *knowledge* of what's best. Knowledge alone has no motivational power. Karnazes didn't start running because he knew it would change his life. He did it because he wanted to *feel* something.

We are motivated not predominantly by knowledge but by *emotions.* Part of the reason you brushed your teeth this morning, and have every morning, is that you're *afraid* of the dental visits that will be required if you don't. You're probably also *worried* about morning breath. Emotions like fear and anxiety compel us to behave in ways that knowledge, on its own, cannot.

In the case of Karnazes and every other person who sacrifices something — anything — to work hard toward some uncertain accomplishment, the motivation comes from one emotion in particular. It's the emotion that motivates us to do all the things we do to become the kind of person we want to be. We choose work over play, we neglect friendships and relationships, and we give up easy pleasures — from drinking beer and playing video games to watching TV — because we want to feel more than simple pleasure; we want to feel pride.

In the Western part of the world, people have known for a long time that pride is important. It's something that almost all of us North Americans quite explicitly care about, a lot. We know, without any doubt, that pride is something we want to feel — in our jobs, our children, our ideologies and our belief systems, our sports teams, our country, and, most centrally, ourselves.

But the question of whether humans everywhere feel this way — whether pride and the drive to attain it is a universal human experience — has become a topic of scientific inquiry only within the past decade. Until recently, scientists didn't think of pride as a significant force in human lives, or even, for that matter, as an emotion — at least, not a fundamental, universal emotion that all humans share, like fear, anger, sadness, or joy. In fact, for a long time, scientists didn't think much about pride at all.

Yet this question of whether pride is universal has profound implications. If pride is experienced by people in certain cultures only, it would mean that pride is *not* a fundamental part of human nature but is socially constructed, a product of those cultures where it exists. It would mean that the feeling that drove Dean Karnazes to become an all-night runner and that drives so many of us to work our hardest at whatever it is we care most about is something imposed from the outside — by parents, teachers, friends, and coworkers — not something that's part and parcel of our species' internal, innate biological system.

If, however, pride is an intrinsic human emotion felt by people in every culture on our planet, then pride is a part of our biological makeup, our genetic heritage; part of our human nature. And if that's the case, it's almost certainly because *Homo sapiens* evolved to experience pride; that pride has adaptive benefits we've never fully understood. As a result, answering this question — the question of whether pride is universal — is the necessary first step toward achieving a new understanding of this powerful emotion, the impact it has on our lives and our species, and the ways in which we might use it more purposefully.

Although humans vary enormously — many of us, for example, would rather sleep at night than run — we also have a great many qualities in common. To take a few obvious examples, our hunger for food and our thirst for water, our aversion to pain and our desire for pleasure, our preference for a warm (but not too hot) climate, and our need for at least 21 percent oxygen in the air we breathe — these are all universal and biologically endowed features of the human experience. While it might seem less critical, our shared capacity to feel and express emotions is also a universal part of what it means to be human, and it's a part that has shaped our nature in significant ways.

Emotions are biological and psychological responses to events that our species has encountered again and again throughout its history, situations that have posed challenges to humanity's well-being and even its survival. Thanks to natural selection, emotions evolved in humans to prepare us to cope with these challenges in the most adaptive ways possible — that is, in ways that are most likely to ensure that an individual survives long enough to reproduce his or her genes.

Take, for example, the complex network of neurons, synapses, muscles, and blood vessels that work together to create the emotional experience of fear. This system is triggered by any event that places us (or those we care about) in potential danger. Our brains instantly interpret these events as threatening, and this appraisal sets off a cascade of mental and physical responses that, collectively, we call fear. These include physiological changes like increased heart rate and sweating; cognitive changes like heightened alertness and attention oriented toward the source of the threat; and behavioral changes like sudden freezing and a distinct wide-eyed facial expression that allows us to visually acquire more information and simultaneously send a quick signal informing those around us that danger lurks.

When fear is activated, there is also, of course, a change in our subjective experience — we *feel* afraid. But this feeling is just the tip of the iceberg, the most superficial part of the emotion. It's the part we're often most aware of, but it's only one small piece of the body's solution to whatever challenge it's confronting. And all of these changes are oriented toward a single goal: converting the fearful human into the most capable threat-avoiding machine he or she can be.

Even now, many millennia after humans developed the capacity for emotion, the effectiveness of this evolutionary tool can still be felt, viscerally and without warning. Next time you wake up to something that's gone bump in the night — and before you bound out of bed to investigate — take a minute to notice the state that your body and mind are in. Moments ago, you were completely unconscious. Now, seconds later, you're more awake than you've felt in days. Your heart is pounding; your mind is racing as you mentally analyze the objects in your kitchen to figure out if one was inadvertently left in a precarious position; your muscles are tensed, ready to spring to life.

Evolution made you this way; it is responsible for the rapid and dramatic physical changes you experience in moments like these. By creating within humans a highly functional fear response, natural selection ensured that our species was well equipped to deal with any threats encountered, both now and in our ancient history, from saber-toothed tigers to toppling dishware. To be sure, the specific nature of these threats has changed fairly drastically over time. A modern human is much more likely to feel fear in response to the sound of glass breaking in the middle of the night than to a surprise encounter with a lion. But the fear that we experience now is much the same as what our ancient ancestors felt, and, in both cases, it's the body's way of coping with the threat.

Fear is only one of a small set of emotions that are functional in this way, that evolved to motivate humans to do things that are good for us and avoid things that are bad for us, and, in the process, increase our likelihood of surviving long enough to reproduce. This is what it means to say that these emotions are adaptive; they have, for many millennia, helped members of our species survive the onslaught of predators, a frequent lack of food and water, and an often harsh environment long enough to conceive and bear children. In more recent times, they've helped humans survive much, much longer.

And, while helping us survive, these emotions have also made us who we are. They are part of our human nature, which is to say that we acquired them through genes we inherited from our parents and their parents before them. Like the rest of our biology and psychology — from bodies that can walk upright, run from predators, and forage for food to the massive cognitive apparatus inside our heads that allows us to distinguish safe berries from more dangerous ones and create computers, airplanes, and nuclear weapons — our emotions are part of what make us human. Thanks to our species' tendency to experience fear in response to potential danger, our ancestors escaped saber-toothed tigers, set aside poisonous berries, and successfully reproduced. Because of this same tendency, we are a species that will often err on the side of caution, become obsessed with our mortality, and appreciate the humor of Woody Allen.

This understanding of emotions as an evolved part of human nature is a relatively recent intellectual accomplishment. Fifty years ago, the dominant academic ideology of the day, which held forth across the social sciences and the humanities, was social constructivism. The proponents of this view believed that emotions, like most of the rest of human psychology, fell outside the purview of the natural sciences and could be fully appreciated only with an eye toward cultural relativism. In order to understand a given psychological experience, constructivists argued, one would need to examine that experience within the context of the experiencer's own cultural history. Natural evolutionary processes could explain human biology below the neck but not above it. According to constructivists, emotions were not a product of an innate and evolved human nature but instead were learned from other members of one's culture — parents, teachers, friends, and siblings.

This belief, that emotions are culturally specific phenomena, was itself a reversal of a prior understanding. About a century earlier, in 1872, the world's most famous anticonstructivist, Charles Darwin, published *The Expression of the Emotions in Man and Animals,* a book with the central goal of arguing that emotions are natural and biological. Darwin was no emotion researcher, yet he devoted an entire book to the topic of emotion expressions. He did so because he wanted to take his theory of evolution beyond the obviously biological to the more deeply psychological. Darwin believed that emotions provided the best entry point because, he argued, emotions are manifested *visibly* in the body, and therefore cannot be only a part of the mind.

This claim — that emotions are both mental and physical states — is one we now take for granted. Unlike so many aspects of human psychology that occur entirely inside our heads — our capacity for rational thinking, complex decision-making, and moral judgments, for example — emotions occur both in our minds and out. Emotions are internal psychological processes — we *feel* fear and anger as mental states, just like we feel hunger and thirst — but emotions are also expressed outside the mind, through the facial and bodily movements we make, automatically and often unavoidably, when we experience them. When we're happy, we smile. When we're angry, we purse our lips and frown. When we're scared, we tense up, widen our eyes, and prepare to fight or flee. This makes emotions visibly and blatantly different than mental thoughts we can't observe. Because of this difference, emotions provide a means of comparing human psychology with the psychology of other animals, who, unlike (most) humans, can't talk about their feelings.

One of Darwin's most impressive skills was his observational ability; close surveillance of various plant species is what initially led to his formulation of natural selection. So in seeking evidence for evolution at work in the human mind, Darwin turned to a part of the mind that he could witness, a part that could be directly observed in both humans and other animals who, he thought, must share a common ancestor. Emotion expressions provided a way of demonstrating that humans inherited at least one part of their psychology, because, as

Darwin could plainly see, these expressions were visibly similar to the emotional behaviors displayed by animals.

This is something that anyone who's spent substantial time in the primate section of a zoo can attest to. Look closely at any species of monkey, and you'll quickly find something eerily familiar about those furry creatures. Their humanlike fingers and toes contribute to the impression, but it's their faces — and the expressions they make — that have the greatest impact. Darwin noticed this too, and he filled *The Expression of the Emotions in Man and Animals* with examples of such striking cross-species similarities. He wrote, for instance, of an acquaintance who kept a monkey "in his house for a year; and when he gave it during meal-times some choice delicacy, he observed that the corners of its mouth were slightly raised; thus an expression of satisfaction, partaking of the nature of an incipient smile, and resembling that often seen on the face of a man, could be plainly observed in this animal." Darwin also went further, taking his argument beyond primates. Dogs, for example, were said to approach each other with "erected ears, eyes intently directed forwards, hair on the neck and back bristling, gait remarkably stiff, with the tail upright and rigid. So familiar is this appearance to us, that an angry man is sometimes said 'to have his back up.'"

How can we explain these similarities between the facial expressions of humans and many other species if not through processes of evolution by natural selection? How could human expressions of emotion look so much like the expressions shown by other animals if humans had not inherited these expressions from our ancestors — who, long ago, *were* other animals?

Nonetheless, Darwin's claim — that human emotions are inherited from our nonhuman ancestors in the same way that human ears, eyes, and noses are — was slow to catch on. The idea was particularly bold (and particularly hard to defend) because, at the time, the best evidence Darwin could rally in support of it were these anecdotal observations: scientists who happened to notice that their pet monkeys and dogs looked a lot like people in moments when the animals appeared to be especially emotional. And the deep entrenchment of the constructivist view that soon took over much of academia ensured that Darwin's idea wouldn't be taken seriously — or seriously studied — anytime soon. In fact, it would be nearly a hundred years before scientists attempted to seek out more solid, empirically based evidence to support Darwin's claim.

But finally, in 1967, a thirty-three-year-old clinical psychologist named Paul Ekman decided to try to do just that: resuscitate Darwin's theory of emotions by finding cold, hard evidence in support of it. Ekman had read Darwin and was frustrated by the social constructivists' quick dismissal of his more controversial ideas. But how could he prove that Darwin was right? Ekman obviously couldn't go back in time to test whether prehistoric humans showed the same emotion expressions as their modern-day counterparts. Instead, he would have to find a modern subject pool on whom to test Darwin's theory.

Talking with anthropologists — scientists who study groups of people living in what are known as traditional small-scale societies, communities where the current lifestyle is similar to that of many of our prehistoric ancestors — gave Ekman an idea. If Darwin was right and human emotion expressions were biologically encoded, passed down in our genes from our nonhuman ancestors, then they should be the same not only in ancient humans but also in modern humans *everywhere*. Emotion expressions should be universal across our species. But if Darwin was wrong and emotions were socially constructed, then they would necessarily differ by culture. The likelihood that different social groups spread all over the world might have *constructed* the same emotion expressions purely by chance was minuscule.

This insight led to a study that became one of the most famous in all of psychological science. Ekman realized that the best way to test Darwin's claim would be to find people who had no knowledge of Western cultural norms or emotions. If he could study people who had never encountered Westerners and had no access to American or European films, television, or magazines, Ekman could test whether American emotion expressions were universal. If people who were entirely culturally isolated from the West were shown pictures of American emotion expressions and identified them in the *same way* that Western-ers do, it would have to mean that these expressions were a universal part of human nature rather than learned through one's culture. It would require a coincidence of epic proportions for two entirely sepa-rate populations, each with its own cultural norms and values, to have spontaneously developed the same facial expressions for each emo-tion. The most parsimonious explanation for a finding of successful emotion recognition in a cultural group of the sort that Ekman had in mind would be that emotion expressions are evolved, that people ev-erywhere attach the same meaning to smiles, frowns, and grimaces *be-cause it is human nature to do so.*

Ekman chose as the subject of his study a tribal group of people known as the Fore, a traditional small-scale society in Papua New Guinea. They were, at the time, a preliterate culture, meaning that their language had no written form. Some spoke a pidgin version of English, but most spoke only local dialects. By the end of the 1960s, the Fore had been visited occasionally by anthropologists, but never by tourists. Ekman described the group as "a stone-age culture" — a label we'd avoid today partly because it's politically incorrect, but also because it's inaccurate, given that the Fore of 1968 had undoubtedly changed somewhat from Stone Age times. Still, Ekman's description effectively conjures up how he must have felt upon arriving on this small island to find a group of people who almost certainly had had no exposure to American emotion displays.

To test Darwin's claim, Ekman compiled a set of thirty photos (culled from over three thousand that he and his collaborators had taken or found, all without the help of the Internet!) of people dis-playing six facial expressions that seemed to be associated with dis-tinct emotions in the Western world: anger, disgust, fear, happiness, sadness, and surprise. He showed these images to the Fore and asked them to identify the emotion expressed in each.

The results of this study provided the first empirical evidence in support of the Darwinian view of emotions. For almost all of Ekman's photos, the large majority of Fore participants correctly identified the emotion displayed. Speaking statistically, the frequency of participants who responded correctly was significantly greater than what would be expected by chance (that is, if participants were guessing randomly among the response options Ekman gave them).

Now, "significantly greater than what would be expected by chance" might not sound particularly impressive. You might think that we should observe 100 percent agreement that a sad expression conveys sadness if the expression is universal. But even among highly educated American college students — psychology majors who participate in research studies all the time — researchers never achieve 100 percent agreement about *anything*, be it the emotion expressed in someone's face, the name of the first African American president, or whether Justin Bieber should be deported to Canada. In any study that relies on human responses, there will be humans who respond atypically, because they aren't paying attention or they want to mess with the experimenter or they genuinely hold an idiosyncratic perception of the stimulus or the world at large.

In fact, Ekman's statistically significant results allowed him to conclude that the six emotions he had examined were universally associated with distinct facial expressions. But his results also did much more than that. They demonstrated that Darwin had been right to draw parallels between humans' displays of emotions and those of animals. If people all over the world identify the same emotions in the same observable expressions, this knowledge must be something humans possess because we evolved to do so; it must be part of our nature. Emotions — core mental phenomena previously relegated to the domain of the humanities — had observable behavioral components that could not be a product of cultural learning and so had to be part of a shared human biology. These findings made a strong argument — perhaps the strongest out there — for rejecting the social constructivist theory of the mind and its contention that our feelings are nothing more than artifacts of our culture.

It is no understatement to say that Ekman's study completely changed the way psychological scientists understood emotions. Before Ekman's research, most psychologists viewed emotions as culturally learned and therefore as belonging more within the province of anthropology than psychology. The few psychologists who disagreed with this position tended to be psychoanalytically oriented theorists who, following Freud, saw emotions as pathological instincts — largely about sex — that people spent most of their time defensively guarding against. The new understanding brought forth by Ekman's research was that this is simply not the case. Emotions are not entirely culturally distinct or products of socialization. Instead, they are a universal part of human nature, both psychological and biological, part of our genetic heritage and a natural and even healthy part of humans' endowed experiential and behavioral repertoire. This new knowledge prompted a major shift in the orthodoxy. Psychological scientists began studying emotions, and emotion research (or affective science, as it's often called) became a major subdiscipline of the field.

By the end of the millennium, emotions had become such a central part of psychology's focus that many scholars viewed emotions as the motivational force guiding almost all of human behavior. Today, many psychological scientists agree that any decision we make, any relationship we pursue, any *thing* we want — all these judgments, behaviors, and desires are influenced by emotion. Even those decisions we believe are shaped by rationality or logical principles about what is right or good are in fact more often triggered by a gut emotional response. We tell ourselves that such decisions aren't driven by our emotions, that we are relying on the mind's most sophisticated reasoning processes, but research shows that we are very good at coming up with "sophisticated" reasons to justify what we want to think, and what we want to think is almost always shaped by how we feel.

Thanks in large part to Ekman's research among the Fore, emotions have come to be regarded as a massively important feature of the human mind. But there is an important caveat to this statement: it applies to *some* emotions, but not all. Ekman found that six — and only six — emotions have universal expressions. As a result, these six emotions have come to hold a special status in the psychological literature, and particularly in the subfield of affective science. Because Ekman could show that they are universal — associated with distinct, observable behaviors that people everywhere display and recognize in the same way — anger, disgust, fear, happiness, sadness, and surprise came to be seen as "basic emotions," meaning that they are fundamental to human nature. Each of these emotions is more than its facial expression alone, but the expressions provided scientists with a window, a way of objectively measuring the emotion through systematic observation and demonstrating that it's not simply a feeling that some people in some cultures say they experience.

In other words, the universality of the expressions that signal them had to mean that these six emotions are universal too, and therefore evolved — but some scholars, including Ekman himself, took this further. The six basic emotions, he argued, are *the only emotions* there are. If an emotion failed to pass the test of having a universal expression, it might be interesting, even potentially worth studying, but it could not be considered a real *emotion*.

Pride — the emotion that drives Dean Karnazes to run hundreds of miles at a clip and that made me leave my barista job to start a graduate career in psychological science — was not one of Ekman's basic six. Could this mean that pride is not part of human nature? Or is it possible that Ekman's groundbreaking, paradigm-changing work left something out?

As a child, I remember being curious about my father's late-night reading habit. I had an instinctive belief that everything anyone did — whether it was going to school (me), going to work (my parents), or shopping for groceries (one of them, *always* with me, much to my great eight-year-old annoyance) — must have a purpose. The purposes behind shopping for food and going to school were fairly obvious; you needed to eat to live, and school taught you what you needed to know to get a job, which was also necessary for life, albeit some future adult life. But the reasons behind many other things people did on a very regular basis were much more difficult to figure out. My dad spent hours every night after dinner sitting in his rocking chair, reading a book and drinking a cup of instant black coffee. I could tell from the intense look on his face and the plentiful underlining he performed that his books weren't light beach reads; they were deeply intellectual material, often in the form of literary criticism. What was the point of that?

I remember asking my dad why he spent so much time doing something that didn't seem to have a clear purpose. His answer was that it was part of who he was. He stayed up late reading literary theory each night because his books gave him a sense of meaning and identity he failed to find in his real estate job.

My mom, meanwhile, was busy studying for a PhD in English literature, something that I knew, even then, required far more schooling than anyone really needed to get a job. When I asked her why, she told me that she'd spent the majority of her childhood reading every book in her local library, and she was getting a PhD so she could spend the rest of her life in a career that paid her to do the thing that was most important to her.

What my parents' answers helped me realize is that the needs, or emotional motivations, that drive people to do everything we do fall into two different categories. First, there are the basic emotional motivations — those that *directly* get us to do what we need to do to survive, including all those mundane but necessary everyday tasks like shopping for groceries and earning a paycheck. When our basic survival needs are threatened, we feel basic emotions like fear and anger, and these emotions motivate us to do what's needed to change the status quo. When these needs are met, we feel happy, an emotion that tells us all is right with the world and motivates us to keep at it.

In fact, these survival-enabling emotions are the six that Ekman found to be universal: anger, disgust, fear, happiness, sadness, and surprise. Their motivational power directly propels us to make sure we meet our basic survival and reproduction-oriented needs, and this power is the reason they exist; it's why our species evolved to experience them.

But there's also a second category of emotional motivations, the ones that drive us to figure out who we are and to fill our lives with meaning. The distinction between these two categories of needs was made quite eloquently by Eep, the Neanderthal protagonist of the 2013 animated film *The Croods.* Shortly after discovering the *Homo sapiens* way of life, Eep tells her father, Grug, that their Neanderthal focus on survival alone "wasn't *living!* That was just not dying! There's a difference."

The emotions that give shape to these two distinct categories of motivations and needs — the need to survive, and the need to feel good about ourselves while doing so — are different. Ekman's six universal emotions are, without a doubt, essential to the persistence of our species. They help us survive in a complex and constantly shifting world. They influence many of the decisions we make every day. But they do not explain what we choose to *do* with our lives to make them meaningful. None of Ekman's six basic emotions motivate us to do all the things we do that are about more than just surviving.

For us *Homo sapiens,* emotions motivate us to do much more than not die; they help us to *live* — to find a greater sense of purpose beyond survival alone. The resulting human desire for identity and meaning explains why my mom pursued a PhD and why my dad spent much of his free time reading. These behaviors cannot be explained by anger or fear or even simple happiness. Behaviors like these make it abundantly clear that humans care about more than just staying alive. We have another motivation: we want to feel good about ourselves. Or as Dean Karnazes explained at the end of his memoir, "I run because it's my way of giving back to the world by doing the one thing it is I do best."

Make no mistake: the emotions that propel us on this quest for identity and meaning *also* increase our chances of surviving and bearing offspring who survive. Just like the six emotions that Ekman identified, these other emotions too must be the result of evolutionary processes, because they too are part of human nature. The motivation to live a life of meaning is something we all share.

In fact, as we will see, building a sense of oneself, finding an identity that fits, and creating a meaningful and purposeful life is, ultimately, adaptive. Those who are most successful in this pursuit are rewarded with dense social networks, feelings of well-being, and even longevity.

But building an identity is adaptive in a different way than fending off a deadly virus is. As far as a strategy to ensure the survival of your genetic material goes, it's much less direct than, say, making sure there's food on the table or that your family has a warm and safe place to live. At times, it may even be counterproductive to some of those survival-oriented needs. Think of Paul Gauguin's decision to become a starving artist instead of a well-off suburban dad. In the search for identity and meaning, humans often do things that would make no sense if our only goal were to stay alive or even to increase pleasure and reduce pain. We frequently forgo pleasure and subject ourselves to pain; we work and suffer much more than we need to. We do not simply get by; we strive, often desperately, to create lives that make us feel good about ourselves.

Self-esteem — the extent to which people feel good about themselves, or, in more technical terms, the extent to which people see themselves as having worth and value — is tremendously important to our species. It's somewhat surprising, then, that for many years, emotion researchers almost completely neglected this basic human need. Just as surprising, the Ekman view on emotions — that they are discrete evolved entities with important differences among them — was, until recently, missing from the research literature on the self. Self-esteem researchers knew that people with high self-esteem feel good about themselves and that people with low self-esteem feel bad, but that was about as far as they went. Whether good or bad meant happy, angry, afraid, or some other potentially fundamental emotion was largely unexamined.

The two emotions that are most obviously relevant to the self are pride and shame. These are the emotions we feel when we think about ourselves — about who we are, who we want to be, and whether we're becoming or failing to become that kind of person. Yet according to Ekman's universality findings, these two emotions aren't worth acknowledging. As a result of Ekman's work, many scientists agreed that pride and shame are not basic, evolved emotions.* They do not have universally recognized facial expressions. Yes, pride might be an emotionally tinged experience that occurs among certain peoples in certain cultures, but the scientific dogma is clear: if it is not associated with a universal expression, it can't be considered an evolved emotion.

Think about what this means. The emotion we feel when we feel good about ourselves — the emotion that motivates us to do so many of the things we do to feel as if our lives are worthy — is *not a universal human emotion,* according to the school of thought that's dominated this field of study since Ekman's day. How can this be? Pride is what prods us to put off easy pleasures and play the long game, to figure out how to be the best we can be. As a result, this emotion has to have had a major impact in shaping human nature. Almost by definition, this emotion *must* be an evolved part of that nature.

But if that's the case — if pride is adaptive and shared by all humans — then according to the scientific dogma, it should be universal in some visibly apparent way, such as having a cross-culturally recognizable, nonverbal expression. And maybe it does. Just because no one has found one yet doesn't mean it doesn't exist. Instead, it might mean that we've been looking in the wrong place.

What does your face look like when you feel good about yourself — that is, when you feel pride? If you saw that expression on someone else's face, would you recognize it as pride?

If you think the answer is no, you're not alone. Indeed, all existing scientific evidence suggests that pride does *not* have a universal facial expression. If it did, Ekman would have found it. Prior to traveling to Papua New Guinea, he'd spent more hours than anyone else, ever, doc-

---

* Although this book is focused on pride, shame is an important supporting character. The opposite of pride in every way, shame motivates many of the same outcomes as pride but does so in a prevention-oriented, rather than promotion-oriented, way. We seek to avoid feeling shame in the same way we seek to feel pride, and often these two searches combine into one. However, for the sake of staying on topic, in most cases I'll restrict my discussion to the pride side of things.

umenting every muscle movement that the human face made when it was being expressive.

It's difficult to imagine what a pride facial expression would look like — how it would look different from simple happiness — but then again, humans are not free-floating faces. We have bodies too. And when people feel pride — when they experience success — their appearances *do* change. It's a change that involves their faces, but also their bodies, often working in concert.

When people feel pride, they smile, as they do when they feel the basic emotion of happiness. But something else happens too. Proud people stand a little taller; they spread out their arms and make themselves bigger. Darwin himself made this observation back in 1872, writing in *The Expression of the Emotions in Man and Animals:* "A proud man exhibits his sense of superiority over others by holding his head and body erect . . . he makes himself appear as large as possible; so that he is said to be swollen or puffed up with pride."

Could this shift in body posture constitute an *evolved* basic emotion expression? Could the tendency to push out your chest and hold your head up high when you feel good about yourself be part of human nature?

After migrating to graduate school, I decided to try to find the answer to this question. My graduate adviser Rick Robins and I asked friends, colleagues, other grad students, even undergraduate drama majors to pose this hypothetical pride expression while I took their photos. I then projected these photos onto a large screen and showed them, slide-show style, to darkened rooms of undergraduates at the University of California, Davis, where I was a grad student. The undergrads looked attentively at each image and indicated what emotion they thought it conveyed.

Once again, Darwin was right. Almost all of our research participants identified almost all of the photos we showed them — like the one in figure 1.1 — as pride. Recognition rates ranged from 73 percent to 95 percent — all far greater than what we'd expect by chance — with an average of 83 percent. The best-recognized photos were ones we had taken pains to make as pride-like as possible by telling our friendly posers exactly how much to tilt their heads back or where to put their arms. In fact, there was one permutation that seemed especially well recognized: the combination of expanded posture, a small smile, head tilted slightly (but not too far) back, and arms held akimbo with hands on the hips (see figure 1.2). But we also found solid recognition rates (greater than 70 percent) for two other versions: the one featured in figure 1.1, with arms raised above the head and hands in fists, and the one in figure 1.3, with arms folded across the chest, CEO-in-a-business-meeting-style.

Figure 1.1. A prototypical pride expression

What these results mean is that there is an expression (or expressions) that, college students agree, conveys pride. People — or, at least, UC Davis undergrads — can recognize pride from a particular combination of body and facial positions, and they can distinguish it from similar emotions, like happiness or excitement.

What these results do not prove, however, is that this pride expression is universal, or part of human nature. In fact, if you showed UC

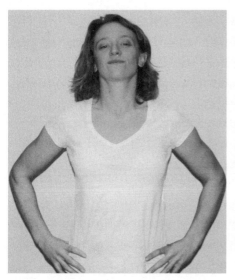

Figure 1.2. Another prototypical pride expression, typically very well recognized among American undergraduates

Figure 1.3. Yet another prototypical pride expression, also known as CEO-at-a-business-meeting-style

Davis undergraduates photos of the classic American thumbs-up sign, you'd probably find 95 percent recognition for that too. There are plenty of expressions — better known as gestures — that are instantly recognizable within a particular cultural group, but *only* within that culture. Think of waving hello, winking, or prominently displaying your middle finger. These can all be safely performed within most American social groups — safely, that is, if your goal is to communicate, though not necessarily if your goal is to avoid getting punched. But the fact that Americans recognize these expressions does not mean that they are evolved emotion displays; after all, many of these gestures would not be recognized by people who belong to other cultures. Like language, gestures are communicative only within certain cultural contexts, and as anyone who's tried to fist-bump someone over the age of eighty-five knows, they are far from universal.

If this pride expression, which appears to be well known among American — or, more precisely, *Californian* — college students is a human phenomenon and not just a cultural one, it should also be recognizable among people who, like Ekman's Fore, have no knowledge of

Californian culture. But finding research subjects like that is not an easy feat. It was not easy when Ekman did it, and in some ways it's even more difficult today. At the point of this writing, all but a handful of known remaining traditional small-scale societies have been studied, at least to some extent, by Western anthropologists. As a result, it's now exceedingly difficult to find anyone in the world over the age of ten who has never seen a white person or a product of Western culture like a Coke bottle (as was the case for a particularly curious Kalahari San tribe member in the 1980 film *The Gods Must Be Crazy*). Papua New Guinea has become a regular anthropologists' stomping ground since Ekman's visit, and many of the people living in traditional small-scale societies there now have not only met and spent time with Westerners but even participated in American research studies.

However, there is a population of humans who, like the Fore of Ekman's era, are not particularly familiar with American college-student gestures but who, unlike the Fore, are easy to locate in California: young children.

Although children are well known to be sponges who very quickly pick up on everything and anything to which they're exposed, we can still safely assume that they've acquired considerably less cultural knowledge than college students. My colleagues and I theorized that if young children could recognize this pride expression we'd found, it would at least rule out the possibility that the expression was unique to California college-student culture. And, sure enough, by the time kids reached the age of four, we found, they could recognize pride — well above chance levels and at about the same rate as they recognized the expression they know best: happiness.

But this finding, that Californian children — like Californian young adults — recognize pride, still doesn't answer the question we really wanted to ask: Do people from other cultures recognize pride? This is *the* question that needs to be answered in order to know whether pride is part of human nature. And the only way to know for sure whether the pride expression is not simply an artifact of American culture is to test for pride recognition outside of American culture.

Bologna, Italy, lies about six thousand miles outside of California —

and, as anyone who's traveled to Italy might expect, adult Italians living in Bologna were also found to recognize pride with ease. This tells us that pride recognition is not restricted to U.S. soil, but this finding is not as informative on the question of universality as it might seem. Despite its geographic distance from North America, Italy is really not all that far from the United States culturally speaking, and, of course, there are certain Italian gestures that have become readily recognizable to segments of American society (*Capisce?*). Furthermore, both countries are Western cultures; Italy might even be considered a seat of Western civilization. Italians could have invented the pride expression and transmitted it to North Americans, along with Roman architecture, Caesar haircuts, and pizza.

The only way to determine conclusively whether the pride expression is universal is to test whether it's recognized by people living in a remote part of the world — people who, unlike the Bolognese, have little or no familiarity with Western culture. If people like that could recognize the pride expression, it would have to mean that pride is universal and, perhaps, that pride has an evolutionary purpose scientists haven't yet fully understood.

People like the Fore who populated Papua New Guinea fifty years ago are hard to come by these days, but a close equivalent — at least in terms of isolation from Western cultural influences — can perhaps be found in the rural countryside of Burkina Faso. An African country landlocked between Ghana and Mali (and formerly known as Upper Volta), Burkina won its independence from France in 1960 and has suffered a series of military coups and revolutions since then. Like the citizens of many other West African nations with no tourist industry or major exports, the large majority of Burkinabé live in extreme poverty. The United Nations Human Development Report regularly ranks Burkina among the three poorest countries in the world. Only about 25 percent of the population is literate in French, the national language. Instead, most Burkinabé speak and understand local dialects that have no written form. In the country's more remote villages, residents have no electricity (and hence no TV or Internet), can't read, write, or speak a Western language, and have never left their country. The odds that such people might somehow have been exposed to an emotion expression that is unique to Western culture are slim at best.

This was my hope, at least, as I headed to Toussianna, a tiny village in the western countryside of Burkina Faso that looked like it could be featured in a *National Geographic* spread. Toussianna seemed like the perfect setting for the ultimate pride-expression universality test. Mud huts with thatched roofs dotted the countryside. Chickens roamed free. Our Burkinabé research collaborator Jean Traore, a government bureaucrat and sometime village chief, had spread the word among the local villages that something was "happening" at his home in the center of the village. In exchange for the Burkinabé CFA franc equivalent of several dollars and five kilos of rice per person, forty people hiked to Jean's home from neighboring towns, some as far as five kilometers away, to participate in our pride-recognition study.

The women wore traditional African clothing — brightly colored dresses and headscarfs — and most carried a child in a local version of the Baby Bjorn: a large scarf that tightly wrapped the child to the woman's midriff. Most also carried heavy loads on their heads — precariously balanced buckets of potatoes or cassavas. The men were as likely to be dressed in jeans and T-shirts obtained from NGO airdrops as in more traditional homespun tunics and loose pants, but, other than the car we arrived in, this was the only indication of a contemporary Western cultural presence that my fellow researchers and I observed anywhere in the area.

One by one, a male or female interviewer, also dressed in traditional garb but carrying a clipboard with our study's questionnaire, approached each participant and led him or her to chairs set off from Jean's house. There, participants were asked to identify the emotion conveyed in a series of laminated photos. These featured our expert posers displaying pride, along with other expressions.

The result? Of the forty Burkinabé participants Jean managed to recruit, 57 percent recognized pride.

That rate, 57 percent, was a good deal lower than the recognition rates we had previously found in American undergraduate samples —

about 75 to 85 percent, on average — but also *much* higher than the chance-guessing rate, which was 12 percent in this study. Just as important, the Burkinabé participants were no worse at recognizing pride than any of the other emotion expressions they viewed, except for happiness — which, at 84 percent, was better recognized than anything else. For every other expression, recognition rates ranged from 58 percent (for surprise) to 30 percent (for fear), making pride one of the best-recognized expressions.

The interviewers also asked the Burkinabé participants a second set of questions. To empirically verify their lack of exposure to Western culture — the critical assumption behind the research — we devised a quiz to test their knowledge of major Western cultural icons. If our participants failed to identify certain famous Westerners — people like movie star Tom Cruise, soccer star David Beckham, and President George W. Bush (this was 2003) — it would be a good sign that they lacked even a minimal familiarity with Western culture. And, in fact, no one accurately identified any of these famous Westerners. In contrast, almost three-quarters of the sample recognized a photo of the Burkinabé president (who, at the time, had led the country for sixteen years) — indicating that they understood the questions we were asking.

The finding that a fairly substantial proportion of our Burkinabé research sample did recognize the pride expression can mean only one thing: pride — an emotion previously assumed to be culturally relative — is universally recognizable. A statistically significant number of participants living in a remote, non-Western, traditional small-scale society accurately identified the pride expression. The observed recognition rate was higher than most of the rates Ekman had found for his six basic emotion expressions in Papua New Guinea thirty years earlier. Given the time that had passed, our Burkinabé participants were almost certainly not as isolated from the rest of the world as Ekman's Fore had been, but they were still a group of people who had no formal education, lacked the financial resources to travel far from their village, and understood neither French nor English — the languages most likely to be spoken by any Westerners with whom they came into contact. These were people who couldn't recognize the current American president or Tom Cruise, but they knew pride.

The results from Burkina Faso prove, as certainly as scientists can know anything, that pride recognition is a universal human ability not learned through one's culture. If it were — if American four-year-olds recognized pride because they'd been taught to do so — then our Burkinabé participants who had never had that lesson would not show accurate recognition. The fact that these individuals could recognize this expression means that the emotion that makes us feel good about ourselves and that motivates us to do all the things we do to feel good about ourselves looks the same everywhere.

But just because pride *looks* the same everywhere does not mean that pride *is* the same everywhere. The studies in California, Italy, and Burkina Faso demonstrate that a diverse range of people recognize expressions of pride portrayed in photos of other people, but not that an equally diverse range of people *display* their feelings of pride in this way. The people in the photos were, after all, striking poses in exactly the way we'd instructed them to. The question, then, is whether people in Burkina Faso — or anywhere else in the world, for that matter — *show* the same expressions that Americans do when they feel pride.

There are theoretical reasons to expect that they might — that people everywhere should manifest pride in the same way. Years ago, Ekman argued that his findings of universal emotion recognition necessarily had to imply that those recognizable expressions are also universally displayed. How else could we explain the fact that people everywhere can identify these expressions in the same way if not for the fact that people everywhere regularly see these expressions *displayed by others around them* in the same way? It might be that recognition itself is an innate adaptation, that the brain comes hardwired with an automatic ability to perceive the meaning of these six distinct emotion expressions. Or it might be that the tendency to display these expressions in emotional situations is what's innate, and recognition is learned by virtue of growing up in a world where such displays are shown on an hourly basis. Either way, evidence for universal recognition logically has to entail universal display.

But there is a flaw in this logic. Although we might not know why, it's possible that emotion expressions could be universally recognized yet *not* universally displayed. They could be universally known prototypes: ideal, exaggerated exemplars of a concept that people understand, but not because they represent behaviors that are actually shown. Think of the once widespread yet clearly incorrect belief that the sun rises and sets because it's orbiting the Earth, rather than the other way around. The ubiquity of this belief might have been used as evidence for its truth, but that would have led to a deeply flawed conclusion. Although it's difficult to explain how universal emotion recognition would exist if these expressions were not universally displayed, that failure of imagination does not rule out the possibility.

The question of whether pride is a universal human emotion — and thus whether it's likely to be an evolved part of human nature — essentially boils down to the question of whether people all over world show the critical pride behaviors when they feel pride. Head tilted back, chest expanded, arms raised; finding these nonverbal behaviors *actually displayed* among a vast diversity of far-flung humans, rather than simply testing their reactions to posed expressions, is the best — and maybe the only — way to know whether pride is part of our nature.

Imagine that you're paying a visit to Mecca, the Saudi Arabian holy city regarded as the spiritual capital of Islam. Millions of people visit this sacred site each year, so you are surrounded by faces and languages from every corner of the world. Unless you speak Arabic, you have no way to communicate with the vast majority of the people around you — at least, not using words.

Emotions, by contrast, would come in handy on a trip to Mecca. Even in the absence of a shared language, you would be able to recognize the smile of a fellow pilgrim as a sign of happiness, and the frown of another as a sign that you'd accidentally stepped on his foot. Straightforward nonverbal signals like this would be an invaluable tool for you as you navigated such a complex, multicultural environment.

Until recently, scientists assumed that any display of pride in one of your fellow pilgrims might be unrecognizable to you — but our research in Burkina Faso overturned this assumption. We now know that other pilgrims who see your pride expression will immediately understand what it means and perhaps come to assume that you've reached the pinnacle of your journey. But none of the studies I've mentioned thus far tell us whether anyone, anywhere in the world, actually *displays* these expressions during a prideful situation. If you bump into a Saudi sheikh on the annual haj, would he in fact convey to you with his body language alone that he was a mighty royal, rather than an ordinary pilgrim like yourself?

To answer this question, I turned to a unique set of research participants: world-class athletes competing in the 2004 Olympic Games judo competition. My collaborator David Matsumoto had obtained photos taken by an official Judo Federation photographer who was on the mat with each competitor, snapping away. We thus could examine images of every movement made by every athlete during the ten to twenty seconds immediately after every match, the moments when the winners of this group might be expected to feel a fairly extreme level of pride.

By coding the behavioral movements shown by these athletes, we could measure the actual expressions displayed by people who were feeling pride — probably the most intense pride of their lives. Because these photos were from the Olympics, we could do so for people from all over the world.

We had photos of eighty-seven athletes participating in a total of fifty-five matches. For each match there were about ten to fifteen photos of the two athletes who'd been competing. Using a set of scales I provided, my research assistants coded all the behaviors they observed from both athletes in each series of photos; rating, for example, how much head tilt each athlete demonstrated on a scale from 1 to 4. The coders quickly reached a high level of reliability — meaning that they agreed with one another about what the appropriate code was for each behavior; for instance, exactly how much chest expansion constituted a rating of 4 rather than 3. This is important, because it indicated that their codes were picking up on something real, something objective that could be perceived by multiple independent people, rather than

something each coder saw differently depending on his or her own idiosyncratic way of viewing the world.

Once all the photos had been coded, I performed a simple comparison: Did the athletes who'd won their match display pride-expression behaviors — tilting their heads back, expanding their chests, and
raising their arms — to a greater extent than the athletes who'd lost?
By comparing winners and losers in this way, we could determine
whether people from all over the world were more likely to show the
pride expression in response to success — a situation that, at least according to my own Western cultural norms, should elicit pride — than
in response to failure.

In fact, this is exactly what we found. Match winners displayed *every*
behavioral component of the recognizable pride expression — chest
expanded, head tilted up, shoulders pulled back, arms extended out
from the body, and smiling — considerably more than losers. These
differences were not just statistically significant; they were huge. This
was probably due in part to the fact that losers tended to be doing the
exact opposite: displaying typical shame behaviors like slumping their
shoulders and lowering their heads — the antithesis of the pride expression.

The same results emerged across gender. Male and female athletes
were equally likely to display pride in response to success. Next, the big
question: Would this result hold across cultures?

There was good reason to think that these athletes' nationality
might influence their tendency to display pride. A large body of evidence from research on cultural psychology has shown that while we
individualistic Westerners love to self-enhance — we do anything and
everything we can to feel good about ourselves, and often successfully
convince ourselves that we're better than most others around us — collectivistic Easterners are more likely to self-efface. This cultural diver-
gence is nicely captured by the difference between the Western adage
"The squeaky wheel gets the grease" and the comparable Asian sentiment "The nail that stands out gets hammered down." Pride is, undoubtedly, much more about squeaking for attention and standing out
than getting hammered down; we feel pride when we feel good about

ourselves, and displaying the pride expression tells others how great we think we are. A cultural psychologist might therefore expect to find a difference between the pride displays shown by Asian and American athletes.

But despite the vast cultural variation among the athletes in our study, the winners all displayed the same pride expression. We had photos of individuals from thirty-six countries on six continents, yet there was no relation between an athlete's culture and his or her tendency to display pride; Chinese, Japanese, and Korean winners were just as likely to show the pride expression as Americans, Canadians, Estonians, Mexicans, and Austrians. To really push the issue, I divided the sample into categories based on how collectivistic or individualistic each athlete's home nation was according to collectivism and individualism scores available for every country in the world. I then re-ran my basic comparison — pride displays of winners versus losers — within each subsample. The same pattern emerged. Even looking *only* at athletes from highly collectivistic countries (which, based on the previously derived worldwide scores, were Brazil, Bulgaria, China, Greece, Iran, Japan, South Korea, Portugal, Russia, and Taiwan), winners were still significantly more likely to show pride than losers.

This result tells us that the pride expression is not simply a readily identifiable icon that people all over the world are familiar with. It is a behavioral response that people all over the world *actually display* after a success.

But all of this evidence for the universality of pride displays is still not quite enough to prove that humans everywhere display pride following a success *because* doing so is an evolved part of our nature. Recall how important it was that we made sure our Burkinabé participants had minimal exposure to Western culture. Here, we were examining behaviors shown by Olympic athletes — people who'd spent plenty of time observing the nonverbal displays of other athletes from all over the world. Their prideful responses to victory might have been a result of their biologically endowed human nature, but they might also have been a result of learning. Showing your pride is, after all, what you're supposed to do when you win an Olympic medal.

How to surmount this last hurdle? Essentially, the only test subjects who could tell us that pride displays are innate rather than learned were people who had never seen a Western pride expression. If people like that responded to success by displaying exactly that expression, it would prove, fairly conclusively, that pride is a universal human emotion.

Fortuitously, Matsumoto had exactly what we needed: a new set of photos, taken by the same official Judo Federation photographer, but this time featuring *blind* athletes competing in the Paralympic Games. Some of these individuals had acquired their blindness late in life, but we focused on the small subset of athletes who were congenitally blind and so had unquestionably *never* seen a Western — or any culture's — pride expression. These were people who *could not have learned to show pride from watching others.* Though this was a tiny group of only twelve competitors, six of them happened to be match winners, and six were match losers. Comparing the behaviors shown by these two groups of six revealed that after winning a match, congenitally blind athletes broke into that same reliably recognized, chest-expanded, shoulders-back, smiling display. As can be seen from figure 1.4, the pride expression shown by a born-blind athlete is indistinguishable

Figure 1.4. Pride displays spontaneously shown in response to victory at the Olympic and Paralympic Games by a sighted (left) and a congenitally blind (right) athlete

from that of an athlete who's seen that same expression many thousands of times.

Together, the results from these studies leave little room for doubt. Pride *is* part of human nature. The emotion that motivates humans to do the things we care most about and that make us feel like our lives have meaning is part of our species' naturally evolved repertoire. The reason that Dean Karnazes runs, that my dad reads, that Gauguin painted, and that I quit making lattes is that we are all driven by a powerful internal force that compels us to seek out more — to do whatever we need to do to experience pride. We are hardwired to feel this force, and it propels us to become people we can feel good about. In the long run, following our pride has adaptive benefits; as we will see, the identity and meaning that pride helps us find is, ultimately, good for our genes.

But first, we need to ask: What exactly *is* this emotion that carries so much weight in the daily lives of humans everywhere? What does it mean, really, to say that you feel proud of yourself? Try saying it out loud: "I'm proud of myself." It's a bold statement — a claim that makes many uncomfortable — and, partly for that reason, it's a much more complicated statement than it may at first seem. As we will see in the next chapter, although pride is universal and ubiquitous, it has more than a single simple meaning and, as a result, more than a single simple effect on human lives.

2

A Virtuous Sin

WHAT IS THE first word you think of when you think of pride? If your mind jumps immediately to your last big accomplishment — maybe you secured a new client at work or finally finished an important and time-consuming project — your answer might be something like *achievement,* or *accomplished,* or even *confident.* And, in fact, these are apt descriptions for the thoughts and feelings that accompany typical experiences of that seventh basic emotion.

But it's also possible that, when asked this question, you think first of that time you were, perhaps, a little *too* proud of yourself. Maybe it was after you beat a good friend at an intense game of chess and felt the need to victory-dance around the room. Or maybe the question prompts thoughts not of yourself, but of someone else — for instance, that colleague at work who always makes sure to point out his successes and take credit for every team triumph. If *these* are the images that spring to mind when you're asked this question, then the first word that comes into your head might be less commendable and desirable — and less obviously adaptive — than *achieving* or *confident;* perhaps instead you think of a word like *arrogant,* or *conceited,* or even *cocky.*

In fact, the various words that people use to talk about pride are not all simple synonyms, like *fearful* and *afraid*, or variants of the same emotion that differ in degree, like *anger* and *rage*. There also seem to be many more words for pride than for these other emotions. If I ask a roomful of college students to identify the nonverbal expression of pride and label it with any words they choose, I might find myself with a hundred different responses. There would be words like *achieving, accomplished, confident,* and *successful* — all positive states that most people want to feel — but also words like *arrogant, pretentious, conceited,* and *smug,* states that can be pleasurable but that many of us try to avoid, or at least don't readily admit to feeling.

All these words have something in common: they all describe how people feel when they feel good about themselves. But they also differ from one another in a clear-cut and seemingly meaningful way. And they differ from one another much more than the collection of words we typically use to describe other basic emotions like anger or fear. Pride, it seems, is more complicated to define than the other universal feelings.

In other languages, the complexity of defining pride is even more apparent. Take Italian, which has *two* translations for *pride: fierezza* and *orgoglio*. These are not synonyms, nor do they connote a distinction in intensity. No, these are actually two different emotional experiences — two different ways of feeling proud. *Fierezza* is a bold and excited kind of pride, the term stemming from the same Latin origin (*ferus*) as the English word that's been widely adopted by fashion reality-show hosts — *fierce*. *Orgoglio,* which stems from the Germanic root *urgol* (meaning "distinguished"), is more negative. Italians don't typically use the word *orgoglio* to refer to themselves; they more often apply it to someone else who seems proud, and they don't mean it in a nice way. This same distinction exists in many other languages too. For the French, it's *fierté* and *orgueil*. In Arabic it's *al-kibr* and *al-fakhr*. Spanish has only one word for *pride* — *orgullo* — but that word alone has two distinct meanings; one is, roughly, a sense of accomplishment, and the other is the appearance of egotism or vanity.

English, like Spanish, captures all these nuances — accomplished, fierce, bold, distinguished, and arrogant — with the single word *pride*. This is a word with origins in eleventh- and twelfth-century Old French, which used *prud* (or *prouz*) to mean "brave" or "valiant." At that time, the term apparently had no negative connotations; the Norman knights of the era applied it to themselves, and proudly. Later on the Anglo-Saxons used the same word to (more negatively) describe the army that was invading them.

Consistent with this multiplicity of meaning, *Merriam-Webster's Dictionary* lists two definitions for the English word *pride* — and two that could not be more antagonistic. The first is "inordinate self-esteem/conceit." The second? "A reasonable or justifiable self-respect." So, pride is about self-esteem or self-worth — feeling good about oneself — but, according to our most respected dictionary, that same word refers to both a reasonable amount of those good feelings about oneself and an inordinate or *excessive* amount of those feelings.* This makes *pride*, for lack of a better word, weird. If you look up *anger* in the dictionary, you won't find two definitions, one for when it's justified and one for when it's out of hand. In both cases, anger is anger.

In fact, this complexity has been part of the emotion's history since the dawn of Western civilization. A first glance at ancient intellectual history points to a straightforwardly negative view of pride, consistent with the dictionary's "inordinate conceit" definition. Much of this negativity comes from religion; Christian thinkers have long associated pride with the sin of refusing to respect God's power. In addition to the famous biblical proverb "Pride goes before destruction, a haughty spirit before a fall" (Proverbs 16:18), many of the best-known early Christian scholars — Saint Augustine, Thomas Aquinas, and Pope Gregory I — characterized pride as, variously, "the queen of sin," "the beginning of all sin," and "the root of all evil." For Dante, pride was the deadliest of the seven deadly sins. In his *Divine Comedy*, the pun-

---

* Consistent with earlier views, the original 1828 dictionary by Noah Webster placed much greater emphasis on the first definition. The second definition, which is more consistent with contemporary Western views of the word, is largely a modification made by the Merriam brothers.

ishment for pride was carrying a stone slab on one's neck, forcing the head to turn downward and preventing the sinner from standing upright or puffing out his chest in a classic pride display.

But ancient Christians were not the only early scholars to hate on pride. Buddhists referred to pride as one of the "ten fetters" that shackled an individual to samsara, an endless cycle of suffering. Chinese philosopher Lao-tzu, author of the *Tao Te Ching,* described pride as a recipe for failure and death. For ancient Greeks like Plato, Homer, Aeschylus, and Herodotus, pride was hubris — a force powerful enough to destroy the political order.

But despite this overwhelming negativity, there was one early philosopher who expressed a more positive view of the emotion. According to the famous Greek thinker Aristotle, pride was a virtue, not a vice. Aristotle argued that proud people were those who had the perspective to appropriately appreciate and acknowledge their own greatness. In his view, to be proud was to be great *and* unafraid to say so.

Much later, French philosopher Jean-Jacques Rousseau also proposed a more nuanced account, distinguishing between what he called *amour-propre* and *amour de soi.* The latter, Rousseau argued, was a "natural sentiment which inclines every animal to watch over its own preservation." Even in the uncivilized state of nature, humans would experience *amour de soi.* It's our survival instinct — the thing that makes (some of) us willing to cut off an arm or eat other humans, if times get really tough. *Amour-propre,* in contrast, is "a relative sentiment, artificial and born in society, which inclines each individual to have a greater esteem for himself than for anyone else." That might sound like the dictionary's "inordinate conceit" definition, but Rousseau went further. He suggested that *amour-propre* "is the true source of honor" — it's what motivates people to *care* about how others see them and how they see themselves in comparison to others. This is the pride that makes people want to be "good" — or, as Rousseau understood it, valued by society. So maybe *amour-propre* is excessive pride, but, according to Rousseau, in order to flourish in the company of others, we need it.

Taken together, these prescientific conceptualizations present a somewhat confusing picture of pride. To the religious thinkers, pride is sinful, but to the philosophers, it's a necessary evil, or maybe even a good in itself—a positive force for society. Turning back to the dictionary, perhaps the answer depends on whether a person's pride is excessive or reasonable, on whether it's unwarranted or merited.

What we need in order to clear up this confusion is science. Theologians and philosophers can argue all day long about what pride *should* be or how we should understand it, but empirical data, of the sort that psychological scientists collect, can tell us what pride actually *is*.

So how have psychologists conceptualized pride? The truth is, for the most part, they haven't. Prior to 2000, there was almost no psychological research on pride. In the 1990s, this meant fewer than three published papers a year. That's not nothing, but given the many tens of thousands of psychology research articles that appear annually (179,032 in 2013, according to the PsycINFO database), it's an extremely small number. By comparison, in the same time frame, there were about twenty-six published articles a year on anger and forty-one on fear. Psychologists were devoting a great deal of research attention, time, and money to their newly founded field of affective science, but one affect, in particular, got left behind.

Fortunately, though, plenty of psychological scientists in the 1990s *were* studying a topic very much related to pride: narcissism. And as we will see, their efforts to understand this often-dysfunctional set of personality processes laid the groundwork for current research into pride, an effort that commenced in full force at the beginning of the new millennium.

In 1976, a twenty-eight-year-old Arnold Schwarzenegger told *Rolling Stone* magazine, "Around the time of grammar school I had this incredible desire to be recognized . . . I didn't care about the money, I thought about the fame, about just being the greatest. I was dreaming about being some dictator of a country or some savior like Jesus. Just to be recognized."

This statement suggests a fairly extreme — even delusional — level of self-regard, but a level that's not unusual for individuals who, like

Schwarzenegger, fit the personality profile known as narcissism. We all know the type. It's not just that they feel good about themselves; it's that they have a seemingly insatiable need to demonstrate how *great* they feel about themselves, all the time. And as the rest of us can see, the way these individuals see themselves doesn't match up to reality. Narcissists think they're better than they actually are, and — even more annoyingly — they think they're better than everyone else around them too.

To be clear, narcissists are not losers — in fact, in certain domains, like politics, narcissists tend to be quite successful. Bill Clinton, who never missed an opportunity to extoll his successes in office, was determined on the basis of personality ratings made by 121 presidential experts to be only the seventh-most-narcissistic president in American history (Lyndon B. Johnson was the first). Narcissists also aren't simply arrogant boors — they can be charming and engaging, even the life of the party. The narcissist is that person in your social circle who always seems to take control of the conversation and demonstrates an almost desperate need to stay at the center of attention. (If you can't think of any narcissist in your circle, I've got bad news: it's probably you.)

While psychologists in the 1980s and 1990s were *not* studying pride, they *were* devoting a great deal of research attention to narcissists — a group of people who seem to feel, on a frequent and intense basis, something that strongly resembles pride. Narcissism looks a lot like one definition of *pride* in particular — the one characterized by words like *arrogant* and *cocky* and that, to Italians, is *orgoglio.* Narcissists are people who radiate the dictionary's first definition of *pride* — "inordinate conceit."

What is it that makes narcissists behave the way they do — charming and extraverted on the one hand, but off-putting and aggressive on the other? And how do others respond to these behaviors? Do narcissists get away with their excessive arrogance or do they face social punishment? Psychologists in the 1990s became fascinated by these questions, and the psychology of narcissism became (and continues to be) a blooming area of research. These experiments were not geared toward understanding pride, per se, but their findings are nonetheless informative for the question of why pride seems to sometimes mean arrogance.

In one illuminative study, small groups of students were gathered together for twenty minutes each week over a period of seven weeks to chat about various topics, things like their friends and families or their deepest worries and concerns. In the early weeks of the study, the students who scored high on a measure of narcissism (a measure that asks people to endorse items such as "If I ruled the world, it would be a much better place") were well liked — even admired — by the others in their group. They were perceived as friendly, agreeable, hard-working, and psychologically well adjusted.

By the end of the study, however, the group had done a 180. After seven weeks of getting-to-know-you conversations, the narcissists' peers came to see these individuals as disagreeable and aggressive, prone to fits of anger and anxiety, and not so well adjusted after all.

This change of heart makes sense. Early on, narcissists take control and lead the conversation when no one else will. Even though their favorite topic is themselves, others don't mind; listening to a narcissist brag is often preferable to an awkward silence, and a group member who can be relied on to run the show is a valuable asset. These traits make narcissists popular and powerful, as witnessed in American presidential politics; not only is a narcissist more likely than a non-narcissist to become president, but those presidents who are most narcissistic tend to win more of the popular vote and pass more legislation.

Eventually, though, things change. Engaging and commanding at first, narcissists reveal a different side to those who stick around long enough to get to know them well. Over time, narcissists become hostile, insulting, and aggressive. These behaviors are particularly pronounced when others question their overweening self-views — something that probably doesn't happen often to a Clinton or a Schwarzenegger but is a regular occurrence for the more average narcissist. And even for the Clintons among us, narcissism can be a risk factor. Despite their initial popularity, the most narcissistic presidents are also the ones most likely to face impeachment.

In a study documenting the narcissistic tendency to become angry and aggressive when faced with criticism, college students were assigned to write an essay that took a position on one of the hottest topics of the day: a woman's right to abortion. The researchers told these participants that they would receive feedback on their essays from another person in the study, an individual whom they had never met and never would meet. In actuality, there was no such person, and all feedback was predetermined by the researchers. Some participants thus found their returned essays covered in negative red marks along with the comment *This is one of the worst essays I've ever read!* Others received more positive ratings and the comment *No suggestions, great essay!*

Participants were next told that they'd be playing a computer game against the person who had just either criticized them or heaped on the praise. The goal of the game was to respond to images that appeared onscreen more quickly than one's opponent. For each round they won, participants could press a button that would blast the loser with punishing noise. They got to set the volume of the noise, and the researchers used this setting — how loudly participants wanted to blast their opponents — to measure the participants' desire to hurt the person who had just insulted or complimented them.

Not surprisingly, subjects whose essays had been criticized blasted their imaginary opponents more loudly than did subjects whose essays had been praised. No one likes to be insulted. But, much more interestingly, this tendency was particularly pronounced for the narcissists in the group. For these individuals, the anger they felt at being challenged made them want to lash out and aggressively punish the challenger.

This general principle — that narcissists react to perceived threats against their ego with intensified anger and aggression — has been replicated many times. Narcissists who feel criticized will not only blast loud noise to retaliate against a perceived offending party but also give that unlucky person a large dose of extra-spicy hot sauce. One study found that narcissists would dose another participant with hot sauce even when they'd been informed that this particular individual didn't

like spicy foods and *especially* if the participant had written on a preference sheet, *Don't be a jerk and give me something I don't like!*

Now, you might be thinking, why *shouldn't* narcissists behave this
way? These are people who believe that they're better than the feedback they're getting suggests, and that has to be frustrating. Indeed,
narcissists often *are* every bit as smart, creative, and successful as they
think they are; Clinton and Schwarzenegger are good examples. But
this isn't always the case. Narcissism is not intrinsically linked to being
talented, smart, or skilled in any particular way, and narcissists are just
as likely to be great as not so great. Furthermore, narcissistic aggression is not tied to objective measures of competence or intelligence;
it's not that narcissists become especially angry when they're insulted
in domains where they clearly deserve better treatment. Rather, narcissists simply can't deal with any negative feedback — in any domain
they might have staked their ego on — at all.

A better explanation for the narcissistic tendency to go on the attack when faced with threat comes from psychoanalytic theory — the
school of psychological thought initiated by Sigmund Freud. According to psychoanalysts, narcissistic aggression is best understood as a
Freudian defense mechanism known as *reaction formation*. The basic idea is that one very powerful way to cope with a threatening belief is to deny it and simultaneously espouse its opposite — often ve-
hemently. Think of the closeted gay politician who votes for antigay
policies, or the guy who's planning to propose to his girlfriend but decides he's dodged a bullet when she breaks up with him first. In the
case of narcissism, the theory of reaction formation would suggest that
narcissists' extreme arrogance is *not* a genuine expression of high self-
regard. No, according to this theory, narcissists don't fight when they
feel attacked because they so strongly believe that they're smarter and
better than their attacker. Instead, they fight because they *actually believe the opposite*. Narcissism, the psychoanalytic view holds, is a defensive strategy used to counter unconscious insecurities. The pride
that narcissists feel is false; it is psychologically manufactured to help
bury feelings of shame.

This might sound counterintuitive (in fact, much of psychoanalytic

theory *is* counterintuitive), but think about it for a moment. If someone you've never met insults an essay you spent about five minutes
writing as part of a study you're participating in purely for the sake
of getting some extra course credit, would you really care enough to
want to cause this person intense ear pain? Might you instead think to
yourself, *What does he know?* Or even *I guess it wasn't such a great essay
— after all, I spent only five minutes on it.* To put it another way, what
would make you want to lash out with a blast of especially loud noise
or extra-spicy hot sauce?

As it turns out, a good deal of evidence supports the idea that
narcissism is, at least in part, a reaction to deep-seated insecurities.
Those who feel the need to attack their challengers tend to be driven
by something other than a genuine and staunch belief in their own
greatness. Although narcissists overtly express an overbearing sense
of grandiosity and arrogance, at an implicit — or unconscious — level,
they demonstrate the opposite: low self-esteem. One study found that
while narcissists scored high on measures of explicit self-esteem —
measures asking people to endorse items like "I take a positive attitude
toward myself" — they simultaneously scored *low* on an implicit measure of self-esteem, which assesses how quickly people associate words
like *me, myself,* and *I* with words like *cockroach* and *vomit.* In fact, the
worse narcissists felt about themselves on an implicit level — that is,
the quicker they were to associate *me* with *cockroach* — the better they
claimed to feel about themselves on an explicit level.

This is exactly what Freud would predict; it's a perfect demonstra-
tion of reaction formation. The worse narcissists feel about themselves unconsciously, the more they exaggerate how great they are
consciously. This explains why narcissists regularly express excessively
positive self-perceptions yet also have an excessive need to make sure
everyone else around agrees with those views. It also explains why narcissists respond defensively — by becoming aggressive — when their
greatness is questioned. Deep down, at an implicit level, narcissists feel
bad about themselves, and any indication that others might feel the
same activates their worst fears.

The unconscious nature of these feelings is exactly the problem.

If narcissists were more aware of their implicit low self-esteem, they would not display the same kind of aggressive response to ego threats. People with *explicit* low self-esteem — those who tell researchers that they do *not* "take a positive attitude" toward themselves — don't lash out in anger when they feel challenged. Similarly, people who genuinely believe in their own self-worth also don't become hostile when others insult them. They may decide that those others are wrong and choose not to befriend them, but they feel no need to physically harm them. The best explanation for narcissists' fierce motivation to punish people who threaten their grandiose self-perceptions is that these perceptions are the only thing protecting narcissists from deeply hidden feelings of shame.

In short, narcissists' extreme arrogance is a cover-up. It's an emotional tool that's used to counter unconscious insecurities. The pride that narcissists experience — a pride that's best summed up with words like *arrogance, conceit*, and, in Italy, *orgoglio* — is not about feeling good; it's about *avoiding feeling bad.*

To be sure, there are people out there — many people — who feel good about themselves in a way that's *not* defensive. On average, just over half of the world population agrees with the statement "I have high self-esteem." Some of these individuals are narcissists, but most authentically like themselves and aren't overexaggerating their positive self-perceptions in order to defend against implicit insecurities. While narcissists also agree with statements like "I know that I am good because everybody keeps telling me so," those with high self-esteem are more likely to simply say, "I feel that I'm a person of worth, at least on an equal basis with others."

High self-esteem is exactly that — the feeling of being "good enough." The old *Saturday Night Live* skit where Al Franken played fictional self-help guru Stuart Smalley nicely captures this sentiment. In his daily affirmations, Smalley would try to boost his self-esteem with a motivational mantra (spoken aloud into a mirror): "I'm good enough, I'm smart enough, and, doggone it, people like me!"

People with high self-esteem clearly feel pride, but it's not the same kind of pride that narcissists feel. This is the pride that's best represented by words like *accomplished* and *productive*, or even *confident* and *worthy*. It's the pride that Italians call *fierezza* and that the dictionary defines as "reasonable or justifiable self-respect." People who feel this kind of pride, quite simply, like themselves.

Studies have shown that there are enormous benefits to this kind of genuine self-liking. Adolescents with high self-esteem grow up to be adults who are happy and healthy and unlikely to suffer from obesity or heart or lung disease. They go on to college, become successful in their careers, and end up financially well off. On the flip side, thirteen-year-olds with low self-esteem are more likely to grow up to lead a life of crime. Feeling genuinely good about yourself — feeling that fierce, confident, and achieving version of pride — is good for you, and it's clearly much better for you than feeling not so good, or even bad, about yourself.

In contrast to people who are genuinely high in self-esteem, narcissists experience pride in a way that's problematic. It makes them arrogant and aggressive and can cost them friends and relationships. This is a very different set of outcomes from those encountered by the high-self-esteem set, whose pride allows them to become healthy, happy, popular, and successful. It would seem, then, that there are two drastically different ways of responding to the same emotion.

Perhaps the answer to the question of what pride is and why it's been conceptualized in such different ways throughout history lies in *this* distinction. If pride is the emotion underlying narcissism — that is, the core motivator of narcissistic behaviors — then pride promotes aggression, hostility, and general jerkiness. But if pride is the emotion that shapes high self-esteem, then pride should motivate achievement, success, and healthy living. Which is it? Or could the answer be that *pride is two different things?*

Most people have heard the myth that the Inuit (sometimes known as Eskimo) have one hundred different words for *snow*. Although it's an exaggeration — many scholars argue that the Inuit have roughly the same number of root words for *snow* as English speakers do — it's repeated often because it makes an important point. We create the language we need to talk about the things that matter in our lives. For the Inuit, snow is much more than just some cold white stuff that leads to canceled school days, bad driving, and a merry Christmas, so the Inuit need more than a single word to talk about it. By paying attention to these words, we can learn about what matters most in daily Inuit life.

In the same way, the words that people use to describe their feelings provide a telling window into how they think about these feelings. If a feeling is important, we'll have a word for it. If it's very important, we'll have many words for it. And if it's important in more than one way, we'll have distinct sets of words for it.

To figure out how people — not theologians and philosophers, but ordinary folks — think about what pride *is,* my graduate school adviser Rick Robins and I decided to study the way they talk about it. We asked a sample of undergraduates to write down every word that came to mind when they thought about what pride means and how it feels. Posing this question to several hundred UC Davis students, we found ourselves with a massive list of 795 different words and phrases. We cut out all the words that were mentioned by fewer than 2 percent of the sample, to get rid of the more idiosyncratic suggestions (for example, *enlightened*). This got us down to sixty-five.

Now, this does not mean that the English language includes sixty-five different ways of feeling pride. What's much more likely is that many of these words cluster together to form distinct categories of meaning. In the same way, although Inuit languages provide a quick and easy means of verbally distinguishing between snow that's falling, new snow that's lying softly on the ground, and hardened snow that leaves a deep icy hole when you step through it, Inuit people — like most Northeastern and Midwestern Americans — are readily aware of the similarities between these various snow forms and can make mental categories on that basis. While the Inuit may benefit from a language that allows them to indicate with a single word that it's currently snowing, they also recognize that the fluffy stuff coming down is the very same stuff that backcountry skiers are desperate to shred. Put simply, even though Inuit people can use distinct words to describe distinct forms or states of snow, they also know that these forms are not entirely separate and that some are more interrelated, or overlapping, than others.

The same is likely to be true for the sixty-five pride words our research participants generated. The large majority of these words are almost certainly related to one another in some systematic way. To figure out how people intuitively associate or categorize these words, we asked a new sample of undergrads to rate how similar each word was to every other word. We then plugged their ratings into a statistical program that spit out a "pride map" — a visual representation of these students' assessment of the semantic interrelatedness of the words we had entered (shown in figure 2.1 for twenty pride words). In this map, words that are closer together are semantically more similar.

If you look closely at this figure, something interesting quickly becomes apparent. The twenty words pictured here seem to cluster into two distinct groups, one on the top, and one on the bottom, and

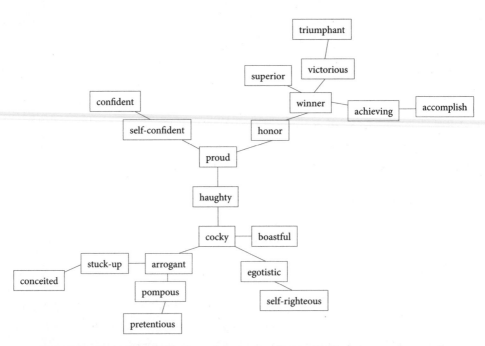

Figure 2.1. Semantic similarity among 20 pride words. Only 20 words were included in this study, reducing the number of ratings participants were asked to make to 190 (the sum of all possible pair combinations for 20 words).

they're separated by that central word *proud*. And the words that appear in the upper half of the figure suggest a concept that is notably different from what's suggested by the words in the bottom. Looking even more closely and with an eye toward figuring out what binds the words in each cluster together, you might be reminded of the distinction between narcissism and more genuine self-esteem, or between the dictionary's two definitions of *pride*.

Together, these twenty words characterize the feelings we'd expect of people who have high self-esteem *and* the feelings we'd expect of narcissists. But that central word *proud* demarks a major semantic separation between these two sets of feelings. All the words in the top half fit well with a classic understanding of high self-esteem, *fierezza,* and *Webster's* second definition. All the words in the bottom half could readily be applied to a narcissist, someone who is feeling *orgoglio,* or *Webster's* first definition. What this map tells us, then, is that, at least in terms of the way people understand and think about pride words, there really are two different kinds of pride, and they appear to break down into roughly positive and negative categories.

But this conclusion is based on a map of people's semantic representations — how people *think* about pride. It doesn't necessarily mean that people also *feel* pride in these two different ways. Thoughts and words are a useful window into reality, but that window can be distorted. When it comes to felt emotional experiences, cognitive conceptualizations are only one source of information. It's possible that people think about pride in terms of two separate things but during actual pride experiences — *pride feelings* — these things come together with no real distinction between them.

To address this possibility head-on, we asked undergraduates to think about a time in their lives when they had *actually felt* pride and then to relive it by writing about the events surrounding the experience. This is a well-honed psychological research method for eliciting emotions; it turns out that simply asking participants to describe in great detail a past emotional event reliably produces within these individuals a re-experience of the feelings that went along with the event, often even including emotion-related physiology like increased heart rate when writing about a fear-inducing event or increased finger temperature (as blood rushes to the extremities, preparing for action) when writing about an angering event.

In our study, asking undergraduate participants to recall a time when they had experienced pride led them to write about events such as this one: *I was awarded the All-League Honor. I had worked hard to play well, and when the Honor was announced, I felt proud of myself. The years of practice and hard work had paid off.* After writing short narratives like this, our participants viewed a long list of emotion words — including all sixty-five pride words we had collected — and rated, on a scale from 1 (meaning "not at all") to 5 (meaning "very much"), the extent to which each word characterized their feelings.

Our question was whether our participants' emotion ratings would reveal a similar pattern to what we'd found in other undergraduates' semantic associations. Would someone who gave a 5 to a word like *accomplished* also give a high score to a word like *confident*? And would she be just as likely to give a high score to a word like *cocky*? We used a statistical approach known as factor analysis to quantitatively determine which words most often co-occurred — that is, clumped together — in participants' descriptions of their prideful memories.

The results were striking. Participants' pride feelings elicited by their memories of past pride experiences formed exactly the same pattern as these words did in other students' ratings of their semantic similarity. Once again, two separate categories of words emerged. And the content of those categories was becoming more than a little familiar. Words like *achieving, accomplished,* and *productive* always occurred together, along with words like *confidence* and *self-worth*. Words like *arrogance* and *egotism* formed a separate category, along with words like *conceited, cocky, smug,* and *pretentious*.

What this means is that the distinction between these two kinds of pride is not just a result of the way people *think* about pride; the distinction is intrinsic to *what pride is* and how it feels. Using these results, we could differentiate between participants who tended to endorse the *achieving-accomplished-productive* feelings and those who were more likely to report the *arrogant-egotistical-smug* feelings. The participant who wrote about winning the All-League Honor had a no-tably high score on that first dimension. But other participants scored higher on the second. There was, for example, the young woman who wrote, *I felt very proud of myself when I got a 4.0 GPA. I would initiate conversations by asking groups of people how they did last quarter. After hearing their response, I would obviously mention my success.*

The way that these two students — the All-League Honor winner and the perfect-GPA achiever — talked about their pride could not have been more different. Yet both were responding to the same ques-tion; both were writing about a relived pride experience.

The results of our analyses explain how this can be. Pride is not one thing. It is two things, and two things that are distinct in a meaning-ful way. The two dimensions we'd found in our factor analyses were only slightly positively correlated with each other, meaning that the tendency to feel one of the two prides was not particularly related to the tendency to feel the other. When people feel pride, they are just as likely to feel one type and not the other as they are to feel both together.

But this doesn't mean that we can't differentiate between the kinds of people who most typically feel each. Using the words that best rep-resented each pride dimension (for example, *accomplished, confident,* and *successful* versus *arrogant, conceited,* and *stuck-up*), we developed scales, standardized tools to assess any person's tendency to experience one form of pride or the other. Confirming our suspicions, partici-pants who received high scores on our scale measuring the confident and achieving kind of pride also tended to have high self-esteem. Par-ticipants who scored high on the arrogant and egotistical pride were more likely to be narcissistic and low in self-esteem. The kind of pride a person regularly feels, in other words, is linked to the kind of person-ality she has.

Of course, we can't know from these correlations whether pride causes these personality differences or is merely associated with them. Theoretically speaking, although there is good reason to think that frequent experiences of authentic pride would foster long-term self-esteem while experiences of hubristic pride would forge a narcissis-tic personality, it's just as likely that the causal relationship goes in the other direction, that having a narcissistic personality makes certain people prone to experiencing hubristic pride, while those who can maintain a more genuine sense of high self-esteem regularly experience authentic pride instead. But what is certain is that the kind of pride that's linked to self-esteem is different from the kind of pride that's linked to narcissism, and this tells us that pride — or, more accurately, the *distinction between the two prides* — is at least one of the things that separates these two personalities. Even if we don't know why — that is, what causes what — we now know that one critical difference between narcissists and people with genuine high self-esteem is the way these people experience pride, the emotion that's central to both dispositions.

If only we were more like the Italians, we'd be able to easily talk about and understand this distinction between the pride that's linked to self-esteem and the pride that's linked to narcissism. These two prides *are* different, that much is clear — yet in English, they bear the same name. This presents a problem for anyone who wants to learn more about pride, be it a psychologist like myself or someone who'd simply like to steer clear of the narcissistic pride and seek out the more positive kind. We probably don't need one hundred words for pride, but two would be helpful.

In many ways, the perfect name for the more arrogant form of pride already exists, because the ancient Greeks came up with it thousands of years ago: *hubris*. The Greeks applied this word to people whose overweening self-perceptions led them to forget that they were mere mortals; the classic example is the mythic Icarus, whose father built him wings that he used to fly too close to the sun. *Hubristic pride* perfectly captures the emotion that's conveyed by the words that cluster in this category. And, fittingly, psychologists have now largely settled on this term as the handle for the more negative, narcissistic form of the emotion.

Unfortunately, though, the other, more positive kind of pride defies such easy labeling. There is no mythologically meaningful, non-hubristic equivalent for the kind of pride that's linked to self-esteem. *Ar-*

istotelian pride has the requisite Greek connotations and nicely nods to Aristotle's conceptualization of pride as an accurate assessment of one's own worth, but understanding the significance of this label requires a fairly detailed knowledge of ancient Greek philosophy, making it a somewhat pretentious (and potentially hubristic?) option. There's also the fact that *Aristotelian* doesn't exactly roll off the tongue.

But there is a word that emphasizes the distinction between this kind of pride and the narcissistic origins of hubristic pride. It's a label that makes a theoretical point: that this other kind of pride is based on relatively accurate — rather than enhanced — assessments of one's self and thus on a genuine and authentic perception of one's self-worth. *Authentic pride* is the term that has come to be an accepted label for this other category of pride.

These two labels — *hubristic* and *authentic* — suggest that the distinction between the two kinds of pride is about much more than words. It's a distinction in how the experience feels and how it makes people feel about themselves and others. It's even about the kind of people they are. In fact, those who regularly experience authentic pride tend to have a very different personality profile than those who regularly experience hubristic pride. The authentic pride–prone are outgoing and friendly, agreeable, calm and anxiety-free, creative, and popular. They want to help and advise others and often volunteer their time to do so. They are generally communally oriented, meaning that they place a high value on their relationships and friendships. Perhaps as a result, they tend to be very satisfied with these relationships and with life in general.

In contrast, those prone to hubristic pride are not only narcissistic and low in self-esteem but also vulnerable to bouts of shame. They can be disagreeable, aggressive, hostile, and manipulative, and, perhaps as a result, they tend to have fraught relationships and few close friends. They're more interested in derogating and taking advantage of others than helping them. They also experience social anxiety and in some cases even clinical depression.

But despite these arguably massive differences, people who tend to experience one or the other of the prides also have a few things in common. Both demonstrate a desire to get things done and have an impact on the world. Both seek and pursue rewards and strive to get what they want. But even these similarities — this shared drive to get ahead — play out differently for the authentically proud than they do for the hubristically proud. Those prone to authentic pride have a high level of self-control and an ability to avoid acting impulsively — two traits critical to actually accomplishing one's goals. Those prone to hubristic pride are more impulsive — motivated, perhaps, by their outsize egos instead of a rational assessment of how and when to act — and thus have a harder time regulating their attention and behavior. Think of that colleague at work who has big ideas and big plans but somehow fails to produce big results.

The two prides are also linked to different ways of dealing with failure and success. Those who tend toward authentic pride can put their failures in perspective. They acknowledge them but treat them as temporary setbacks and are soon ready to tackle new goals. Those prone to hubristic pride do not respond as smoothly. Their problems begin with a tendency to set unrealistically high goals, consistent with their often-desperate desire for fame and fortune (think of Schwarzenegger's aim of becoming like Jesus). Although they typically fail to achieve these absurd heights, they disregard those failures and distract themselves by interpreting any minor success — or even any ambiguously positive event — as a sign of their excellence. They endorse questionnaire items like "When an attractive person smiles at me, I can tell it means she is hot for me" and "If someone praises the way I express something, it makes me think of writing a book."

Obviously, the tendency to feel authentic pride is very different from the tendency to feel hubristic pride. But it's not clear whether these different pride feelings are the *cause* of these different personalities; that is, whether authentically proud people are caring, friendly, and hardworking *because* of their authentic pride. As every student of behavioral science knows, correlation does not equal causation. Indeed, it's almost certain that things go in the opposite direction, at least some of the time — that a person's stable personality influences which kind of pride she regularly experiences. But we might still wonder whether feelings of authentic pride could directly motivate prosocial behaviors, and whether hubristic pride could motivate the antisocial hostility and even aggression that tend to characterize people who regularly experience this version of the emotion.

Though it seems unlikely that a single pride experience could trigger prosocial or antisocial behaviors, we decided to test this possibility. If the links between pride and personality *are* due in part to the motivational impact of pride — that is, if pride causes a specific personality — then single, momentary experiences of each kind of pride should lead people to engage in different kinds of behavior. Feelings of authentic pride might make people behave in a more prosocial way. Feelings of hubristic pride might make people more antisocial.

Because we wanted to establish a particular causal direction — to know whether pride *causes* certain behaviors — we experimentally manipulated pride experiences. We again used the relived emotion task — the one where participants write about a past event in which they felt pride — but this time we induced in these individuals specific kinds of pride, either authentic or hubristic. Some were assigned to recall "a time when you felt like you had succeeded through hard work and effort, reached your potential, or achieved a goal." Others recalled "a time when you behaved in a self-important manner, or felt pretentious or stuck-up."

Next, all of these participants were placed in a situation where they could choose to be prosocial (kind and empathic) or antisocial (hostile and derogating). Specifically, we asked them to make evaluations about members of ethnic groups that were different from their own. People belonging to different groups — and particularly those that are different in a way that's stigmatized by mainstream society — are easy targets for individuals looking to boost their own self-worth by putting others down. This is a form of prejudice, and it's one that narcissists regularly engage in.

We wondered whether hubristic pride might be the emotion that drives this process, that pushes narcissists to make prejudicial judgments against these easy targets. Hubristic feelings of superiority and arrogance might convince individuals that they *are* better than others, especially if those others belong to a group that's already a target of animosity. Add to that the feelings of shame and anxiety that tend to accompany hubristic pride and the defensiveness triggered by those feelings, and we might reasonably expect hubristic pride to prompt normally nonprejudiced individuals to take advantage of any opportunity they can find to insult those who are different from them.

Authentic pride, in contrast, should have the opposite effect. The genuine feelings of self-worth and confidence that come with authentic pride should reduce any need to defensively attack others. And because authentic pride is linked to a prosocial and compassionate attitude, it might even motivate people to want to help those who are different. Authentic pride could increase empathy for stigmatized others and consequently promote *less* prejudice.

To test this theory, we asked an all-white sample of students at the University of British Columbia, in Vancouver, Canada (the university where I work as a professor), to complete what they were told was a "population survey." The survey asked them to estimate the proportion of Caucasians and Asians in the Canadian population who could be characterized by certain traits, some negative (hostile, aggressive) and some positive (friendly, likable). Because participants were simply making estimates about the presence of certain traits in certain populations, they didn't realize that, really, this survey was a measure of racism. By asking people to estimate how many Asians are hostile and aggressive and how many are friendly and likable and then comparing those "estimates" to similar "estimates" made for white people, we objectively determined participants' willingness to insult members of an ethnic outgroup.

Although it's difficult to imagine the typical politically correct and liberal-leaning white west-coast Canadian university student expressing a racist attitude simply because the researchers made him feel hubristic pride, *that's exactly what we found.* White participants who'd been randomly assigned to write about a time they felt hubristic pride rated Asians more negatively than they did Caucasians. White participants who wrote about authentic pride did the opposite; they rated Asians more *positively* than people of their own race.

These results are compelling; they tell us that the two prides can shift people's beliefs about stigmatized others. But the measure of prejudice we used in this research is a measure of attitudes; it tapped into prejudicial beliefs but not prejudicial behavior, like discrimination. Would hubristic pride motivate people to actually discriminate against others? To address this question we conducted a second study, again manipulating the two prides but this time measuring discriminatory behavior: the biased application of punishment for a crime.

We asked participants to read a police report about an arrested criminal; their task, we told them, was to assign bail. The criminal was a prostitute — a purveyor of a crime that's often considered victimless (although in some circles, the criminal is also thought to be the victim). Because prostitutes tend to be pitied as much as they are blamed, asking participants to decide how to punish a prostitute places them in a situation where there is no clear answer. As a result, their judgments are malleable and thus potentially vulnerable to the impact of hubristic or authentic pride.

Recall, though, that in our first study, pride didn't make people generally hostile or compassionate; it evoked those feelings specifically for members of an ethnic outgroup. So, in this new study, rather than ask participants to set bail on any old prostitute, we asked them to set bail on a prostitute who, we thought, would be a particularly likely target of stigma: a gay male prostitute. (Though a small minority of participants in this study — students at the University of North Carolina — were likely to be gay men, we assumed that the large majority was not, making a gay male prostitute a clear outgroup member.)

Sure enough, the brief experiences of hubristic and authentic pride we manipulated influenced the amount of bail participants set. Those who were made to feel hubristic pride forced the gay prostitute to endure a harsher sentence than did those made to feel authentic pride.

These findings are consistent with our predictions, but they're still somewhat surprising. On the basis of being randomly assigned to write about a time when they felt pretentious and superior versus a time they felt confident and accomplished, college students became more or less willing to engage in prejudice. Momentary experiences of hubristic pride led ostensibly prosocial individuals to express offensive attitudes about Asians and to harshly punish a gay prostitute.

If there is a silver lining in this research, it's our finding that momentary experiences of authentic pride led individuals from this same population to become more prosocial. And, in a final study, we added a measure of empathy and found that authentic pride makes people care more about others, in stark contrast to hubristic pride, which makes people care less. According to the results of a statistical analytic tool known as a test of mediation, it is this change in empathy that causes their subsequent prosocial or antisocial (and racist or homophobic) judgments.

The story behind these effects is clear. People who feel authentic pride differ from people who feel hubristic pride at least in part because of the impact these emotions have on their judgments of others. As a result, authentic and hubristic pride influence prejudicial attitudes and behavior in opposite ways. That in itself has major implications; it suggests that the kind of pride experienced by people in power — politicians, employers, and administrators — may contribute to how these people treat those who rely on them or need their help.

But the difference between the kinds of behaviors engendered by each of the two prides goes well beyond prejudice. As we'll see, authentic and hubristic pride are powerful motivators of a broad range of social behaviors. In-group favoritism and outgroup derogation — social sciences terminology for ugly phenomena like racism and homophobia — are just two examples (albeit particularly pernicious ones) of how the two forms of pride can have a pronounced effect on human behavior, for better or for worse.

We can seek to understand the causes of an emotional experience — or any psychological phenomenon, really — at an ultimate level or a proximate one. Ultimate causes are answers to the big whys: Why do humans seek lifelong mates? Why are men and women different? Why are children dependent on their parents? The answers to these questions require an examination of evolutionary history (if we want to un-

derstand humans in general) or of particular social and cultural histo-
ries (if we want to understand people within a specific group).

One of the goals of this book *is* to answer the ultimate question of
why humans evolved to feel pride. But first, we need to tackle the more
proximate question. Proximate causes are more concrete explanations;
they are answers to the smaller whys, questions about what caused
particular events to occur within a given context or at a particular moment. At a proximate level, we want to understand what it is, exactly,
that makes people in a certain situation feel pride — and, especially,
what makes people feel one kind of pride versus the other. What determines whether people respond to events that make them proud with
a sense of superiority and arrogance as opposed to confidence and accomplishment?

Emotions are caused by specific interpretations — or *appraisals* — of
events. We feel fear not when something scary happens but when our
brains come to *see* that thing as scary. Fear occurs when we appraise
an event as threatening: when we hear a sound in the night we can't
identify or see a bearlike creature in the woods. This appraisal triggers
a cascade of responses: physiological arousal, tense muscles, a readi-
ness to run, and the feeling of being terrified.

In the case of pride, the critical appraisal is not of possible danger
but almost its opposite: that something good has happened. But that's
just the first step. The second step is deciding that the cause of this
good thing is *you*: a good thing happened because *you* made it happen.
Most of us make this kind of appraisal on a daily — even hourly — basis. Often it's justified; you credit yourself quite deservedly for cooking
a delicious meal, coming up with a great idea, telling a funny joke, or
checking items off your to-do list. At other times this appraisal is perhaps less legitimate; you credit yourself for receiving a great hand in a
game of poker or for a friend's promotion at work. Justifiable or not,
appraisals in which we give credit to ourselves — known as "internal
attributions" — are necessary for pride. You feel pride when you decide
that *you* are the cause of the good thing that happened but not when
someone or something else is.

But do internal attributions elicit both kinds of pride? To find out,

Rick and I turned to the narratives we had collected from undergrads who were asked to recall their proudest moments. We asked research assistants to carefully read each, paying close attention to the way these participants had interpreted the situations that caused their feelings. Not surprisingly, almost all the narratives involved an internal attribution; participants believed that *they* were the cause of the things that made them feel pride. But much more interesting, participants who wrote about an experience of authentic pride described *a different kind* of internal attribution than those who wrote about hubristic pride.

Authentically proud participants wrote about positive events that were caused by something they *did* — the hard work they put in to make the success happen. Hubristically proud participants, in contrast, credited some larger aspect of their identities, something about who they *were,* like their abilities and talents or their stable personalities.

This is the difference between a student who believes she aced an exam because she studied hard and one who believes she aced it because she's naturally smart (and who, perhaps, didn't study much at all). The former belief is an attribution to a cause that's internal but *controllable.* We can control how much effort we put in and how hard we work. The latter belief is an attribution to a cause that's also internal but *uncontrollable.* We can't control how smart we are, no matter how hard we try.

This difference — between feeling pride for reasons that are controllable and action-based, as opposed to reasons that are uncontrollable and identity-based — seems to be crucial to the psychological distinction between the two prides. Authentic pride is the emotional response to successes that are hard won and that people know occurred as a result of their own efforts. Hubristic pride is the emotional response to successes that are perceived as less effortful and thus less controllable, events that, people believe, occurred simply because of who they are.

No wonder authentic pride is associated with feelings of achievement and accomplishment while hubristic pride is linked to egotism and arrogance. If you think you succeeded because of your hard work, you should feel confident, productive, and accomplished. And if you believe you succeeded because of who you are, well, then it makes sense that you'd feel pretty great about yourself in a manner that could be described as conceited or smug.

To test whether these results go beyond the mere correlational — whether these distinct appraisals *cause* the distinct pride feelings — we conducted a study experimentally manipulating attributions; in other words, we laid out for participants a specific reason they might feel pride. We asked undergrads to read hypothetical scenarios about succeeding at an important school event: performing well on a class exam. This is an event that mattered a lot to these students, and it was something they could all relate to, even if, for some of them, it was a rare experience. They were asked to read two scenarios and imagine how each would make them feel. One read: *You recently had an important exam and you studied hard for it. You just found out that you did very well on the exam.* The other read: *You've always been naturally talented (i.e., smart). You recently had an important exam and you didn't bother studying much for it, but it still seemed very easy to you. You just found out that you did very well on the exam.* Our hypothesis was that the first scenario would lead students to report strong feelings of authentic pride resulting from that hard-won success, whereas the second scenario would lead to greater reports of hubristic pride, caused by a success that had little to do with one's own controllable effort.

In fact, as we had predicted, when participants read about succeeding because of their hard work, they reported greater authentic pride than when they read about succeeding because of their abilities. Conversely, success caused by abilities led to greater hubristic pride than success caused by effort. This means that these appraisals — whether success is attributed to effort or ability — are a proximate causal factor determining which kind of pride people experience. Making one kind of appraisal or the other when interpreting a given success causes the momentary experience of one kind of pride or the other. And what determines whether people attribute their successes to their efforts or their abilities? That gets us back to personality. Narcissists tend to make internal, uncontrollable attributions for positive events, while those with high self-esteem tend to make attributions that are internal but more controllable.

Together, all of these studies demonstrate that authentic and hubristic pride are very different emotional experiences. They involve distinct sets of subjective feelings. They are associated with almost completely opposing personality profiles. They're elicited by different appraisals about the causes of success. They trigger different social behaviors.

Importantly, these distinctions are not an artifact of American cultural understandings of pride or of the way the English language uses that word. In fact, the distinction between the two prides is much more explicitly embedded into other languages, like French and Italian. Furthermore, studies in China and South Korea replicated our results, even though Asian cultures hold more negative attitudes toward pride in general. In these countries, pride tends to be devalued and self-enhancement discouraged, yet people still make the same distinction between authentic and hubristic pride and report experiencing both.

In fact, both authentic and hubristic pride are part of what it means to feel pride. Both are typical responses to the question "What is pride?" Both are felt during relived pride experiences. And both are associated with the pride nonverbal expression.

This last point — that authentic and hubristic pride look largely the same — was made in a set of studies that asked participants to view different versions of the pride expression (for example, in some, posers reached their arms high up above their head while clenching their fists, and in others, they kept their hands on their hips) and decide whether each conveyed authentic or hubristic pride. Participants were *unable* to reach a clear decision. For almost all the expressions we showed them, about half the participants chose authentic pride and about half chose hubristic.

Now, this doesn't mean that people can't ever tell whether someone is feeling authentic or hubristic pride. When we showed participants these pride expressions and gave them other information about the expresser — that she was known to be arrogant, for example, or that he'd just experienced a success and attributed it to his hard work and effort — participants voiced a clear opinion about which kind of pride was conveyed. Context helps. The way people talk about their pride says a lot about which pride they're feeling. When Donald Trump says, "Let me tell you, I'm a really smart guy. I was a really good student at the best school in the country," we can guess which kind of pride he's experiencing, even though we probably wouldn't be able to figure it out from his nonverbal expression alone. Likewise, when Academy Award winners emphasize how humbled they are "just to be nominated," we know what kind of pride they're feeling — assuming we believe them.

In sum, the research evidence for a distinction between the two prides helps us solve a puzzle that's plagued most attempts at understanding pride for over a millennium. Philosophers, theologians, and even novelists (think Jane Austen's *Pride and Prejudice*) have long observed that pride is both good and bad, both a "crown virtue" and a "deadly sin." We now know how this is possible.

Pride is not just one thing, and it's not simply good or bad. In fact, pride is too complex to be characterized along the dimension of good versus bad. To understand pride, we need to understand the distinction between self-esteem and narcissism. And to fully understand that distinction, we need to tackle a more complicated problem still.

To understand why we, as humans, have pride — the ultimate *why* question — we need to understand the human self, the complex psychological entity that's capable of feeling good in two very different ways. Pride, regardless of which form it takes, is the emotion each of us most wants to feel about that self, and it's what motivates us to mold ourselves into the kind of people we want to be and to develop an identity we feel proud of. Fear or anxiety might have made Dean Karnazes seek out a stable, well-paying job, but the desire to feel pride is what made him one of the strongest and most inspirational ultramarathoners in the world.

In the next chapter, we will closely examine the uniquely human self. In doing so, we'll take the first step toward addressing the ultimate *why* question of pride: Why did humans evolve to experience this emotion, in all of its two-sided glory?

3

Me, Myself, and I

PSYCHOLOGISTS, anthropologists, primatologists, and biologists, even philosophers and economists, have often posed the question: What is the one, crucial thing that separates humans from every other species of animal? What makes us unique?

Some say it's our ability to think ahead and make forecasts for what we'll want and how we'll feel in the future. Others say it's our ability to build and share cultural knowledge; to learn basic skills from others so that, as a species, we can make innovative advances far beyond what we could each figure out alone. Still others say it's our opposable thumbs.

The fact is, *none* of these traits (except, perhaps, the thumbs) would exist without an even more fundamental and distinctly human capacity — our uniquely human sense of self. Without the human self, our species would not have been able to do or become all the things that make us different from other animals. And the emotion we most want to feel about our selves — pride — is what motivates us to do and become all these things. Pride is what makes us want, often desperately, to find or to be our best selves.

But the relationship between pride and the self does not go in only one direction. Pride gives us the motivational kick we need to make ourselves great, but the possession of a human self is what makes pride possible. Pride and the self are mutually reinforcing psychological phenomena, two adaptations that go hand in hand and whose joint evolutionary development has allowed our species to become what it is today.

With that said, it may be self-evident that the self almost certainly preceded pride in the march of human evolution. After all, the reason we experience pride — both the authentic and the hubristic variety — is that we have selves that we can feel good about. Pride is what we feel when we think about who we are and decide that we like what we see. When we like who we are because we see ourselves working hard toward some accomplishment that carries meaning for us, we feel authentic pride. When we like who we are because we see ourselves as better than others or as possessing some special abilities that give us an inherent superiority, we feel hubristic pride.

What this means is that without a self — without the ability to come to know the kind of person we are and then evaluate that individual — *we would not feel pride.* And so, to understand why we experience pride at an ultimate, evolutionary level, we need to understand what it means to have a sense of self.

The human self is different from the self of every other animal out there, which explains why we experience pride, while — as far as we know — monkeys, dogs, and earthworms do not. But this is not to say that we are the only species with any kind of self-concept. All organisms — even single-celled amoebas — possess a self, in the sense of having a rudimentary ability to distinguish between themselves and everything else. And for all organisms, the self is motivational; it's what makes every animal spend a good part of its life protecting itself from all things nonself or finding ways of eating nonself while avoiding eating self.

But many species go far beyond simply knowing where the self ends and nonself begins. Some develop rich networks of knowledge about how the self relates to nonself. Chimpanzees and orangutans, for example, can calculate the self's place in the dominance hierarchies that shape most of their inter-ape relationships. Humans do the same; in every group we belong to, we know our social standing relative to others.

But the human's sense of self goes much further than that of all our ape cousins. At only eighteen months of age, humans have already achieved the pinnacle of self-awareness found among adult chimps: the ability to look in a mirror and realize that what we're seeing is a reflected image of ourselves and not some other tiny primate. By adulthood, the human self has become a complex set of cognitive and emotional capacities that are unique to our species and that, together, allow us to achieve, learn from others, create and innovate, and behave morally.

What, exactly, is this uniquely human self? To begin with, it's important to understand that the self is not a single, simple entity. The philosopher William James was the first to make this point, distinguishing between two major components of self that he referred to as the "Self as Knower" and the "Self who is Known." This is a distinction between the subjective *I* self and the objective *me* self. If you happen to be grammatically inclined, you can remember this distinction by thinking of the difference between the subject and the object of a sentence. Just like a sentence's subject, the subjective *I* self does the acting, while the objective *me* self is more likely to be acted upon.

What this means is that the first part of the self — the subjective *I* — is what does everything and thinks everything. It's the tiny metaphorical homunculus inside the brain that processes all information and controls all behavior. It's the person you're talking about when you say something like "I want ice cream" or "I'm on my way to work."

The *me*, in contrast, doesn't do, think, or want anything. The *me* is more like a set of knowledge structures — a book of information — about who each of us is. The *me*, in essence, is your identity; it's the self you're thinking about when you think about yourself. It includes all the knowledge you possess about who you are, including your personality, your competencies and abilities, what you know, and what you look like. It's who you mean when you say something like "I'm five foot seven" or "I'm good at basketball."* Everything you know about yourself, you know because you have a *me*.

But — and this is where things get complicated — the *me* cannot exist without the *I*, because you can have a sense of who you are only by virtue of using the *I* to look at it. This becomes readily apparent if you ever find yourself in the existentially odd position of looking at yourself without self-awareness — that is, without the self-conscious knowledge *That is me*. If placed in such a situation — one that is admittedly quite unusual — the person you are looking at can be perceived only as something *other* than *me*. The novelist Jorge Luis Borges illuminated this point with a poignant hypothetical: "Pete is waiting in line . . . [at] a department store, and he notices that there is a closed-circuit television monitor over the counter. . . . As he watches the jostling crowd of people on the monitor, he realizes that the person over on the left side of the screen in the overcoat carrying the large paper bag is having his pocket picked by the person behind him. Then, as he raises his hand to his mouth in astonishment, he notices that the victim's hand is moving to his mouth in just the same way. Pete suddenly realizes that *he* is the person whose pocket is being picked!"

Pete's sudden realization prompts a major shift in perception — the *I* moves instantly from observing some other person to observing *me*. Even though Pete was in fact watching *the same person* throughout the entire story, that sudden recognition of *Hey, that's me* changed his experience completely.

This is what it means to be self-conscious. It's the capacity to look at yourself and know, without any thought and certainly without any doubt, *That's me* — and to feel completely different about the object you're looking at as a result. It's a capacity that's fully present, as far as we know, in our species alone, and it's the capacity that has made our species the way it is.

· · ·

---

* Or, to use the appropriate I-me terminology but much less typical phrasing, "That's me who's good at basketball."

The fact that we humans are able to know who we are — to use our subjective *I* self to obtain a (relatively) clear sense of our objective *me* self — is remarkable, if you think about it. This is something that no other animal can do — at least to the extent that we can — and it's something that affects almost everything else we do, from eating, drinking, and sleeping to making new friends, finding a career, or flirting with a date. Try to imagine accomplishing a task as simple as grabbing an afternoon snack without knowing something about the kinds of foods you like, not to mention other snack-related goals and concerns you probably possess within your body of self-knowledge: considerations of healthfulness, your dinner plans for the evening, and your feelings about gluten. We know a great deal about ourselves, and we use that knowledge to inform every decision we make. But how do we obtain this information in the first place?

In 1902 the sociologist Charles Cooley coined the now-anachronistic term *looking-glass self* to address this question. Cooley's idea was that our sense of our self — our identity — comes from the reflected appraisals of other people around us. We figure out who we are by closely monitoring how others react to us. As Cooley put it, much more poetically, "Each to each a looking-glass; reflects the other that doth pass."

It's a notably counterintuitive approach. Cooley's view was that, rather than forming one's identity through deep thought and introspection, a person *infers* what she must be like on the basis of how she affects those around her and how she imagines they see her. If others laugh when you talk, you decide you must be funny. If others avoid you, you start to see yourself as unlikable. Eventually you build an entire identity on the basis of the reflections you observe bouncing off all the people you interact with. Importantly, though, the resulting *me* is not an actual mirror of other people's perceptions of you; it's more like a fun-house mirror — distorted by your own often-misguided ideas about what others must think.

Cooley's looking-glass account places a much larger emphasis on the impact of others in forming one's own identity than many of us would like to believe. Part of becoming an adult is deciding that it doesn't matter what others think; *I* know who I am and who I want to be, and no one can tell me otherwise. But the fact is, it would be difficult to maintain a view of yourself as funny if the people around you didn't laugh at your jokes. We all look to others to figure out how to define ourselves. We *choose* those others — the goth teen shapes her identity (and her piercings) based more on what her goth friends think than on what her parents think — but it's undeniable that our friends, partners, social groups, and, yes, even our parents influence our identity. And for young children who are first developing their *me* selves, these others are essential.

Early on, young kids don't make any distinction between how their parents see them and how they see themselves. Only around age two does a child begin to use his *I* self to realize that he has a *me* that's separate from others. It's a frightening epiphany. A toddler suddenly becomes aware that others can look at him, and his first thought is to hide — most typically by burying his face in a parent's lap. These kids seem embarrassed, but it's not the same kind of embarrassment that adults experience, the emotion you feel when someone catches you walking smack into a glass wall or when you spill soup on a colleague. Early childhood self-consciousness is more like what's felt by the adult recipient of the spilled soup — the colleague who, despite her utter innocence in the spillage incident, feels undeniably self-conscious about her soupy state. Like the two-year-old, the soupy colleague knows that others are looking, and — unfairly, of course — evaluating her (*She seemed so professional until I saw her covered in soup*). For anyone with a *me* self, this is not a comfortable feeling.

Self-consciousness — the recognition that my *me* self is different from yours and might be evaluated by you — is the first part of identity development. The second part is learning what it takes to obtain a positive or negative evaluation. At the same time as they're becoming self-conscious, children are learning the rules and standards of their society, rules that determine which behaviors are appropriate and which are not. Tying these two lessons together is the third part of identity development — the understanding that *my* behaviors will be judged according to my society's standards.

The first three steps of identity development happen relatively quickly, during the first few years of life, but there is a fourth step that happens more gradually, over a longer period in childhood. During this fourth step, kids start to internalize external evaluations from parents, teachers, and peers and convert them into self-evaluations. This is a critical switch, from *Mommy is happy when I wash my hands* to *I'm a good girl when I wash my hands.* It's the switch that changes an emotion like joy into an emotion like pride; the child moves from feeling a shared happiness with her parent toward feeling a sense of accomplishment *in her own self,* along with an ability to congratulate herself for it.

For younger children, every decision about how to behave is pitted against an adult's feelings about that behavior. But as kids grow older and become increasingly socialized, they take their parents' rules and regulations and make them their own. They measure themselves against internalized standards, and when they fail to meet those standards or when they surpass them, they end up experiencing the same emotions that adults feel when we compare ourselves to our own expectations and beliefs, the "self-conscious emotions" of guilt, shame, and pride. Without the presence of internalized social standards and the cognitive capacity to evaluate oneself on the basis of them — that is, without an ability to use the *I* to see one's *me* self and judge whether it is good or bad according to the local norms — there would be no pride.

This process of internalizing social norms by incorporating them into the *me* self occurs over several years. While second graders talk about guilt as a feeling of being afraid that "others won't like me anymore," for fifth graders, guilt becomes "I feel stupid." The fifth grader — like the adult who loses an important deal at work or forgets an anniversary or throws plastic into the trashcan instead of the recycling bin — doesn't need to think about how his parents will evaluate him in order to feel bad about himself. The good news is, this cuts both ways; most adults also don't need to think about their parents to feel proud of themselves for closing an important deal at work, knitting a sweater, or building a bookshelf.

The successful internalization of social norms — allowing these norms to partly determine the kind of self one becomes — is perhaps the most important prerequisite for becoming a social being: a fully capable adult member of any human society. The anthropologist and existentialist sage Ernest Becker equated this process to a performance in a dramatic play, but one with severe consequences. "If we uphold our part in the performance, we are rewarded with social affirmation of our identity, [but] if we bungle the performance, we are destroyed — not figuratively but literally."

Although Becker's suggestion that successful identity development is a matter of life and death might seem extreme, he's right. A person who fails to develop an identity that meets his or her society's standards faces certain social rejection, a fate that, in human evolutionary history, *would* have meant literal death. For this reason, we evolved to internalize our society's norms and make them our own.

There is also a fifth developmental shift, and it occurs as a result of the internalization of social norms: self-conscious emotions — guilt, shame, and pride — start to *drive* behavior. Prior to internalizing norms, kids need to think about how their parents will evaluate their every behavior in order to decide whether to enact it. But once kids can evaluate themselves according to their own internalized norms, they no longer need to think about how others will judge them to decide how to behave. They choose to do the right thing — that is, the thing their society wants them to do — not because they know it's what their parents want but because *they* want to be considered good, and their *emotions* tell them that following social norms is the best way to do that.

Developmental psychologists have demonstrated this shift by asking five- and eight-year-olds to imagine themselves in two socially complicated situations: crashing into a friend's bike, or learning that they did well on an exam. These children were then asked to imagine how they would *feel* in these situations and how they would *behave*. For five-year-olds, the amount of guilt or pride they expected to feel was not particularly predictive of their behavior. Some of these young kids said they would behave in appropriate ways — offering to pay for bike repairs, giving themselves gold stars for their exam success — and some did not, but their emotions had little to do with it.

For eight-year-olds, however, a different pattern emerged. Many of these older children still behaved inappropriately, but those who did the right thing did so *because of the emotions* they felt. Eight-year-olds who felt more guilt from the bike accident were more likely to pay for repairs, and those who felt more pride gave themselves more gold stars.

The implications of this study are clear: Older children, like adults, choose to enact the behaviors that make them feel good about themselves. As a result, these emotions — the desire to feel pride and to avoid feeling guilt — motivate people to do all the things we do because our society wants us to, things that make us "good" people.

In other words, because your *me* self is, to a very large extent, an internalized reflection of what others think about you, combined with an understanding of societal norms and rules, pride is what you feel when the *I* recognizes that the *me* is doing what society wants of it. The *me* captures what it means to be a social being, to know one's place in society. And pride is an internal barometer, telling you whether you're meeting society's expectations, the extent to which you are being or becoming a "good" person, where *good* is defined according to what your social group wants.

As a result of its barometer capacity, pride can motivate us to behave in ways our society wants us to. And we're most likely to successfully do that when we're reminded of what our society wants of us — that is, of the kind of person we want to be, the ideal *Me* self. Numerous studies have demonstrated this point. People are most likely to behave in ways their society values when they are reminded of their identities — who they are and who they want to be.

In one example, developmental psychologists rewarded seven- and eight-year-olds for wins at a bowling game with prizes that could go either to themselves or, if they chose, to other kids who were less fortunate. All of these kids knew that they should share at least a few of their prizes with other children who needed them more, and when they did so, an experimenter told them either "Gee, you shared quite a bit. I guess you're the kind of person who likes to help others whenever you can. Yes, you are a very nice and helpful person" *or* "Gee, you shared quite a bit. It was good that you gave some of your marbles to those poor children. Yes, that was a nice and helpful thing to do."

If you read those two statements quickly, you might have missed the difference between them. Even if you read them slowly, it's still not obvious why that very subtle difference would matter. In both experimental conditions, kids were praised for their generosity. But in that first condition, kids were told that generosity was part of their *identity* — "you are a very nice and helpful *person.*" In the second condition, kids were encouraged to instead see their generosity as a one-time behavior — "that was a nice and helpful thing *to do.*"

What the researchers found was that the kids who received the first message, about their identity, were later more willing to share another valued resource — colored pencils that the researchers gave them — than were the kids who had been praised merely for their behavior. In fact, the kids who received behavioral praise were no more generous later on than kids in a third experimental condition, a group of children who'd received no feedback at all. This suggests that simple reinforcement, or praise for a single behavior in one domain (helping the poor), was not at all effective at shaping future behavior in a slightly different domain (sharing colored pencils with classmates). Shifting kids' perceptions of their *me* selves, however — encouraging them to see themselves as the kind of person who tends to behave generously — was an effective means of changing their ongoing behavior for the better.

Telling kids who they are makes them want to behave accordingly because the *me* self is the object of one's pride, and much of a person's behavior is oriented toward making sure she feels pride every chance she gets. Telling a kid that she did something well on a single occasion might make her feel pride in that one-time behavior, and it might even persuade her to engage in that same behavior again. But if the goal is to encourage her to generalize beyond the single behavior — to not only give prizes to poor children during one bowling game but behave generously across many situations and contexts — we need to make the kid see her *me* self as a generous person. If she's like most humans, she'll then want to do what it takes to feel pride in that identity.

But does this same process work for adults? Most grownups already hold fairly stable identities — we know our *me* selves pretty well — so it's not clear that the provision of identity information from some external source would have much of an effect on behavior.

As it turns out, adults, too, are influenced by subtle suggestions about who we are, although the process is different for us than it is for kids. The key difference is that, for adults, the information provided needs to be a *reminder* of what we already know, not something new. An adult can't easily be persuaded to believe that he is someone he's never thought himself to be. But he can be reminded of how much he values certain aspects of himself — how much the various parts of his *me* can be a source of pride. And when this happens — when an adult is encouraged to focus the *I* on certain parts of the *me* — his desire to feel pride in those parts of himself make him want to behave in the way those *me* parts would want him to.

The motivational power of the adult *me* self can be seen from a study conducted immediately prior to the 2008 U.S. presidential election. Randomly selected California voters were asked a few questions about their voting plans. Some of these individuals saw questions implying that voting might be part of their identities, like "How important is it to you to *be a voter* in the upcoming election?" Others saw questions that instead referred to voting as a behavior: "How important is it to you to *vote* in the upcoming election?"

Despite the seemingly minuscule linguistic difference between these questions — and to be clear, the italics you saw were mine, not the researchers' — they led to very different behaviors. An almost shocking 96 percent of participants who received the identity manipulation — that is, who were asked whether it was important to *be a voter* — went on to vote in the election, compared to 79 percent of registered California voters overall and 82 percent of participants in the behavior condition (a rate not significantly different from the overall turnout).

The difference we're talking about here — shifting the voting behavior of 14 to 17 percent of participants — is more than enough to change the course of almost any highly contested election if applied to the entire electorate. As the authors of this study noted, this finding has major implications for basic democracy. But it also has major implications for the importance of the *me* self — and the pride each of us wants to feel in that self — in shaping behavior. Those participants who were asked whether it was important to them to vote but chose not to do so were not bad people. They were registered voters who almost certainly had incorporated into their identities a representation of "*me* as voter." But if that self-representation wasn't activated by the researchers' reminder, then other aspects of the *me* — perhaps "*me* as parent" or "*me* as hard-working employee" — were salient and more likely to guide their behavior on that day.

Indeed, within each *me* is not just one set of internalized social norms but many constellations of norms — one for each social group we belong to. As a result, focusing the *I*'s attention on the *me* does not always promote behavior that's good for us or for all of our communities. Unlike the norm of being a good citizen who votes, some of the social norms that shape our pride-motivated behaviors can be problematic. Think of the norms that are typical of a society of inner-city drug dealers. Some of these, like loyalty and a strong work ethic, might be good for both the individual and his society. Others, like increasing one's customer base by introducing dangerous and addictive drugs to children, are much more problematic for society — at least, the larger society that encapsulates the drug-dealer subculture and within which the dealer also lives. Still others, like carrying a firearm and using it against rival gangs, are problematic for both the larger society and the individual.

Because a person's identity can incorporate both positive and negative social norms, reminders of more negative identity-relevant norms can trigger corresponding problematic behavior. Think of Paul Gauguin, who, in order to feel pride in the *me* he most wanted to embrace, traded in the norms of his bourgeois Parisian society for those of the bohemian art world — which meant abandoning his wife and children and forming questionable relationships with teenage women.

Supporting this point, studies have demonstrated that identity reminders *can* lead to less-than-ideal outcomes, depending on one's constellation of social norms. In one example, psychologists reminded a group of middle-school children who were low in socioeconomic status and part of a minority racial group about their minority status — a major component of the *me* self for anyone who belongs to a socially stratified society. The researchers then asked these students to take a quiz assessing their health knowledge. Kids belonging to racial or ethnic minorities tend to view health-promoting behaviors, like eating well, getting enough sleep, and exercising, as "mostly a white, middle-class way of being" — so, normative for a society they don't belong to. For this reason, when these kids were first asked to complete sentences designed to focus the *I* on the racial/ethnic *me* (for example, "I am _____," followed by boxes indicating various races/ethnicities), they displayed less health knowledge than kids *who shared the same minority status* but had not been reminded of it before completing the quiz. In other words, being reminded of an aspect of the *me* that didn't fit with healthy living prompted these kids to behave in the way that *me* would want them to — they literally forgot what they knew about how to be healthy.

The desire to feel pride in each and every component of the *me* — or at least those components that are currently on our minds — can promote behaviors that are problematic and even maladaptive for other components of the same *me* self. This is because we are most proud of ourselves when we act consistently with our ideal *me* self. When we're reminded of that identity, or a particular piece of it, we become particularly inclined to behave like it. The net result is that we do things that make us most like whatever aspects of our identity are currently on our minds, regardless of whether these behaviors are good or bad for the rest of our selves.

Thanks to socialization, though, the kind of person we want to be is, quite often, the kind of person our society or societies want us to be. For most of us, that means respecting group norms — following laws and rules of social conduct and treating others as we wish to be treated ourselves. The majority of the time, most people in any given society do what it takes to follow that society's rules, because doing so makes them feel good about themselves. But social groups don't only want people to be good — however the group defines *good*. Sure, being a good or generous or loyal group member is enough to make a young kid proud (usually). When we become adults, however, our societies expect more of us, and as a result, we expect more of ourselves.

Most of us want to be good, yes, but we also want to be *great*. We want to be impressive, competent, and accomplished. We want to achieve. Just as our *me* selves — and that burning desire to feel pride in those selves — can lead us astray, depending which component of our identities we are currently focused on, they can also help us find success.

There may be no other country in the world where success is as-sumed to be as attainable by anyone as it is in the United States, the so-called land of opportunity. But of course, the vaunted American Dream is much closer to some people's grasp than others'. One of the many disturbing testaments to this fact is the large gap in achievement that exists between white and African American students. Study after study has shown that no matter what performance measure you use — grades, standardized test scores, dropout rates — white students in the United States consistently do better than African Americans, and often by a wide margin.

Numerous policies have been implemented in an attempt to reduce this disparity, but one potentially promising direction comes from re-search on the *me* self. Pushing students to think about their *me* selves' most important values, and allowing them to feel pride in those values, can decrease the race-based achievement gap.

This remarkable idea is the brainchild of a team of psychologists who, in one study, asked seventh graders to write a paragraph about a value that was either very important to them — something like spend-ing time with friends, playing sports, or connecting with family — or *not at all* important to them. This short exercise, performed a sin-gle time in a single class, had a major impact on the final grades of the African American students in the class. Those who wrote about something they valued — something that was important to the *me* —

showed a .26 to .34 grade increase (based on a 4.0 metric), an effect large enough to turn a B into a B+ or an A– and to slice in half the proportion of students who received a D or worse in the course.

As for the European Americans — the white kids — in the study: regardless of whether they wrote about their important values or their unimportant ones, their grades were unaffected. As a result, this simple exercise reduced the achievement gap between the African Americans and European Americans in the class by a whopping 40 percent.

According to the authors of this study, the reason this exercise worked so well is that it encouraged African Americans to focus, while in an achievement setting (that is, at school), on aspects of their identities that were unrelated to negative stereotypes about African American achievement — stereotypes that these students are all too frequently bombarded with. Unfortunately, and unavoidably in many parts of North America, these stereotypes have become part of this group's identity — the part of the *me* that is "*me* as an African American student" — and because we all behave in ways that are consistent with how we see ourselves, they shape behavior. Many studies have shown that reminding minority-group members of a stereotyped aspect of their identity produces behaviors consistent with the stereotype, whether it's African Americans performing worse in school, women performing poorly on a math test after being reminded of the stereotype that women are bad at math, or Christians performing worse on a test of logic after being reminded of the stereotype that Christians are bad at science.

What the value-affirmation study showed, though, is that the same self that lies at the root of these problematic behaviors can be used to reverse them. When African Americans were reminded that their academic identity was more than just the stereotyped part — and that the stereotyped part was far from the most important part of who they are — they became motivated to overcome the negative impact of the stereotype. Reminding these students that they have every right to feel proud of their academic *me* selves was all it took to push them to overcome the default, stereotype-consistent behavior they were otherwise prone to engage in. This is because the human desire to become a certain kind of person — the kind of person our society has made us want to be — influences not only moral, civic, and health behaviors, but also the behaviors that help people get ahead: their achievements. Your *me* is a person who is good — however your society defines *good* — but also a person who has social value, who can accomplish things that the group cares about. For students, this means that the ideal *me* is someone who works hard and does well at school.

All humans share this basic desire to see ourselves and be seen by others as good, moral, and *competent*. According to psychologist Mark Leary, this fundamental motivation is ultimately shaped by an even deeper one: the drive to feel a sense of belongingness with one's group. People want to feel pride in the *me* self and have high self-esteem, says Leary, because it's our way of knowing whether others like us and want to keep us around.

Leary uses the term *sociometer* to describe this process; his idea is that self-esteem works in the same way as a thermometer or a car's fuel gauge. When your self-esteem is high, you know you're in solid social standing. When your self-esteem is low, it's a signal that you're in trouble — in danger of being rejected by your group. And because in human evolutionary history, group rejection meant literal death, the desire to have high self-esteem is adaptive; it's a way of ensuring that people do whatever's needed to stay safely included within their groups. Being rejected by one's group today is not nearly as problematic as it was several millennia ago, as most of us now live in close proximity to hundreds — and, thanks to the Internet, thousands — of other groups we can join, providing rejected individuals with at least a few alternatives to death due to isolation. But because of our biologically inherited sociometer, rejection still feels awful, and there are people who will choose death over it.

In research supporting his self-esteem-as-sociometer account, Leary has shown that undergraduates who are made to feel excluded — they're told that other students who had just gotten to know them don't want to have anything to do with them ever again — feel awful.

Rejection hurts. And it hurts in a specific way. According to Leary's findings, it makes people feel less worthy, competent, smart, valuable, confident, and *proud*.

Leary's argument is that these feelings — which he calls "lowered self-esteem" — are functional. In the same way that feelings of fear alert us to the possible presence of a bear, feelings of low self-esteem alert us that we're in danger of being excluded by our group. Leary's point is that the ultimate evolutionary cause of self-esteem is to tell us when we need to shift our behaviors to cope most effectively with that impending threat.

This does *not* mean that the desire to be included by others in our social group is the *proximate* — that is, the direct and immediate — cause of our desire for high self-esteem. At the proximate level of our day-to-day behaviors and motivations, we don't seek high self-esteem because we want to make sure we're in good standing with our social group, just as we don't seek sex because we want to reproduce (in the large, large majority of cases). We do these things, in the moment, because they feel good. But at an ultimate level, evolution has made these things feel good because they are good for us, or for our genes. Sex has historically been the best way to pass on our genes, and lowered self-esteem, according to Leary, is the best way to get us to change our behaviors so we stay safely included.

Supporting this account, studies have found that the pain of rejection is as real as physical pain — the body's signal that you're in danger of attack from an adversary, predator, or disease. When humans experience physical pain, the body responds in a number of adaptive ways, many of which are instigated by increased activity in the brain's anterior cingulate cortex (ACC), its neural "alarm system." To demonstrate that a similar process occurs for social pain — that is, that the pain of rejection sets off the sociometer warning signal in the same way that touching a hot stove sets off a physical-danger warning signal — a team of neuroscientists forced participants to endure the more social kind of pain while the researchers monitored their brains using an fMRI scanner.

Each participant in this study lay inside the scanner — a tube with

Figure 3.1. Visual depiction of the computer game Cyberball

a circumference just slightly wider than a human body — and played a computer game known as Cyberball. The subjects watched on a screen as three avatars — one of which they controlled — tossed a ball back and forth (see figure 3.1). Following standard social norms, upon receiving the ball, most participants immediately passed it to the avatar they didn't receive it from, to keep all three players in the game each round.

But then the researchers changed things up a bit. After a few minutes of group play, the two other avatars — which, the participants were told, were controlled by others also in the study — stopped passing to the participant's avatar. No reason was given, and nothing was said; all of a sudden, the participant simply found his or her avatar excluded — turning its sad little hand icon toward the ball holder with each play, hoping to receive, but always in vain.

While this might seem like a far cry from Mark Leary's favored method of rejection induction — being told that real people whom you've met don't ever want to see you — it worked. Participants who were suddenly ignored by the other avatars felt excluded *and*, according to the scanner, showed greater activity in the ACC region of their brains than participants who played a fully three-way game of Cyberball. In fact, the more their ACCs became activated, the more distress the rejected Cyberballers reported. What this means is that social pain is orchestrated through the same part of the brain as physical pain, the part that is the brain's warning system. Both kinds of pain send a signal telling the human in charge that something needs to change or she will face serious danger.

The sociometer alarm system keeps us safely included within our social groups, and it works, in part, because of pride. Pride is the prize that motivates us to avoid setting off the alarm. It's what Leary's socially *included* participants felt — it was even one of the items he used to measure their momentary shifts in self-esteem. It's almost certainly what those value-affirming African American students felt and what those Californians who'd been reminded that they were voters wanted to feel.

Pride may have been the underlying motivational factor in all of these studies, but because until recently psychologists rarely thought about pride (see chapter 2), none of these researchers (other than Leary) directly measured pride in their studies. There is, however, one study that examined the motivational power of pride and did so by targeting this particular emotion. This is the study that shows that feelings of pride *are* what motivate people to be the best kind of self they can be. It makes clear that when we feel pride, we come to know that we are on track for maintaining an ideal *me* self (the *me* our society most wants of us), and we respond by doing whatever we can to keep it up. The message pride sends you, in shorthand, is to keep on truckin' — keep doing whatever it is you're doing, because that's the thing that is getting you toward the *me* self you want to be.

In this study, undergraduates were asked to spend some time working on an extremely boring task: estimating the number of dots in images that appeared on a computer screen. The students were told that this task was a test of their "cognitive abilities" — a vague term that sounds definitively important for college students' future success. Next, to experimentally induce feelings of pride, an experimenter told some of the participants, "You received a score of 124 out of 147, which is the ninety-fourth percentile. Great job on that! That's one of the highest scores we've seen so far!" Other participants — in a control condition — were also told that they'd gotten a solid score in the ninety-fourth percentile but not that this was anything particularly impressive or pride-worthy.

All participants were then asked to switch over to a different but equally boring task that required a similar skill set as the prior one. This time they received the following instructions: "Please work on this task as long as you like. Do not feel as if you must finish all of the exercises provided. In fact, it is not possible to complete the entire set in the time provided for this experiment, so please continue doing this task until you feel as if you would like to stop."

What participants didn't know was that the researchers were interested in precisely *how much time* they chose to spend working on this second task — and, more specifically, whether those of them who had been induced to feel pride would spend more time on it than those who hadn't. Sure enough, the researchers found that those participants who had been made to feel pride voluntarily chose to work almost *twice as long* on the new task as participants who had been informed of their performance but not encouraged to feel proud of it. Feelings of pride made the former students want to keep on truckin'.

What's particularly interesting about this evidence for the motivational power of pride is that, in both experimental conditions, participants knew that they had succeeded. But it was only when they felt pride in their success that they became inclined to repeat that performance. This is important, because it tells us that pride has a causal impact on behavior; it made these participants want to persevere. It also tells us that the motivational effect of pride goes above and beyond that of simply *knowing* that one has done well.

This is an argument I made in the first chapter of this book: To influence outcomes and shape behavior, we need emotions — not just knowledge. Knowledge — be it of threat or of one's own competence — has little motivational power; rather, it is the emotions triggered by this knowledge that motivate human action. In the case of a hard-earned success, this means that it's the pride we feel in that success — and not only the success itself — that begets future success.

This research suggests that pride is the emotion that sets off the sociometer and compels us to act according to the feedback it's provided. Pride lets us know when we need to change our behavior to make sure we maintain solid social standing, and it gives us the motivational push to work hard toward socially valued successes: the outcomes that keep us in that solid standing. In short, pride looks out for the *me*.

The desire to feel pride, and to keep feeling it when we already have it, gets us to do what we need to do to feel good about ourselves. And because the ultimate function of the *me* is to provide an internalized mental representation of what our various social groups want of us, pride motivates us to do everything we do to meet our societies' standards. Sometimes this means being generous, altruistic, and helping others; other times it means being a good citizen who votes; and in still others, it means working hard to achieve.

Understanding how the *me* self shapes our behavior — and gives us an ideal to try to live up to — is thus the first step toward answering the ultimate *why* question about pride: Why did humans evolve to experience this emotion? The first part of the answer is that pride pushes us to become the kind of person our society wants us to be. And becoming that person — developing a *me* self that meets societal needs and goals — ensures our continued inclusion in our social groups and helps us avoid potentially deadly social rejection. It's an emotional system that works. When people are encouraged to feel proud of themselves — when, for example, they're reminded of who they are and why their values are important to them — they become better people; they strive to live up to those standards. The self is an almost constant reminder of the kind of person you want to be — which (most of the time) is also the kind of person your society wants you to be.

Pride thus helps to ensure your continued group inclusion — but this is only the first part of the story. Pride is, after all, about much more than being liked. Being included and avoiding rejection is an important first step for surviving human social life, of course. But pride gets us beyond survival. Mark Leary has argued that the sociometer is all about group inclusion; its job is to make sure we are constantly surrounded by people who will take care of us when we need it and work with us in our basic animal quest to survive and reproduce. But what if our desire to not only feel okay about who we are but to feel *pride* in who we are is about more than that? What if the ultimate reason we are so desperate to feel good about ourselves is that pride not only tells us whether we're liked but also whether we're on track for attaining a position of status?

Being liked is undoubtedly important, but being respected and admired — reaching a place in society where we have the power to influence others and get what we want — arguably has an even greater potential for an evolutionary payoff. Indeed, raising one's status may be the ultimate goal of the self and its protective sociometer, and also of pride, the emotion that guides both.

In the next three chapters, we will see how pride unleashes a string of outcomes that allow humans to navigate our complex social environment. Hierarchically structured human societies, and the cultural wisdom embedded within them, are one of the most noteworthy adaptive features of our species. Pride, it turns out, is the key to understanding how we use our groups' social-rank stratification and accumulated cultural knowledge to our advantage. This single emotion explains not only how we get by in society but also how we climb the various social ladders placed before us and use the shared wisdom of those around us to become smarter and more innovative. In short, pride gets us status and lets us create.

4

Like a Boss

O N MARCH 2, 2004 — a date better known in American political circles as Super Tuesday — Senator John Kerry won the Democratic Party's nomination for U.S. president. Kerry's decisive victories in nine states that day combined with earlier wins in thirteen others made it impossible for any other candidate to beat him, and his final competitor, Senator John Edwards, conceded. By that point it wasn't a particularly close race; Kerry had been the clear front-runner since the very first primaries in Iowa and New Hampshire. But it was, nonetheless, an important milestone for the Massachusetts senator — probably the most important in his career. At that moment, Kerry achieved something that only a handful of people in history had, and he was closer to becoming the most powerful political leader in the world than he ever would be, in all likelihood, at any point in his lifetime again.

Before Kerry began to speak to the throngs of supporters that had gathered before him at the Old Post Office Pavilion in Washington, DC, he paused, silently reflecting on the significance of the event. The usually reserved senator stood before an audience that was cheering wildly for him and smiled. He lifted up his head and broadened his

Figure 4.1. The 2004 Democratic Party nominee for U.S. president, John Kerry, after learning that he had won the primary election

chest. He raised his arms above his shoulders, clenched his fists, and gazed upward. In that moment, Kerry displayed an unmistakable expression of pride — the same nonverbal display that is reliably recognized by villagers living in rural Burkina Faso and spontaneously shown in response to Olympic victory by athletes all over the world, including those who have never seen it displayed.

Kerry was preprogrammed by evolution to display that expression in that moment. But *why* is that the case? Why has John Kerry, along with every other member of our species, evolved to display pride in this type of situation? The finding that pride displays are universal in humans means that displaying pride and observing the pride displays shown by others around us is almost certain to help us (or, more specifically, help our genes) survive and reproduce. What we don't know from the universality evidence alone is *why*. Why is displaying pride adaptive?

This is not a question of why we *feel* pride. As we saw in the previous chapter, our human desire to feel pride ensures that we do right by our *me* selves, which in turn ensures that we stay included in our social groups. And as we will see in the next chapter, the desire to feel pride also gets us further, helping us not only to stay included in our groups, but also to take control of them. Later on, we will see that feelings of pride and the desire to experience those feelings — often at any cost necessary — motivate us to do whatever's needed to attain power and influence over others.

But understanding why we *feel* pride doesn't explain why we also *show* pride to others with this particular nonverbal expression. Why, at an ultimate, evolved level, do people all over the world respond to their greatest successes by spontaneously breaking out into that reliably recognized display?

To answer the question of why we display pride in the way we do, we need to trace the ancient history of the pride expression. And that history is older than you might think. Because the expression is universal and innate in humans — meaning that it occurs in people everywhere, reliably, and without learning — it most likely originated sometime prior to our own species' beginnings.

In fact, the evidence is sparse, but primatologists have observed nonverbal displays that look a lot like pride in several of our nonhuman primate relatives. Perhaps most famous is the chest-beating drum performance of mountain gorillas made famous by that supersize cinematic gorilla King Kong. But confident or self-congratulatory behaviors like this have been documented in other primates too. Dominant catarrhine monkeys have been described as standing a bit taller and conveying a "strutting, confident air." Some of our closest ape relatives — chimpanzees — are also known to take on an expansive expression when in the presence of a subordinate. Primatologists call this a bluff display and note that it has the effect of making the animal appear larger; he stands upright on his hind legs, raises his shoulders, and makes himself as tall and wide as possible. There's even an involuntary, biological component that adds to the overall enlarged appearance: piloerection, or shoulder hairs standing on end, making the chimp look

Figure 4.2. A chimpanzee showing the typical bluff display
alongside a more subordinate companion

like he has the chills or just stuck his finger into an electric socket (see
figure 4.2).

The bluff display is about as similar to the pride expression as a
nonverbal display shown by a different species whose members walk
on four legs and are covered in thick furry hair can be. If we take this
similarity to suggest that the bluff is an evolutionary precursor to pride
— meaning that it's the prehuman primate expression that, in humans,
became pride — then knowing something about how the bluff functions in chimp life might provide a means of beginning to answer that
ultimate *why* question — why the pride expression evolved in humans.

For chimps, the bluff is a warning. Chimps bluff when they want
to assert their power; it's their way of telling a rival, *Back off, you don't
want to mess with me!* For a high-ranking chimp, a nonverbal display
that quickly and effectively sends this message is adaptive; it intim-
idates observers who might otherwise want to challenge the alpha
chimp, and — if challengers believe the threat behind the bluff — it de-
ters the need to fight it out. Anytime a fight is avoided, both parties

benefit, making the display functional for everyone. If a potential in-stigator is deterred from challenging a more dominant group mem-ber, the instigator avoids defeat, which could result in injury, worsened subordination, or even death. Meanwhile, the alpha animal benefits by virtue of saved resources, such as metabolic energy and time that would have been needed to recuperate from the battle (chimpanzee fights can be fierce), and also avoids a small but undeniable risk of death.

The particular components of the bluff are well suited to help both chimps involved benefit in this way. The generalized body expansion, erect posture, and piloerection make the bluffing animal look larger, facilitating his assertion of power. The bluff also meets a necessary cri-terion that evolutionary scientists require of displays that are thought to be evolved signals, meaning displays that came into existence for the express purpose of sending messages to observers: the display of such expressions must come at a cost. If the bluff evolved as a nonver-bal signal of dominance, it must be costly — either potentially dan-gerous or downright expensive — for the individual displaying it. This costliness is essential because it's what tells observers that the signal can be trusted.

For some evolved signals, this works because the cost of signaling is so high, the individual simply couldn't afford to send it if it weren't true. Take, for example, the male peacock tail, which is metabolically costly to develop, so only healthy males in peak physical shape are bi-ologically capable of building one. The tail's high cost means that dis-playing it communicates reliably to observing female peacocks that the well-endowed male is healthy enough to maintain it.

For other signals, showing the display under false pretenses is phys-ically possible but expensive. In these cases, the signal is costly to dis-play *if* it's not true. Think of conspicuous consumption — the art of buying the more expensive, name-brand version of certain products, like luxury cars, watches, and handbags, purely for the sake of sending a message about one's wealth. People who observe this signal believe it because they know it would be crippling if the consumer were not, in fact, wealthy enough to afford it. For those who have enough money, conspicuous consumption effectively communicates *I'm so rich, I can spend an extra $80,000 to buy the Porsche instead of the Honda.**

In the case of the bluff, only a chimp with good reason to believe in his own relatively greater power and strength can afford to risk it. Not only is the display an overt challenge, but the specific behaviors involved put the displayer in a risky position. The bluff requires standing up in the less stable two-legged pose and opening up one's body to easy attack. This increased vulnerability may be precisely what convinces onlookers that the bluffing chimp really *is* the baddest around — that he's not, in fact, bluffing. After all, why would he expose himself to potential danger like this unless he was more than capable of mounting a solid defense?

The bluff is a good example of a display that's likely to be an evolved signal, both because it has a clear function (it sends a message that bears adaptive benefits for senders and receivers) and because it meets the criterion of costliness (it poses a major risk to any sender who displays it under false pretenses). The human pride expression looks a lot like the bluff — or at least like the bluff in human form. Can we take this to mean that pride displays function to send the same kind of aggressive and intimidating message as the chimp bluff?

On the one hand, the features of the pride expression that seem most bluff-like, such as erect and expansive body posture, *are* linked to perceptions of high rank in humans. These behaviors make an individual look larger, and people tend to associate size with status. By just ten months of age, babies assume that a large-size rectangle will dominate over a smaller one. Also like the bluff, the pride display includes features that make it costly if the displayer is faking; opening up one's body to expand the posture and tilting back one's head to reveal

---

* It's important to note that wealthy consumers don't actually think through the signal value of their conspicuous consumption; in most cases, they believe they are buying Porsches because of properties inherent to the car. But the difference in cost between a Porsche and a Honda is substantially greater than the difference in quality, and the high social value of the signal that's sent by the Porsche but not the Honda can account for that gap in material value.

the jugular both have the effect of exposing some of the human body's most vulnerable parts.

On the other hand, a human's pride expression clearly works differently than the chimp's bluff. While the bluff is essentially a warning signal, shown in response to an external challenge and *prior* to battle, pride is displayed *after* a success or victory. This means that human pride displays send a somewhat different message than a chimp's bluff. While the chimp's bluff communicates a direct threat or power differential — a chimp version of *Check yourself before your wreck yourself* — pride may be a more indirect signal, informing onlookers that the proud individual deserves a status increase as a result of the accomplishment that just occurred, more along the lines of *Hey, guys, check me out!*

Sending this considerably more complicated message is possible in humans, but not in other apes, because of humans' more complicated sense of self. In animals that lack a highly complex *me* self, with its full repertoire of diverse and multifaceted self-representations, the best a status signal can do is inform others of a threat or current power differential. But in humans, the presence of the *me* changes things.

Humans are aware of shifts in the *me*'s social value; each of us can keep track of events that increase our own social worth. We can also keep track of other group members' shifting social value. We can do this because we have complex selves composed of numerous distinct goals and representations, and each success that we experience or observe others experience is understood within this larger context. If we learn of a fellow human's accomplishment — say, scoring in a soccer game or selling a car — we use that information to help formulate an opinion of this person's status, and we do so while also taking into account the other information we already possess about the person — like how many goals she's scored this season or how long he's worked for the auto dealership. We adjust our perception of our fellow human's status partly on the basis of her current success but also on the basis of everything else we know about her — including her past history of successes and failures, her larger life goals and plans, and the relative importance of this particular success within that context. In short, we humans know and can hold in mind much more about the people we interact with than simply whether they present a current threat to our own well-being.

As a result, humans' nonverbal signals don't serve only to intimidate or threaten; they also can be used to inform of likely shifts in social worth. And because the others we interact with have their own *me* selves, these people are able not only to understand the meaning of the signals we send but also to use them to facilitate their own navigation of the social scene. Observing someone in your group display pride might tell you that she is someone you shouldn't mess with and *also* that she's someone you might be wise to befriend, or follow, or learn from.

In other words, by displaying pride *after* successfully conquering an adversary (rather than before), the proud human tells observers that her status is subtly (or, in the case of John Kerry, not so subtly) shifting, and this is information they would be wise to bear in mind. Sending this message, or successfully receiving it, requires an understanding that the self is a stable entity that has continuity over time; that who I am and what I do now is relevant to who I was yesterday and who I will be tomorrow.

If this account is right, then the pride expression's ultimate evolved function is to communicate an individual's belief that he merits a boost in status — that he is the human equivalent of an alpha chimp: a person of power and authority who should be treated with deference. Like the bluff display, a nonverbal expression that sends a message like this would be a valuable adaptation. Humans who can effectively convince others that they deserve an increase in rank will receive better treatment from those others. They'll be granted a larger portion of shared resources and will benefit more from cooperative enterprises. Group members will defer to them, giving them the power to influence and shape social dynamics and to demand a greater share of the pie, where the pie includes all things valued by society — safe shelter, desirable mates, wealth, and literal pie.

This is the reason that social rank is correlated with evolutionary fitness. Throughout human history, those people who ranked higher than others were more likely to survive long enough to reproduce, and to reproduce again and again. So, if the pride display sends a message that has the effect of increasing the sender's status, it would explain why the expression is a human universal.*

This evolutionary account provides a logical explanation for why people show pride in response to success — why John Kerry felt the need to display it after winning his party's nomination for president. It also places pride within a broader historical context; it connects the expression to the nonverbal displays shown by species that share our ancestry but emerged before us in the lineage. It tells us where pride's origins lie. The question, then, is whether this account is correct. When we see a person display pride, do we readily take her expression to mean that she deserves a raise in social rank?

Imagine that you've just bumped into a good friend, and she's got some exciting news to share. She works for a large advertising agency, and she just found out that her company was granted a major contract for a project that two agents in particular had been working on together — let's call them Sam and Diane. She happens to be friends with both agents, so she heard the story from each of them separately. First she received a call from Diane, who — your friend tells you — is filled with pride about the success. Later on, she heard from Sam, who appeared to be feeling something more like appreciation. Would you be able to guess from this information alone which of the two agents was in charge of securing the deal?

According to one social psychological study, the answer is yes, you would. Researchers asked participants to make exactly this kind of judgment: to guess the relative status of two hypothetical individuals who were experiencing pride and appreciation, respectively. On the basis of this information alone, participants had no trouble figuring

---

* Furthermore, because the display is likely to be costly if it's faked — in addition to risking a quick kick to the jugular, those who display unwarranted pride (also known as behaving like arrogant jerks) face severe social penalties — the display is unlikely to be frequently exploited. That said, this question of how and why the pride expression is costly and thus not easily exploitable is a complicated one, and we will return to it in chapter 7.

out who was the boss and who was the subordinate. The person who responded with pride, of course, had to be higher in rank.

This study tells us that feelings of pride are systematically linked to perceptions of high status. If we know that someone feels pride, we infer that he or she is high in status. And what's an easy way to figure out whether someone is feeling pride? In a flash, before she's even had time to tell you how she feels, you can see it from her face and body. The pride expression is an instantaneous way of informing anyone, anywhere in the world, that you're proud. According to this study, then, seeing a person display pride might tell us not only that she's feeling proud but also that she is a high-status member of her society.

Additional circumstantial support for the conclusion that pride displays communicate high status comes from another study that found that participants who were induced to feel pride before working on a task with others were subsequently judged, by those others, to be high in dominance. Pride-induced group members took charge more than group members not made to feel any particular emotion, and as a result, their group mates came to see them as leaders. Presumably these prideful participants were behaving in dominant ways — telling others what to do, making decisions — but it's also possible that their nonverbal expressions played a role. Perhaps those proud group members were judged by their coworkers to be high in status *because* they showed clearly recognizable pride expressions.

The best way to determine whether pride nonverbal displays in fact promote perceptions of high status is, of course, to test it directly: to show research participants images of people displaying pride and examine whether these observers come to see the displayers as high in status. The problem with this approach, however, is that it allows participants to rely on their intuitive knowledge about what pride means, as well as on their more natural, automatic responses to the expression. A research participant shown a photo of a person expressing pride might judge that person to be high in status because the participant has a spontaneous, automatic response to the display *or* because he knows, as we all know, that people who feel pride tend to have high status. If this knowledge is the causal force underlying the participant's judgment, then we couldn't conclude that the pride expression in itself sends a message of high status; rather, this would mean that the pride expression sends a message of *pride,* and observers use their knowledge about the world to infer that the proud person is likely to be high in status.

But if the pride expression evolved as a status signal from earlier dominance and bluff displays shown by our nonhuman ancestors, then it should communicate status information irrespective of any explicit knowledge perceivers might possess about what pride means. In fact, it should communicate this information *implicitly;* observers should grant status to pride displayers *without even thinking about it.* After all, if interpreting the social message behind pride displays required mental exertion, these displays would not make effective signals. Observers would need to devote deliberative, attention-focused resources every time they saw the expression. Inferring high status from pride would be cognitively taxing, like solving a crossword puzzle, and any observer who happened to be distracted would miss the signal entirely. Equally important, observers who *wanted* to disregard the message easily could; the same kind of conscious thought required to interpret the signal could be used to *reinterpret* it — for example, by convincing oneself that the displayer is just happy or wants high status but doesn't deserve it.

In contrast, an automatically perceived signal — one that's understood unthinkingly with no need for conscious resources whatsoever — would be reliably received by *all* observers, even those who weren't paying attention or didn't want to receive it. It's pretty difficult to talk yourself out of interpreting an expression in a particular way if you don't consciously realize you're making that interpretation.

In fact, studies using what's known as the implicit-association test, or IAT, support this idea and suggest that pride displays are unconsciously perceived as signals of high status. The IAT capitalizes on the fact that when asked to connect words or images, people respond much more quickly to those that are conceptually related than those that are not. If you see two words that are strongly related to each other — for example, *witch* and *ghost* — you can't help but respond quickly (typically by pressing a button on a computer keyboard) when one of these words follows the other, and you can't help but respond more slowly when a completely different word, like *banana,* follows instead. The speed with which people respond to various stimuli is therefore a good indication of how strongly those stimuli are conceptually connected in their minds. Fast responses mean strong associations (tight links) and slow responses mean weak associations, or disassociations. As a result, if researchers don't know how strongly associated two concepts are, a good way to find out is to measure how quickly people respond to them when they are presented in quick succession.

Furthermore, the speed of people's responses to various stimuli says something about their mental representations — the thoughts inside their heads — without anyone having to ask for them. Although asking often works perfectly well, there are occasions when *not asking* works even better. By not asking participants to say whether they think a person displaying pride deserves high status, researchers can avoid calling on participants' conscious knowledge of what pride is all about and instead directly tap into their more primitive, uncontrolled, automatic responses. They can test whether pride displays signal high status in a way that would have been useful throughout our species' evolutionary history — before humans had the ability to talk or think through complex ideas about what emotions mean.

In fact, in research conducted in my lab at the University of British Columbia, Canadian undergraduates were found to respond much more quickly to pride expressions when these displays were viewed in conjunction with high-status words — like *commanding, dominant,* and *prestigious* — than when they were viewed alongside low-status words, like *humble, submissive,* and *weak.* We further found that pride expressions were more strongly associated with high-status words *than every other emotion,* including disgust, happiness, and even anger, a notably high-status emotion in its own right. No matter what pride is compared with (and the IAT only works by comparison; it tests whether one set of responses is faster than another), research participants always showed a much stronger association between pride and high status, and the comparison expression and low status, than the reverse. What this means is that when we see someone display pride, our brains can't help but trigger the concept of high status, and this unavoidable inference occurs more powerfully for pride than for any other emotion.

This finding is consistent with the claim that the pride expression evolved as a status signal, functioning to inform onlookers that the displayer deserves a boost in social rank. But these results are not conclusive proof of that claim. They tell us that pride sends a message of high status, and one that's automatically perceived, but only, as far as we know, by *Canadian undergraduates*. To know whether this automatic perception occurs as a result of our evolution — whether perceiving pride as high status is part of human nature — we need to know whether the expression sends the same automatically perceived message to people outside this narrow population. Ideally, people *far* outside. We need to study people like the Burkinabé, people who are unlikely to have learned about an association between pride expressions and high status that might be specific to the North American culture.

Most Americans, after all, could tell you that North American undergraduates automatically infer high status from pride displays. Westerners know what it means when athletes raise their arms and pump their fists after a big win or when corporate managers sit in business meetings with their chests pushed out and their arms crossed, taking up as much space as possible (the recently invented word *manspreading* aptly describes this behavior). Westerners know that these people are making status claims, and if they think about it, they might even know that they're using pride to do it. But do Westerners in general (and Americans in particular) know these things because of their culture — because the link between pride and high status is integral to their individualistic, high-achieving, self-enhancing cultural heritage? Or do they know these things because pride evolved from earlier prehuman dominance displays and continues to function in humans as an unavoidable, universal status signal?

To answer this question — to know whether the status-signaling function of pride is likely to be a product of humans' evolutionary heritage — we need to find out how the expression is interpreted by people who have little or no knowledge of Western culture, people who wouldn't know that ruggedly individualistic Americans view those who appear to be proud as deserving a status boost. If people who lack that knowledge demonstrate the same automatic associations between pride expressions and high-status concepts, it would suggest that these associations are a result *not* of learning or Western enculturation but rather of evolutionary processes that are universal across our species.

But it's not enough to study the pride expression's signaling impact in some remote group of people who aren't familiar with Western cultural associations between pride and status. After all, because the pride display is a human universal, such people might have developed their own, culturally unique, pride-based status signal. If, for example, we were to study a population that, like the United States', places a high value on self-enhancement and whose people seek to bolster their status any and every chance they get, we'd probably find a similar association between pride displays and high status — but not necessarily because this association is universal. Rather, we'd simply be documenting a cultural phenomenon similar to one that exists in the West, perhaps because, in both cultures, tying status gains to the nonverbal display that occurs after success makes a lot of sense. To truly know whether an automatic association between pride and high status indicates universality, a study would need to examine the expression's impact in a remote, non-Western social group where the local norms *reduce* the likelihood of granting high status to those who show pride. In a society like that, individuals could not have *learned* to associate pride displays with high status, so any association that nonetheless exists must be part of their innate human nature.

The perfect cultural group — one that meets both these criteria — can be found on a tiny island in Fiji known as Yasawa. Just fifteen miles in length, Yasawa Island consists of six villages, each composed of about one hundred to three hundred and fifty people who live off small-scale farming, fishing, and gathering. The island has no public utilities, which means no electricity, television, or computers. There's also no postal service. The nearest town is a day's journey by boat. In short, the Yasawan people have no viable means of obtaining any

Western cultural products or media, making it hard to imagine that they might somehow have acquired knowledge about an association between pride displays and high status that is unique to Western culture.

On top of that, several aspects of Fijian culture make it unlikely that Yasawa Islanders would have developed their own pride-status association. In Fiji, all social relationships are governed by an extremely rigid hierarchical system. The chief, who inherits his position from birth, has total power. Even brothers and sisters don't treat each other as equals — instead, the elder outranks the younger, and all younger siblings grant the eldest authority and respect. Their entire relationship is regulated by a detailed array of social norms about appropriate rank-related behaviors. In fact, Fijians have few relationships that *aren't* influenced by status differences and, consequently, shaped by the social rules that govern these differences. At meals, community gatherings, and rituals, people sit, speak, eat, and drink according to a strict status-based protocol.

Alongside these rules come norms about the appropriateness (or inappropriateness) of behaviors that could be interpreted as status claims. For individuals who are low in status, any behavior that might be perceived as an attempt to brag or otherwise demonstrate a deservingness of high status is strictly prohibited. Interestingly, the same rule applies to individuals who *are* high in status. High-status group members are expected to *avoid* the display of any behaviors that might be perceived as an attempt to lord their higher rank over others. Instead, these individuals must make obvious efforts to downplay their status, in part by smiling frequently and going out of their way to be friendly. This means that high-ranking members of Fijian society regularly display expressions of happiness but *not* of pride.

One result of the Yasawa Islanders' unique cultural system is that there is simply *no need* for individuals to display a nonverbal signal of high status. This is partly because rank differences are determined entirely by a preordained and heredity-based hierarchical system and partly because social norms prohibit any behavior that could be seen as an attempt to convey an individual's sense that he or she deserves higher status. Together, these factors make it unlikely that the Yasawan people would have developed, on their own, a pride display that does just this. For this reason, evidence that these individuals nonetheless associate pride displays with high status would support the evolutionary hypothesis. After all, if their culture prohibits the social construction of such a display, and the remoteness of Yasawa Island minimizes the likelihood that they might have learned this association from Western culture, the only explanation left is that these associations are hardwired into the human brain.

The social norms about status and status signaling on Yasawa Island make it an ideal location to test the universality of the pride status signal, but they also make it essential that we assess the local Fijians' *implicit* status associations with pride. Because the Yasawan people are well aware of the cultural norms that prohibit overt status displays in their society, it's unlikely that they would think, on a conscious level, that displaying pride is a high-status move. In fact, we might expect a dissociation between these people's explicit and implicit judgments of pride. At an explicit level, they should judge pride displays in the way their cultural norms tell them to — as *not* relevant to high status. But if human brains evolved to unavoidably perceive pride as a signal of high status, then at an implicit level, we might still find remnants of an ancient automatic association between pride displays and high status, despite the presence of cultural norms fighting against this association.

To test for this dissociation, my colleagues and I began with a study that measured Yasawa Islanders' explicit beliefs about the status connotations of various emotion expressions. Pride, we found, was *not* the highest-status emotion in town. It was higher status than shame, but that's it. To the Yasawan people, pride displays were no more a signal of high status than neutral displays were, and both were understood to be generally irrelevant to status. Happy displays, however, *were* judged to be high-status indicators. Happiness was, apparently, *the* expression that people in this society expected their highest-status group members to regularly display.

These results are consistent with what we know about Fijian culture. A person who shows an expression like pride, which might directly communicate a desire for high status, is violating an important social rule. As a result, this person is explicitly judged as *undeserving* of high status. In contrast, a person who displays happiness is doing exactly what a high-status person is expected to do: demonstrate friendliness and avoid any suggestion of bragging or lording his or her high status over others.

The question, though, was whether these participants' explicit beliefs about the connection between emotion expressions and status differed from their more implicit, uncontrollable judgments. If the Yasawans' implicit responses were consistent with their explicit beliefs, it would suggest a real cultural difference in the message sent by pride displays; it would mean that pride is not a stronger status signal than happiness within this culture. But if we instead found a difference in their implicit and explicit status associations, it might confirm the hypothesis that pride displays are universally linked to high status — even if only at an unconscious level.

To address this question we again pulled out the IAT, which turned out to be a considerably more complicated endeavor with people who had never previously used a computer. Nonetheless, when we compared Yasawan participants' implicit associations with their explicit beliefs, a notably different pattern emerged between the two. The Yasawans showed a stronger automatic association between pride displays and high status than between shame displays and high status — as had been the case with their explicit judgments — but they also showed a stronger automatic association between pride displays and high status than between *neutral displays* and high status. This is different from what they told us when we probed their explicit beliefs. And this difference suggests that these individuals do possess strong associations between pride displays and high-status concepts — but that these are associations they are not aware of. Comparing pride displays with displays of happiness — the emotion that, based on the Yasawans' explicit judgments, is the highest status of all — we found a tie. Both expressions were strongly associated with high status at an implicit level, and equally so.

Now, this result could be taken to mean that pride is not a unique signal of high status — and, in fact, on Yasawa Island, it's not. Happy displays, quite clearly, serve a status-signaling function there too. But this result does *not* mean that pride displays are not evolved status signals. The finding that these implicit associations were no different, despite the fact that Yasawans explicitly judged happy displays as much more indicative of high status than pride, means that there is a difference — or dissociation — between these individuals' implicit and explicit representations of pride. Explicitly, they do not perceive pride as a high-status emotion; they judge it as substantially lower status than happiness. But probing their automatic responses reveals that *implicitly,* they see pride as higher status than neutral displays and just as high status as the emotion that's considered the highest status of all in their culture — happiness.

The observed dissociation between Yasawa Islanders' implicit and explicit representations of pride is particularly informative because it makes it unlikely that these individuals somehow *learned* to automatically associate pride and high status from their limited contact with Western cultures. It's difficult to imagine how these associations could have become so well learned that they would be automatized — embedded within unconscious knowledge structures — *yet remain absent from explicit knowledge.* The more plausible explanation is that pride displays evolved in humans as universal status signals, such that humans everywhere implicitly know that these displays mean high status regardless of any learning they have or have not had. As a result, Fijians can't help but demonstrate their knowledge of this association — even though it's a knowledge they suppress at an explicit level, thanks to their cultural rules and norms about status signaling.

Although it was conducted far from the Old Post Office Pavilion in Washington, DC, this research provides an answer to the question of why John Kerry ultimately displayed pride after winning the Democratic Party's nomination for president. Even though everyone watching already knew that he'd just experienced a massive victory, seeing his expression did much more than inform the public of his success. It triggered within these observers an automatic mental association they couldn't help but make, even if they had been taught not to. Even the

Fijians among us can't avoid implicitly perceiving a pride displayer as high in status, so American Democrats who until that moment might have been John Edwards supporters probably had the same response.

An American Democrat is one thing, but what interpretation could we expect from someone who didn't see Kerry as an accomplished senator with an impressive war record but instead as a rich liberal who spent his free time windsurfing? If observers know something about the context of the display, in other words — something that tells them that the displayer does *not* deserve high status — would pride still so unambiguously trigger an automatic perception of high status?

This is something the studies I've told you about so far can't answer. In all these studies, people's automatic responses to pride expressions were examined in the complete absence of *any other information.* When observers have nothing else to go on, it makes sense that an emotion expression would powerfully guide their perceptions. But the massive audience that watched Kerry that night had a great deal of other information at their fingertips. And in daily life, when we see people show pride, more often than not, this is how it works. It's rare to see someone show an emotion expression and not know *anything* else about the person. More typically, we possess other information that's relevant to the question of whether the expresser deserves high status. In that kind of situation, does pride carry any weight?

Let's travel back, for just a moment, to that imaginary trip we took to Mecca in chapter 1. Once again, while in the midst of this exciting journey, you find yourself face to face with a Saudi sheikh. This time, though, he's not alone; accompanying him is his most trusted servant. It's easy to tell the two apart even though they're dressed similarly; the sheikh walks ahead and carries nothing, while his servant, several steps behind, is loaded down with bags and seems to be struggling to keep up.

But now add one more detail to this scene. As you approach the two men, you notice that the servant, and not the sheikh, is displaying a classic pride expression. Even as he carries his load, it's clear that he's pushing his chest outward and tilting his head slightly upward.

Meanwhile, the sheikh is ... well, the sheikh is doing something with his body and head that's somewhat unexpected. You squint your eyes to make sure, and — yes, strange as it seems, the sheikh's posture is slumped, and his head is tilted downward. By all accounts, the sheikh is displaying shame.

While this imaginary role reversal may seem far-fetched, it happens. Even the highest-ranking leaders in the world at times feel shame, and the humblest servants at times feel pride. But how do we — outside observers who are well aware of the respective ranks of these individuals — interpret their emotional displays? Do we still make those same automatic judgments solely on the basis of their expressions? Does our universal human tendency to perceive someone who displays pride as high in status really override everything else we know about the displayer, including whether he is a sheikh or a servant? Surprisingly, the answer is yes — at least in certain contexts, it does.

To demonstrate this point, my colleagues and I again made use of the IAT, this time to assess the implicit associations individuals hold between status words and pride expressions under a specific set of circumstances: when the expression is displayed *by someone known to be low in status.*

We told a sample of participants — once again, Canadian undergraduates — that they'd be viewing photos of identical twin brothers who played together on their university's soccer team. One brother, Mark, was the well-respected MVP and team captain. The other brother, Steve, was a much weaker player who rarely saw game time and frequently doubled as the team's water boy. On the basis of this short story, anyone who understands the most basic dynamics of team hierarchies comes away with a clear message: Mark is higher status than Steve. To really hammer it in, the brothers wore T-shirts emblazoned with *Captain* or *Water Boy.*

(In actuality, both brothers were portrayed by the same person; this is the reason we said they were twins. This allowed us to ensure that any differences that emerged between judgments of the two could be attributed to our experimental manipulation, not to something about how the posers looked.)

Our participants' task was to quickly pair photos of one or the other of the twins with high- or low-status words. And, not surprisingly, as long as both twins showed neutral facial expressions, participants were much quicker to associate the captain with high status and the water boy with low status than the reverse. Our participants, like most college students, held implicit associations between captains and high sta-

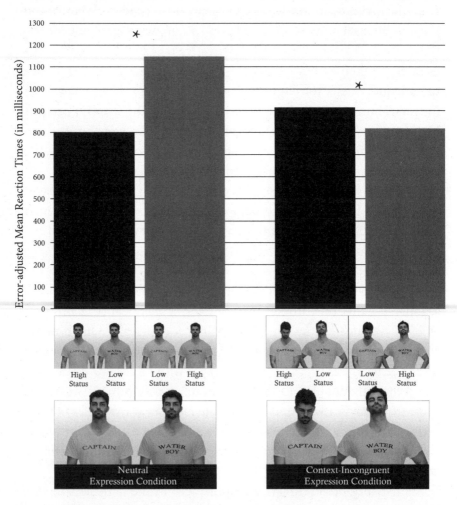

Figure 4.3. Average reaction times (after subtracting errors) in response to images of a captain and a water boy paired with high- versus low-status words. Larger reaction times indicate slower (i.e., delayed) responding. Asterisks indicate statistically significant differences between conditions.

tus and water boys and low status, and these associations drove their automatic perceptions of the twins.

But what about when the twins didn't show neutral expressions? What happened when, instead, they displayed expressions that were incongruent with their social rank — when the captain displayed shame and the water boy displayed pride?

Under these circumstances, we found the exact *opposite* pattern of results. This time, participants were much quicker to associate the water boy with high status and the captain with low status. The twins' pride and shame expressions sent signals about the young men's relative hierarchical ranks that were strong enough to completely overpower the status-relevant information conveyed by the twins' respective roles on the team (see figure 4.3).

These results suggest that the pride expression is a powerful enough status signal to overcome competing information about an individual's status. Pride beats water boy, and shame beats captain.

But these results do not mean that pride displays can be counted on to signal high status in any person no matter what the situation. It's possible that the reason the pride expression overpowered the water-boy T-shirt here is that a water-boy T-shirt isn't all that powerful. In fact, despite their opposing roles on the soccer team, these twin brothers would probably be of a similar social rank in most domains of life outside of soccer. The water boy might even be higher status than his brother in some domains; perhaps he's captain of the chess team (and the soccer captain is the chess team's coffee boy?). Our participants might have been taking into account their broader knowledge of the complex and multiple hierarchies that exist within the social system of the typical college student and, for this reason, became easily swayed by the competing status information that came from the pride and shame expressions.

The way to address this issue, of course, is to manipulate contextual status information much more powerfully so that it doesn't apply to only one hierarchy but instead to the many different social relationships in these people's lives. So we conducted another study in which we again asked participants to make judgments about twin brothers.

This time, though, the twins weren't soccer teammates. Instead, one was a successful businessman with a degree in finance. His brother, sadly, had taken a tougher path through life and was now homeless, living on the streets. The result was a status differential, between a businessman and a homeless man, that is one of the largest that exists within contemporary North American society. Studies have shown that homeless people are considered so low in status that we see them not only as less than us, but as *less than human*. Thinking about the homeless fails to activate the part of the brain that's engaged when we think about other people.

After viewing photos of these new twins, participants completed an IAT, once again with both brothers displaying neutral expressions. Not surprisingly, participants were *much* faster to associate the businessman with high-status words and the homeless man with low-status words than the reverse. In fact, this difference was massive; it was almost three and a half times larger than the difference in automatic status associations between the captain and the water boy when they both displayed neutral expressions.

Given this finding, resulting from the powerful cultural associations that many Americans have with businessmen and homeless people, you might expect that subjects would continue to view these twin brothers as high and low status, respectively, even when they saw the businessman display shame and the homeless man display pride. But, in fact, what we found was that there was *no difference* in participants' automatic status associations with the two very different twins when each showed an expression antithetical to his societally determined status. Our participants responded equally quickly when asked to pair high- and low-status words to both (see figure 4.4).

Now, this does not mean that the pride and shame expressions had no impact on participants' automatic status perceptions in this case. In fact, these expressions *substantially reduced* the impact of the homeless man/businessman comparison. When the twins displayed neutral expressions, the businessman was automatically perceived as *much* higher status than the homeless man. But when the businessman showed shame and the homeless man pride, the two men became *sta-

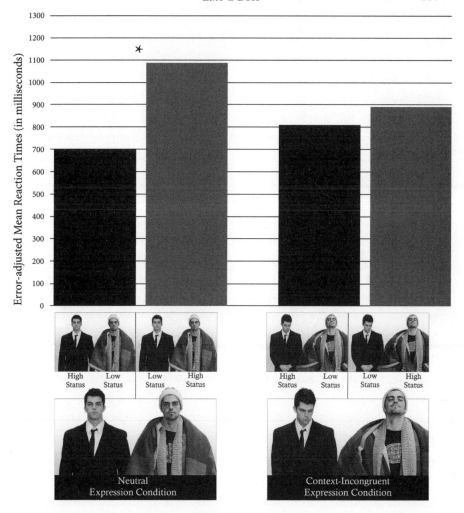

Figure 4.4. Average reaction times (after subtracting errors) when a homeless man and businessman were paired with high- or low-status words. Larger reaction times indicate slower (delayed) responding. Asterisks indicate statistically significant differences between conditions.

tus equals. This means that, although the pride expression is not powerful enough to pull a homeless man higher up the ranks than a businessman, it *is* powerful enough to make him appear *equally high in rank* as an (ashamed) businessman.

So pride does not trump every other status signal, but it comes close. In fact, these studies tell us, pride functions as an effective status signal even when observers possess conflicting information about the expresser's status. Even when we know that the expresser deserves low status, we can't help but automatically perceive him as at least somewhat high in status simply because of his pride. This research therefore indicates that pride is a particularly powerful status signal, and, just as important, it sheds new light on the basis upon which we allocate social rank. We like to believe that we make status-based judgments by carefully collecting all the relevant facts and diligently sorting through them. In fact, these decisions may be guided much more by our evolved automatic reflexes, which can lead us to make snap judgments from powerful emotion expressions like pride.

But is this really the case — do we actually make judgments about the people around us on the basis of whether they display pride? In fact, we can't quite draw this conclusion from the research I've told you about so far. All of these findings are based on automatic perceptions — the speed with which participants press certain buttons when they see certain images. We don't know whether these results have any bearing on actual status judgments made in the real world about real people.

Every day, we make all kinds of decisions that are based, at least to some extent, on inferences of deserved status. These include important decisions like the one Americans had to make about John Kerry — whether to vote for him — but also less consequential decisions, like whom to pick for your team, whom to make friends with, whom to work with, and whom to hire. If the pride expression is an automatic status signal — and one that's difficult to override even when we have contradictory information at our disposal — then displaying it should increase a person's chances of winning the election, being chosen, and getting the job.

But that's only true if the pride status signal affects conscious, deliberated judgments. Few people enter the voting booth, close their eyes, and point. And there are few situations in which a manager must fill an open position so quickly that she can't take a moment to consciously think through her decision. Under these more realistic circumstances — when people have the time and inclination to thoughtfully consider all the relevant information — do pride displays carry any weight? Or, when deliberation is possible, does the available competing and often-contradictory information become more important than a fleeting emotion expression?

To address this question we conducted a study of one of the major status-based decisions many people have to make on a regular basis: the decision of whom to hire. We gave our Canadian undergraduate participants access to the same kinds of data that employers typically have. They viewed video clips of an interview that had been conducted with a prospective job candidate, a person applying for the high-status position of bank manager. This person, either a young man named Kenneth or a young woman named Katherine, was seen seated at the desk of an offscreen interviewer, politely responding to a series of questions. Unbeknownst to our participants, both Kenneth and Katherine were research assistants working for us who had memorized scripted answers to the questions our offscreen interviewer threw at them. And as they gave their answers, Kenneth and Katherine portrayed their best expressions of either pride or shame. When displaying pride, they sat expansively upright in their chairs, taking up as much space as possible. They talked with their hands, at times waving their arms effusively. They held their heads up high and looked directly at the interviewer. When showing shame, our assistants presented a very different picture: slumping their shoulders, keeping their hands in their laps, resolutely gazing down.

Here's a situation where a person's emotion expression is one way of inferring his or her status — a characteristic that's likely to influence employers' judgments about a candidate's qualifications — but it is not the only way. In fact, a much better way to decide whom to hire is by looking at the candidates' résumés. And participants in our study had access to those too. Some saw a résumé that was designed to be excellent; this version of Kenneth or Katherine was extremely well qualified for the position, having graduated from a prestigious Canadian university where he or she participated in numerous impressive extracurricular activities and received strong grades. To top it off, impressive Kenneth/Katherine was fluent in French, a skill Canadians value al-

most as much as hockey. Meanwhile, other participants saw a résumé
that was much weaker. This Kenneth or Katherine had attended a local community college and received only mediocre grades. Weak Ken-
neth/Katherine had no extracurricular or service activities but occasionally participated in pickup sports and reported "some knowledge"
of French.

These résumés conveyed a clear difference between the candidates
and strongly pointed to which one should get the job. And our participants — like actual employers — were not required to make their
decisions quickly or automatically; they had all the time in the world
to watch the videos, read the résumés, and deliberate. Under these circumstances, would pride and shame have any impact? Would our participants be more likely to hire the proud Kenneth/Katherine over the
ashamed Kenneth/Katherine even if they knew that he or she *didn't deserve the job?*

The answer is yes. Participants chose to hire the candidate who displayed pride more often than they chose the candidate who displayed
shame, regardless of the quality of his or her résumé. Displaying pride
in the interview was powerful enough to override the impact of a pretty
terrible résumé, and an impressive résumé couldn't overcome the negative effects of displaying shame. And, lest you suspect that this result
might be due to participants quickly glossing over the résumés, when
we asked them to judge which candidate was more intelligent, their
choice was clear, and it had nothing to do with the candidates' emotion
expressions. Impressive Kenneth/Katherine was judged to be a good
deal smarter than Weak Kenneth/Katherine, regardless of whether the
candidate had displayed pride or shame.

These results could mean a number of different things. It's possible that our participants were put off by displays of shame — slumping
one's shoulders and looking down throughout the duration of a job interview is obviously not a good career move. It's also possible that they
saw the job of bank manager as one where status mattered *a lot,* and
much more than intelligence. But even if both these factors contributed to our results, they don't take away from the basic conclusion we
have to draw: displaying pride in an interview is a solid strategy. Pride

displays are strong enough signals of high status that they can get you the job — even if you don't deserve it.

Together, the accumulated research evidence suggests that the pride expression is not only an evolved emotion expression but also an evolved *status signal*. Humans everywhere display pride after they've experienced a success because doing so sends an adaptive message about their social rank. Showing pride tells others that you deserve a boost in status, and it communicates this information in a way that others can neither ignore nor avoid. Pride displays create an automatically perceived, uncontrollable, and unconscious inference that is powerful enough to overwhelm competing information about the displayer's status and shape real-world status-based decision-making.

Further supporting this conclusion, other studies have found that posing pride displays can have an impact on the subjective experience of those who do the posing; it makes them feel powerful, and may boost their testosterone — a hormone associated with social rank. Importantly, this does *not* mean that posing pride when it's unwarranted is always a good idea. In fact, as we will soon see, it's not. But these findings do allow us to conclude that the pride expression is a universal and powerful status signal that can even influence the expresser's own status perceptions of herself.

This addresses the ultimate *why* question I posed about the pride nonverbal expression; we now know something about why humans universally display this set of nonverbal behaviors in response to a success and universally recognize these behaviors in others as conveying those others' feelings of pride. This research does not, however, address the second part of that question: Why do humans *experience* pride? Why, at an ultimate, evolutionary level, do we *feel* pride when we succeed?

We began to answer this question in chapter 3 by exploring the adaptive consequences of having a human self, but in chapter 5 we will turn to the more specific question of whether pride feelings serve an adaptive function in the same way that the expression that goes along with them does. And this question is complicated by the research evidence suggesting that there are two different ways of feeling pride: an authentic way and a hubristic way. These findings require us to ask whether *both* of these distinct pride experiences are adaptive. If so, it would mean that hubristic pride — the kind of pride that's linked to arrogance, anxiety, and aggression — is good for us, that humans evolved to experience a kind of pride that turns us into narcissistic jerks.

Is it possible that the bad kind of pride is actually good for our species? Could hubris be in our nature?

5

The Carrot and the Stick

O N MAY 2, 2011, Barack Obama called a press conference that was televised across the United States. Millions tuned in as the president confirmed the rumors that had been circulating for hours: U.S. Navy SEALs had raided Osama bin Laden's compound in Pakistan and successfully executed the al-Qaeda leader — the man who had spearheaded the most deadly terrorist attack on U.S. soil in history. In a voice sounding much more triumphant than his characteristically calm intonation, Obama told the world:

Shortly after taking office, I [made] the killing or capture of bin Laden the top priority of our war against al Qaeda. . . . After years of painstaking work by our intelligence community, I was briefed on a possible lead to bin Laden. It was far from certain, and it took many months to run this thread to ground. I met repeatedly with my national security team . . . And, finally, last week, I determined that we had enough intelligence to take action, and I authorized an operation to get Osama bin Laden, and bring him to justice. Today, at my direction, the United States launched a targeted operation against that compound in Abbottabad, Pakistan . . .

For over two decades, bin Laden has been al Qaeda's leader and symbol, and has continued to plot attacks against our country and our friends and allies. The death of bin Laden marks the most significant achievement to date in our nation's effort to defeat al Qaeda.

The speech Obama gave that night was, without a doubt, one of the most important of his career. And although the president did not use the word *proud* to describe his feelings, it is nonetheless blatantly apparent from his confident and assertive manner, along with the words he did use — self-focused pronouns like *I* instead of *we,* again and again — that pride is exactly what he felt.

All humans feel pride in our accomplishments. But for the powerful among us, pride is more than just a good feeling about the *me* self — the set of representations that constitute and define our identities. For these individuals, pride is much more than a good feeling that boosts self-esteem. It's the emotion that helped those in power get where they are. As we now know, pride sends a message about status. When we see people display the pride expression, we can't help but perceive them as high in social rank, and we treat them accordingly — even if we think they don't deserve it. If we don't see a person's expression but still somehow know that she feels pride, that's enough to tell us that she merits high status.

Obama might have been trying to suppress his most overt displays of pride that night, but his feelings still came through — and it's to his benefit that they did. Those who heard or watched the speech immediately came to see Obama as the person most responsible, and most deserving of credit, for bin Laden's death. His popularity ratings surged, and pundits considered the 2012 presidential election all but decided.

To be sure, defeating al-Qaeda and conveying a sense of pride in that accomplishment was not the only reason Obama won the 2012 election (Mitt Romney's "binders of women" might have had something to do with it). But it played a large part. Would these outcomes have occurred if Obama had taken down the leader of al-Qaeda but not followed it up with a public speech exuding pride? Maybe — after all, communicating one's pride is not the only way to climb the social ladder. But it is an effective way. By expressing his pride, Obama made sure that he got the status bump he deserved for his greatest achievement to date as U.S. president.

Countless examples exist of powerful people who've sought to further enhance their status by publicly expressing a sense of pride in a major accomplishment. To take another: Less than a week before Obama told the world about his victory in Abbottabad, real estate mogul Donald Trump called his own press conference. Trump's topic was different than Obama's, but, like Obama, Trump was feeling proud, and he wanted to tell the world. He had been working hard for some time on a project of great importance to him, and he'd finally achieved success. As he explained to the crowd that gathered: "I am very proud of myself. Because I've accomplished something that nobody else has been able to accomplish. I was just informed . . . that our president has finally released a birth certificate."

In many ways, Trump and Obama have a great deal in common. At the time of their respective announcements, they were both high-ranking leaders. Obama was president of the most powerful country in the world, and Trump was CEO and president of the Trump Organization, a massive conglomerate that controls real estate, hotels, golf courses, and television franchises and has a net worth greater than $2.9 billion. And both men reached those heights in part because of their pride. Showing it to others helped tell the world that they were leader material. A desire to feel it motivated them to become the kind of person they each became.

But, as we also now know, pride is not just one thing. There are two very different ways of feeling pride. And it's not difficult to figure out which kind of pride Obama and Trump each felt during their respective press conferences.

Obama's pride is a clear example of the authentic variety. This is the pride people feel from a sense of accomplishment, and it's the pride that makes them care about others. While hubristic pride engenders an almost obsessive focus on oneself, authentic pride fosters a sense of compassion and a focus on others. So it makes sense that, in the midst of taking credit for his role in bin Laden's death, Obama made sure to share that credit with the other people who deserved it — members of the U.S. military and his own advisory team. Authentic pride is also what people feel when they attribute their successes to unstable, controllable causes, like effort and hard work. Obama emphasized exactly these kinds of causes in his speech, meticulously laying out *what he did* to make the accomplishment happen — the steps he took, the effort and work he put in, and the risks he accepted. And, beyond those specific elements of the speech, Obama's personality seems to fit the profile of someone likely to be prone to authentic pride. He's emotionally calm, agreeable, and hard-working. Taking these facts together, there's a strong case to be made for Obama having felt authentic pride that night.

What about Trump — what kind of pride was he experiencing? Unlike Obama, he did not attempt to share the credit for his achievement with others. In fact, he made it quite clear that what he did was something *no one* else was capable of doing — that no one else deserved any credit. This makes Trump's pride excessive, particularly given that the achievement at hand is of somewhat dubious merit. Obama's administration had already released the president's standard short-form Hawaiian birth certificate years earlier, and there was no logical reason to question Obama's birthplace or nationality. But this kind of grandiosity is not atypical for Trump. As famous as he is for his wealth and business acumen, he is equally famous for his unwavering tendency to brag about both. There is no other business leader, corporate titan, or product developer who takes as much care to stake his ego on every accomplishment, giving each building, hotel, restaurant, golf course, and fragrance his own name.

Trump's speech that night perfectly exemplifies what it means to experience hubristic pride, particularly in contrast to the authentically proud Obama. Yet both men have seemingly benefited from their pride, even though it has taken very different forms. Trump may be disposed toward the hubristic variety, but he has reached the highest rungs of his society's hierarchical ladder. In the domain of business success, as in life, Trump is in the penthouse.

What does Trump's success tell us about the consequences of hubristic pride? Authentic pride makes people work hard to achieve and to behave morally — to strive to be a good person. *This* is the kind of pride that should make people leaders. Hubristic pride has a completely different set of consequences. It makes people un-empathic, disagreeable, and even aggressive. Those who experience hubristic pride tend to be impulsive and unconscientious — two traits that make it hard to accomplish one's goals. How could someone who regularly experiences this emotion end up becoming a high-ranking master of his domain? Did Donald Trump really get where he is by virtue of an emotion that's made him, at times, behave like an arrogant jerk?

To answer this question, we need to step back for a moment and delve into the psychology of rank attainment — the study of how people attain high status. We need to ask how our leaders become leaders; what is it that made them rise to the top of the social hierarchy? And, first, an even broader question: What does it mean to have high rank?

So far in this book, I've been talking about status as something that gets people power. Those who have high status are more likely to get the jobs they want or be elected for office. High status means existing at the top of the totem pole; becoming the person who has the best or most stuff; the person who is admired by all and placed on a pedestal; the person who controls what others do, say, and maybe even think; the person everyone is afraid of.

But if we take this fairly fuzzy definition apart and break it down a bit, it quickly becomes apparent that high status is not just one thing. In fact, this definition suggests at least three or four separate things, each of which is part of what it means to be high in rank but none of which fully captures the concept. Having influence over others is not the same as being admired, which is not the same as being feared, which is not the same as having the most resources. These are distinct conceptualizations, but each *is* part of what it means to be high in rank or status.

Like pride, social status is a concept that is much more complicated than it looks at first glance. But, unlike pride, status hasn't suffered from a lack of research. Instead, it's been complicated by just the opposite — lots of researchers from different disciplines seeking to define the term but without talking a whole lot to one another.

Everyone agrees that social rank means social influence, that the people who are highest on the social hierarchy are those who can determine — at least partly — what others around them do. As a result of this power, rank also means resources. Those who are high in rank can, and typically do, use their influence to make sure they get more of whatever's valued by the group, although the resource in question can be anything from food, money, cars, and clothing, to attractive romantic partners, to obedient and deferential followers.

But that's only the *outcome* of high rank. It's the reason why having status is a good thing, something that increases evolutionary fitness and that most people in most societies want. It still leaves open the question of what *leads to* high rank, however. Do people get high rank when others admire them or when others fear them?

Evolutionary psychologists have come up with one answer to this question — an answer that seems pretty solid. Taking a cue from biologists, who built their theories of status on the basis of what happens across the animal kingdom, many evolutionary scientists have conceptualized status as the power obtained from intimidating others and inducing within them a sense of threat. High rank — or *dominance,* as they term it — is, in this account, largely the same in humans as it is in all animals: the ability to win a fight. And there's plenty of evidence to suggest that humans who can effectively dominate others by letting those others know that they must obey, *or else,* end up high on the social ladder.

People who are forceful, assertive, and aggressive tend to acquire high rank, and in some societies they are more likely to become leaders than their fellow group mates who are merely smart but not tough. (This will come as no surprise to those familiar with the social hierarchies that proliferate in many American high schools.) Yes, these people can be jerks, but they still get ahead, and we all know it. In fact, this shared understanding dates back to Machiavelli's famous tract *The Prince,* in which he advised Italian rulers who wished to stay in power that it was "far safer to be feared than loved."

Problem solved? Well, no. As it turns out, there's another, completely different perspective on social rank out there, a view that we also need to consider. This one, coming predominantly from social psychologists and scientists of organizational behavior, suggests that threat and intimidation are *ineffective* means of getting ahead in modern human groups. In direct contrast to the evolutionary psychology approach, these researchers argue that "individuals do not attain status by bullying and intimidating . . . but [rather] by behaving in ways that suggest high levels of competence, generosity, and commitment."

According to the social psychology perspective, people don't earn high rank by being arrogant and domineering; they earn high rank by being nice and competent. High-status leaders are those who possess the most or best socially valued skills or knowledge. They know how to do things that others want to learn, and they contribute to their group by doing precisely those things, and then teaching others how to do them too. Really, this is the kind of status I've been talking about up to this point (though not explicitly); if pride displays are shown in response to an achievement, and communicate to others a deserved status boost, that's because status is earned from achievements.

This second account of rank attainment, much like the first, fits with what we all know. Social rank is, and should be, awarded to those who deserve it: group members who contribute the most and whose leadership is supported by a consensus. Not only does a rank-allocation system like this put the most capable leaders in charge, it also bestows a sense of fairness and legitimacy to the system, stabilizing the hierarchy and making it more immune to potential uprisings from the lower ranks. And empirical studies support *this* account too. People who are seen by others as competent, wise, generous, and committed to their group are consistently found to have the greatest social influence. On the basis of these findings, several scholars have argued that, in human societies, hierarchical relationships based on intimidation or the threat of force *are simply untenable.*

But how does that strong stance fit with the evolutionary psychologists' account? *Is* status earned through competence and kindness? Or is it forcibly taken through aggression and intimidation?

In 2001, two evolutionary anthropologists, Joseph Henrich and Francisco Gil-White, tried to answer these questions by proposing a unifying framework — an account of what status is and how people get it — that offered a solution to the apparent conflict between the two perspectives on how status is earned, whether through qualities we think of as generous, helpful, and *good,* or through qualities that many of us think of as selfish, cruel, and *bad.*

These researchers based their account on observations that had been made by other anthropologists who'd been studying status dynamics in small-scale traditional societies for years. Even in the most egalitarian of these societies, there always seemed to be some rank-ordering system that guided social relationships. But this system was rarely just one thing. Instead, two distinct principles appeared to organize hierarchical differences in many small-scale societies. There was *dominance* — attaining high rank by intimidating, manipulating, and threatening others. But there was also *prestige* — attaining high rank by demonstrating one's skills, competence, and wisdom, along with a willingness to share the profits of these abilities. To take just one example, among the Tsimane, a small-scale society in the Amazon, high rank is awarded to those who are big and strong — that is, capable of threatening others and invoking fear — but also to those who, regardless of their size, are particularly skilled hunters and generous with the meat earned from their kills.

In retrospect, it seems obvious. If there are two competing and equally reasonable theoretical accounts of how people attain high rank, isn't the truth likely to be that *both* are right? But Henrich and Gil-White's model wasn't just a statement of the obvious. They *derived* their model, in the same way that mathematicians derive formal theorems, from carefully constructed evolutionary logic.

They began by reasoning that humans are animals, so, like all other animals, our species should grant power to others who are, technically speaking, more powerful — capable of winning fights. Sure, physical fights aren't the most typical way that humans today battle it out for higher status, but fights don't have to be physical. We can be induced to feel fear even without believing that the intimidator might beat us up. Think of the boss who threatens to fire her employees any time they question her mandates. All an intimidator needs to do is imply that she can, and will, take away valuable resources.

Many of our most prominent contemporary leaders are known for precisely this kind of governing strategy. Steve Jobs, founder of Apple Computer and the company's CEO for many years, liked to motivate Apple engineers by telling them, loudly and sternly, "You are fucking up my company" and "If we fail, it will be because of you."

But there is also another force at play in human rank dynamics. Unlike every other animal species, we are intensely cultural beings. We rely on cultural knowledge and wisdom in a way that no other animal does. One of the reasons we became the unique species we are is that we don't have to invent the wheel anew each time we need it. Instead, we learn about the wheel — along with many of the other most useful things we know — from others in our society.

Part of what it means to become socialized is to learn your society's body of shared knowledge about how to survive. In the small-scale societies that Henrich and Gil-White studied, this knowledge includes things like how to build a canoe, where to find the best berries, and how to deliver a baby. In modern Western society, cultural knowledge is just as essential but is more likely to include things like how to read and do basic math, how to buy food with money, and how to use computers and smartphones.

Finding a way to acquire the accumulated knowledge of one's culture is critical for every human; imagine the difference in reproductive success and resource acquisition between an individual who learns how to obtain food in her culture and one who does not. The importance — and downright necessity — of cultural learning means that there must have been, in human evolutionary history, an adaptive advantage to those who figured out how to get the knowledge they needed from skilled or wise others. Henrich and Gil-White term these ancient models of cultural wisdom *prestigious*. These individuals would have been group members who weren't necessarily the strongest or wealthiest but instead might have been the smartest or the most competent or especially knowledgeable about one particular culturally valued arena.

One way to get these prestigious individuals to share what they know or the profits they're able to attain is to give them power. Let these experts be in control, make decisions, and take a large portion of shared resources. Giving these models this power — deferring to them in this way — benefits everyone. Models acquire an incentive to share their knowledge or at least to not object when others hang around and try to copy them — after all, doing so gets them power! — and subordinates benefit from what they learn. Plus, putting the people who know the most in charge is a solid group decision; it ensures that these experts' wisdom trickles down to everyone else, and the group as a whole gets smarter.

Now, this does not mean that people or groups strategically grant power to those who know more because they realize that's what's best. The fact is, if the system has adaptive consequences, it doesn't matter what people do knowingly. The system will produce in humans certain evolved motivations — such as the motivation to defer to others who seem like they know what they're talking about — whether or not the humans involved are aware of the likely outcomes. The end result is that prestige becomes an effective means of getting ahead.

In sum, because humans *are* like other animals and also *not* like other animals, human evolution should have created two separate tracks to high rank: one based on ancient principles of conflict, where the bigger, stronger, or richer competitor wins, and one based on cultural learning, where the smarter, wiser, or more competent competitor wins.

This account not only integrates the diverse and contradicting prior views of rank attainment but does so by providing an explanatory framework. It gives the *why* of rank attainment, not just the *what*. And it explains not only why human social groups should feature both forms of hierarchy but also why leaders who attain power through one of the two forms versus the other should behave differently and be treated differently by their followers.

Based on this theory, those who gain power via dominance should be feared — maybe even hated — by the rest of the group. Their status is acquired not because followers *choose* to follow them, but because followers feel like they have no choice in the matter. The result should be a position of high rank that's constantly in danger of revocation by an angry mass — which is the reason fascist dictators surround themselves with well-paid or sadistic associates who are ready, at a moment's notice, to fend off potential rebels. It's a kind of power that doesn't last beyond the leader's ability to wield control. Much like the Wizard of Oz, who lost all authority as soon as he was revealed to be a mere "humbug," dominant leaders who can no longer effectively evoke fear will immediately fall from their position of influence.

Those who achieve high rank via prestige, however, have no reason to be disliked and, in fact, should be admired and loved. These individuals acquire high rank because subordinates *want* to follow them; group members willingly defer to the prestigious. And the more generosity, caring, and compassion these prestigious leaders demonstrate, the more powerful they become; their authority is directly earned from the group's appreciation of their contributions. In fact, as soon as these leaders decide to become domineering or manipulative instead of kind and altruistic, they become less desirable leaders.

This is because the competition for prestige favors cultural experts who not only know a lot or can do a lot but who are willing to helpfully share their knowledge and can-do with others. Group members faced with a choice of deferring to a leader who shares her knowledge generously versus one who shares her knowledge arrogantly will always choose the generous option. That said, however, there are leaders who use prestige to get ahead and then, once at the top of the pack, switch to a dominant strategy. When that happens, their status is no longer based solely on prestige. Steve Jobs is a good example of this profile as well; as a skinny, smart guy, chances are he never would have gotten to a position where he could effectively intimidate his followers if he hadn't, much earlier, had a few great ideas.*

As by now you might suspect, Henrich and Gil-White's model — known as the dominance-prestige model of rank attainment — has the potential to answer the question I posed earlier in this chapter: How can a person who regularly feels and expresses a great deal of hubristic pride, like Donald Trump, attain a similar level of status as a person who exudes authentic pride, like Barack Obama? In fact, dominance and prestige might be the answer to a much larger and broader question as well: Why do humans experience pride in two different ways? Why did we evolve to experience a form of pride that makes us want to achieve and treat others with compassion and also a form of pride that can turn us into arrogant jerks?

The answer may lie in this theoretical model of rank attainment. If both dominance and prestige are viable means of obtaining power or social influence, then it makes sense that humans would have evolved distinct emotions to motivate the behaviors needed to orchestrate each. If dominance is as effective a way of climbing the social ladder as prestige seems to be, then an emotion like hubristic pride — an emotion that might be exactly what's needed to prompt the arrogant, aggressive, and manipulative behaviors that allow individuals to become dominant leaders — would be as adaptive as an emotion like authentic pride, which might be exactly what's needed to attain prestige.

The dominance-prestige model might be the answer that psychologists, philosophers, and even theologians have been looking for since the dawn of Western civilization to explain why pride appears to be both good and bad, both sinful and virtuous. But there is one thing missing from this picture of pride and status. Theoretical models are great, but conclusions about human psychology need to be built on data, not just evolutionary logic combined with observations made

---

* That said, according to two recent films about Jobs — *Steve Jobs* (2015) and *Jobs* (2013) — his early rise to fame was largely due to the fact that he convinced Steve Wozniak, his much less socially skilled but much more technically savvy friend, to design a new kind of consumer-friendly computer.

about cultural groups that seem — at least on the surface — entirely removed from our own.

So what do the research data points tell us? A number of psychology studies suggest that people who are aggressive often get what they want, but that doesn't necessarily mean that the leaders of human societies everywhere can use aggression as a viable tactic to reach the highest rungs of the social ladder. Meanwhile, plenty of other studies support the prestige account. From the perspective of most social psychologists in the first decade of the twenty-first century, it was clear how people got ahead, and it wasn't by being jerks.

The best way to figure out how social rank is allocated — that is, what factors determine a group's hierarchical structure — is to get a group of people together, give them some job to complete, and then sit back and watch. If you've ever participated in a group task with people who at the outset don't know one another and are assumed to be status equals, you know what I mean. The group might start out as equals, but that doesn't last long. Very quickly, someone speaks up and begins to take charge.

Maybe the most assertive person in the group starts by telling others what to do. Or maybe she just makes clear what *she* is going to do. There are many different ways for this process to play out, but in any group of individuals assigned to complete some job, status differentiation will naturally occur. Someone will take on the role of leader, and others will defer, letting the leader make decisions about who does what and how the group gets the project done.

The question is, in groups like this — adults in the modern industrialized world working together on a task, and not villagers in a traditional small-scale society or chimpanzees competing for alpha status — what determines who rises to the top?

To address this question empirically, my colleagues and I put people — college students — in exactly this situation. They were brought to our lab and told that they'd have two tasks to complete. First, they'd be given a problem to solve completely on their own. Next, they'd get a second chance to solve the same problem but this time with the help of four other people they'd never met before, and we'd be video-recording their interactions. At the end of both tasks, these participants were told they'd each receive a financial bonus on top of what we were already paying them — if their group had found the correct solution. This gave them an incentive to work hard and do whatever it took to get their group to come up with the best answer.

In short, we created what we thought was an ideal setup for observing hierarchy formation. These were people who didn't know one another but had to work together on a task they cared about and probably had some established opinion about, given their initial solo attempt. It's exactly the kind of situation that begs for the emergence of hierarchical relationships as individuals decide who should lead the discussion and who should listen, who should make decisions and who should follow orders.

As for the problem the participants in this study were asked to solve, it was one used frequently in social psychological research. Originally developed by NASA, it asks participants to imagine that they are astronauts lost on the moon. They're given a list of items that might be available to them on their spaceship, and their task is to rank these items in order of their usefulness for surviving this perilous situation. The list includes supplies like dried food and an oxygen tank — obvious necessities — as well as supplies with more ambiguous utility, like parachute silk and fifty feet of nylon rope. There are also tricky items on the list, like matches — an item that might seem useful, until someone in the group remembers that the absence of oxygen on the moon precludes the possibility of setting anything on fire.

Of course, for the purposes of our study we didn't care about the actual solution to this problem; we just wanted to see how hierarchies formed as participants tried to figure it out. To do so, we measured each participant's dominance and prestige — the extent to which each individual was perceived by the others in the group as someone who intimidated and domineered to get his or her way or as someone who was helpful, thoughtful, and respectful of others' opinions. This meant that each participant had to decide, for each of the other people in his group, whether he "respected and admired him/her" and whether he was "afraid of him/her." (And although it might be surprising that a college student working with four of his peers on a task that requires him to pretend to be an astronaut could be so intimidating as to actually induce fear, that's what dominance is all about. It doesn't have to be fear for one's livelihood. It could be fear that arguing with this person will make her angry or that she'll erupt in a way that would make others uncomfortable.)

To test whether perceived dominance or prestige determined who got power over the group, we used four measures of social influence. First, participants simply rated how influential they thought each of their fellow group members had been. Second, outside observers — research assistants working for us — watched the videos we'd recorded and rated how influential *they* believed each group member had been. As a third measure, we went beyond perceptions of influence to look at actual influential behavior: how much control each participant had over the group's decision-making. Participants with the greatest influence would be those who most effectively persuaded others to adopt their opinions — that is, those who convinced others to agree with the rank ordering of lifesaving space supplies that they had come up with on their own. By examining which participants' solo solutions converged most with the final group solution, we could figure out which participants were most effective at persuading others to go along with what they wanted.

And, finally, we threw in one other measure. We asked a separate sample of participants — also undergraduates — to watch the videos we'd made while wearing an eye-tracker device (a funny-looking headband with a mini-telescope dropped down to cover one eye). This device recorded the focal point of the wearer's attention along with the scene being observed so that we could later *see* exactly what these individuals had been looking at. In any group, people spend most of their time gazing toward those who rank highest, so the direction of these new participants' eye gaze became an additional indicator of relative status for the participants working together in groups (see figure 5.1).

When we pooled our results across all of these various measures of influence and power, what we found would have surprised many sci-

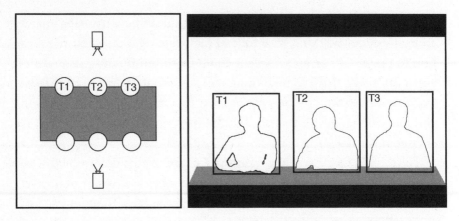

Figure 5.1. Video recordings were made of three target individuals (represented as T1, T2, and T3 in the left panel) seated on one side of a conference table. A new sample of participants subsequently watched these videos while wearing an eye-tracker device, which monitored the extent to which they paid attention to each target by capturing the amount of time they spent focusing on each of the three "regions of interest" — represented by the black boxes in the right panel.

entists from both social and evolutionary psychology. The answer to our question of whether high status was attained through dominance or prestige was . . . both.

Across all four measures of social influence — group members' ratings of one another, outside observers' ratings, actual influence over the group's decisions, and visual attention from eye-tracked onlookers — *both dominance and prestige were equally effective.* Both strategies got people power. Even when group members said that a certain person in the group was dominant — that he used intimidation to get his way — they were still just as likely to grant him control over the group as they were to give it to those they saw as generous or as solid and helpful contributors. Even while acknowledging that they didn't particularly like the dominant group members, participants nonetheless viewed them as influential leaders. And these perceptions were confirmed by the three other measures of social rank.

These findings tell us that the dominance-prestige model of rank attainment is correct — or at least that it accurately accounts for how people attain status in contemporary human groups. The availability of two distinct strategies for climbing the social ladder doesn't apply only to our ancient ancestors or to people living in small-scale traditional societies today. Even in modern-day work groups composed of genial college students, both strategies work. And the strategies *are* very different. The dominant group members in our study were *feared*, not respected. The other participants who had to work with these people did not like them. Yet these people still attained power in the form of control and influence over the group. And they did so *by* inducing fear — even though the society we were studying wasn't one ruled by violence.

These results answer the question of what high status is and how people get it. Just as important, they also begin to answer the ultimate *why* question about experiencing pride: Why do humans feel pride in two drastically different ways? And has Donald Trump managed to get where he is *despite* or *because of* his having one of the most arrogant and aggressive public personas in political history?

We know that pride is what motivates people to do the right thing, to become the kind of person their society wants them to become. The pride expression signals to others that the person showing it is likely to be this kind of person and deserves high status. But the dominance-prestige model complicates things. It begs the question: Which kind of high status are we talking about? On the one hand, if pride motivates people to work hard, cooperate with others, and become good citizens, then pride must lead to prestige. But if that's the case, then why are some people dominant?

A big hint lies in Donald Trump's speech. Trump's message exudes pride — but it is, quite clearly, the hubristic kind. And the form of high status that Trump has attained looks a lot more like dominance than prestige. Trump has, of course, worked hard for his many accomplishments. But as anyone who's watched *The Apprentice* or witnessed one of his political rallies or press conferences knows, he wields his power in a way that is aggressive and intimidating, to say the least. Rich Lowery, editor of the *National Review*, said of Trump, "I've never encountered an American politician at this level that people are literally afraid of — donors are afraid of him." Trump is as good an example as any of a leader who's used a dominance-based strategy to get ahead, and the pride he all too frequently demonstrates is undeniably hubristic. Indeed, in the same way that authentic pride is ideally suited to promote a set of behaviors that should bestow prestige, hubristic pride is the perfect emotion to motivate the kinds of behaviors necessary to attain dominance. Hubristic pride makes people feel superior — they believe that they're better than everyone else around them. It also makes people manipulative, hostile, and willing to derogate others — particularly others who are easy targets. In fact, the arrogance and aggression that goes with hubristic pride might be exactly what's needed to motivate people to treat others as inferiors and to force the weak to do as they say.

My colleagues and I found support for this account with another study of undergraduates. This time our subjects were people who already belonged to hierarchically structured societies: varsity athletic teams. We recruited a sample of jocks — soccer players, baseball players, rugby players, and volleyball players — who not only knew one another well but also knew one another's positions in the team hierarchy. Sports teams have explicit, clearly defined goals (win the game!) and well-established hierarchies to help accomplish these goals. Teams are led by captains, and even if most other players don't have such explicit rank-based titles, there's still a shared understanding about which teammates are leaders and which are followers. For this reason, varsity teammates make an ideal sample for a study of the emotions that underpin dominance and prestige.

We asked these athletes to rate one another on dominance and prestige, and, sure enough, those who reported frequent experiences of authentic pride were the ones whose teammates judged them as most prestigious. These were the people whom others respected and turned to for help. In contrast, individuals who reported frequent hubristic pride were judged by their teammates as dominant. These were people who had control over the group and were seen as leaders, but not because they were well liked. Instead, their teammates were afraid of what would happen if they didn't let these people get their way.

This study tells us that authentic pride may be what gets people to do what's needed to attain prestige while hubristic pride gets people to dominance. And this makes sense. The forceful, controlling, and aggressive behaviors that allow people to attain dominance may be a natural outcome of an emotion like hubristic pride, which tells people they're the best around. The result is a leader who has few close friendships or social connections and who is feared and generally disliked by pretty much everyone.

Authentic pride, in contrast, bestows a sense of confidence in one's accomplishments. It is, in fact, the carrot that motivates people to seek accomplishments. Although individuals can and do feel hubristic pride in their accomplishments — if they attribute those accomplishments to some innate ability or uncontrollable genius — a desire for hubristic pride doesn't typically motivate the hard work needed to attain success (more on this below). But this kind of motivation — prompted by authentic pride — to work hard to achieve, especially in ways one's group values, is exactly the psychological disposition needed to attain a reputation of prestige. Authentic pride is the emotional force that makes people want to do the right thing and be good. It's the pride that fuels the development of a socially accepted *me* self.

To support this point, several colleagues and I collaborated on a study that tested whether authentic pride, *specifically,* was what drove students to study hard for their exams. We expected that high-performing students would regularly feel a good deal of authentic pride and that these feelings would give them the motivational push to keep on working hard and performing at a high level. In other words, we thought that feelings of authentic pride would directly prompt academic achievements by motivating goal-oriented behavior. Students would think, *I feel proud of myself for how well I did on that last exam, so I'm going to keep studying, to make sure I do well on my next exam.*

We were wrong.

Students who perform at the highest levels, it turns out, don't need the motivational push of authentic pride to keep working hard. Most of these high achievers do report feelings of authentic pride in response to their successes, but even the few who don't still work hard and still do well on their next exams.

What we should have realized is that, for high-achieving college students, acing exams is a matter of routine. They don't need to feel a motivating emotion to get them to enact the necessary behaviors, just like you don't need to *feel* the fear of a possible dental visit to be convinced to brush your teeth each morning. Once behaviors are routinized, motivation becomes unnecessary, and, as a result, feelings of pride are not a strong motivational force for students who are already high achievers.

In contrast, for the students in our study who were *not* such high achievers — the people who didn't always ace their exams and for whom studying hard was *not* a matter of habit — a very different pattern emerged. For these students, authentic pride played a critical motivational role. But it wasn't that these students were motivated by feelings of authentic pride to keep working hard — the problem, for these students, was that they didn't typically work hard, so they didn't have much to feel authentically proud about. Instead, it was *an absence of authentic pride,* experienced in response to poor performance on an exam, that gave these students a motivational kick. The lack of pride they felt told them that something was wrong, and things needed to change if they wanted to feel good about themselves. This absence of pride, and a corresponding desire to beef up that experience, pushed these students to ramp up their studying for the next exam, and this change in studying behaviors resulted in an improved future exam performance.

That's right: Students who weren't able to feel authentic pride in their performance on an exam actually did *better* on the next exam *because* they wanted to obtain those feelings! Students who did well on prior exams, in contrast, felt a good deal of authentic pride in response, and therefore weren't motivated to *change* their behavior — they instead inferred from their pride that they should keep on working in the same effective way they had in the past.

In many ways, it makes sense that high-achieving students wouldn't be motivated by pride to change their behaviors by studying harder or putting in more effort. These students could do well again by studying in exactly the same way they had previously. The same cannot be said for the lower-achieving students, however — and for these people, pride can be transformative.

Pride is a carrot, and for the high achievers, it's a carrot they've already eaten. But for those who don't yet have it — those who miss feeling pride, in the same way that Dean Karnazes did before he started running — the carrot prompts a change. These students — the low achievers — responded to the lack of pride they felt by studying harder and, as a result, performed better in the future.

It's noteworthy that in this research, hubristic pride had a similar but much smaller effect than authentic pride. Unlike its authentic counterpart, hubristic pride does not, in general, motivate people to work much more (or less). Because hubristic pride is linked to feelings of greatness that aren't attributable to effort, feeling hubristic pride — or not feeling it — doesn't typically make people want to put in more effort. *Authentic* pride is the kind of pride that influences achievement, an outcome that's essential to attaining prestige but not necessarily relevant to attaining dominance.

So what *does* hubristic pride do? It turns out that it can motivate people to work hard — but only under certain circumstances. While a desire for authentic pride pushes people to put in the kind of work that might earn them higher grades, hubristic pride pushes people to work hard when doing so might *impress others*.

This motivational effect of hubristic pride was made clear in another study, which found that, while college students prone to authentic pride demonstrated high levels of creative thinking simply because these individuals tended to be intrinsically motivated to be creative (i.e., to develop a *me* self that is creative), students prone to hubristic pride demonstrated creativity only if they were *extrinsically* motivated — that is, if they believed their creativity might help them attain some other goal. People who feel hubristic pride will work hard if it's clear that there's something in it for them, something like power or status. But they won't do it for the simple sake of feeling good about themselves.

This finding is important, because it tells us that hubristic pride *can* motivate socially valued behaviors if the proud individual is in the right mindset. Those who feel hubristic pride don't exert their creative energy for the sake of being creative, but they might do so if they think it'll boost their standing in the eyes of others. Or, as the researchers behind this study also found, they'll do it if they're angry and want to show others up. In this research, participants wrote about a time they had felt either happy or angry, and then, while reflecting in the happy glow or angry sulk of memories past, they completed a task designed to measure their creativity. The task was one that couldn't have been simpler; each participant was given two minutes to write down every possible use for a brick that he or she could think of. For some participants — those not particularly well endowed in the creativity department — it was tough to come up with much more than *doorstop*. For others, a vast array of clever and enlightening responses emerged, from *karate chopping* and *murder weapon* to *paperweight* and *mock coffin at a Barbie funeral*.

Among the participants in this study who'd been made to feel happy first, a dispositional tendency toward authentic pride promoted a strong creative performance — these individuals came up with many clever uses for the brick. Happiness is a signal that all is right with the world, so this finding means that people high in authentic pride become more creative when things are going well. In contrast, those in the study who were prone to hubristic pride became *less* creative in the happy condition. When things are going well, these individuals rest on their laurels and bask in their successes rather than putting in more work or creative effort. This difference is part of what makes authentic pride, but not hubristic pride, a good catalyst for prestige.

But what about those participants who were made to feel anger instead of happiness? Anger had little effect on those feeling authentic pride, but for the hubristically proud prone, anger led to the exact opposite of what happened when they were happy. Anger was motivating! In this condition, people who tended toward hubristic pride came up with many more uses for the brick, suggesting that, like extrinsic motivation, there are situations in which hubristic pride enhances creativity.

People who feel hubristic pride can be driven to work hard, it seems, but not by a desire to achieve or be a good person. Instead, they're motivated by a desire to show off or to win a battle against some unknowing competitor. And this is exactly the pattern of motivation that would best befit a person seeking dominance. Dominant leaders don't accomplish things for the sake of contributing valued resources to their group or helping others. They achieve to prove that they are stronger, better, or more powerful than others. Think of Donald Trump's lifelong desire to build ever more and ever bigger buildings, not to mention his more recent aim to take control of the entire United States. Or Steve Jobs's willingness to terrorize his employees into doing whatever was necessary to ensure Apple's rise to the top of the handheld-electronics tower.

Together, this research points to a clear explanation for the prevalence of hubristic pride alongside authentic pride in human societies. The more arrogant kind of pride is ideally suited to promoting and facilitating the behaviors needed to attain dominance. In part, this may work at a deeper, biological level. Although neuroscientists haven't yet found the "pride" region of the brain (nor are they ever likely to, given that most psychological processes are distributed across various neural regions), there may be a pride hormone: testosterone. Testosterone has long been considered the status hormone; human and monkey males both show increases in it following a variety of events that boost their status, from winning a physical fight (for the monkeys) to winning a chess match (for the humans, and the rare very special monkey).

But testosterone isn't only a status hormone; it's also an aggression hormone. As a result, high-testosterone human men tend to be *low,* not high, in *certain kinds* of status. These are men who are not particularly well educated and who typically earn lower incomes, hold blue-collar jobs, and are often unemployed. How can we reconcile this conflicting mix of evidence showing that, on the one hand, testosterone levels rise in response to a status win while, on the other hand, a dispositional tendency toward high testosterone levels is linked to low socioeconomic status?

Having read the first part of this chapter, you probably figured it out: the kind of high status that's associated with testosterone is, quite clearly, not the prestigious variety. High-testosterone men are aggressive, assertive, confrontational, and violent. These are valuable traits for the attainment of dominance, and that may be the reason that these men *do* hold power in many dominance-based hierarchies, such as certain professional sports teams and prisons. But these same traits are counterproductive to the attainment of prestige, and, not surprisingly, prestigious men tend to have relatively lower levels of testosterone.

Of course, there are exceptions: men like Donald Trump who have effectively wielded dominance to attain high levels of socioeconomic status. But on the whole, the aggressiveness that's linked to testosterone may reduce the number of high-testosterone men who reach the peaks of status in many contemporary white-collar workplaces.

If you work at a white-collar job, think about this for a moment. Although you can probably name that one person at work who easily loses his temper and often gets his way simply because others are afraid to fight him, it's probably just one person. In contrast, you may be fortunate to work with several different leaders who are cooperative, helpful, and nice to have around. Dominance and prestige are both effective means to power, but there are differences in which kind of hierarchy tends to predominate in any given society.

Importantly, just because dominance is linked to testosterone does *not* mean that dominance is a male-only strategy, even though women have much lower levels of testosterone than men. Our lab study of hierarchy formation included both male and female work groups, and dominance worked just as effectively in women-only groups as it did among the men. And, perhaps surprisingly, the women's dominant behavior may have been linked to testosterone too.

Although testosterone works differently in women (it is, after all, not only a status hormone and an aggression hormone but also the male sex hormone), there is some evidence that it may be linked to female displays of dominance and perhaps also of hubristic pride. Women with relatively high levels of androgens, one of which is testosterone, tend to judge themselves as higher status than their peers, even while their peers judge them as *lower* status. This sounds a lot like the self-enhancement that's typical of narcissists — individuals who regularly experience hubristic pride. Furthermore, one study found that female prison inmates with higher levels of testosterone were more likely to have been convicted of an unprovoked violent crime than of a nonviolent crime or violence committed in self-defense.

These findings raise the possibility that testosterone is, at least in part, the body's hormonal response to hubristic pride in both men and women. But what about authentic pride? Can testosterone be traced back to that too?

As it turns out, there's probably no hormone that's specific to authentic pride in the way that testosterone seems linked to hubristic pride, but there may be a relevant neurotransmitter: serotonin. Increasing brain levels of serotonin is the goal of the most commonly prescribed antidepressants (Prozac, Zoloft, and all other selective serotonin reuptake inhibitors). Serotonin also plays a key role in status attainment, and not only in humans. High-status male monkeys, as well as high-status male humans, have chronically elevated serotonin levels. But in both species, the kind of leadership these individuals exhibit is different from that observed among those high in testosterone. Serotonin-enhanced leaders are unaggressive and use a friendly approach to gain power.* Artificially increasing serotonin levels in monkeys' brains makes them more social and nicer; they spend more time approaching and grooming others and can often parlay these friendly behaviors into the attainment of higher rank. Similarly, humans given tryptophan — an amino acid that's a precursor to serotonin (and is found, famously, in turkey meat and, less famously, in cheddar cheese) — become less argumentative and more cooperative and also tend to climb in social rank.

In all of these cases, we see something that surprises those biologists who equate high rank with aggression: increased serotonin helps individuals increase in status *while also making them nicer*. If there is a bio-

---

* It's important to note that although these monkeys might attain a form of status that is not based on dominance, it's also not prestige. Because prestige requires cultural learning, nonhuman species that acquire rank through prosocial behaviors may be using a strategy that overlaps with prestige but that did not evolve for the same reasons and does not serve the same function.

logical marker of authentic pride or the motivational force underlying prestige, serotonin is a plausible candidate.

More broadly, what all this research tells us is that we experience pride in two very different ways because it's adaptive — both the good kind and the bad kind. As it turns out, there is a clear-cut evolutionary explanation for arrogance, aggression, and the general jerkiness seen among those who regularly experience hubristic pride. While we'd much rather spend our time with those who tend toward authentic pride, humans evolved to follow people who are dominant too — making hubristic pride an equally adaptive emotion, for better or for worse.

Interpreting evolutionary science can be tricky for the nonscientist, and one common layperson's error in logic, known as the naturalistic fallacy, has gotten many an evolutionary psychologist into deep trouble. It's an easy mistake to make; if we learn that something is part of human nature — our genetically endowed biology — we take this to mean that it must, therefore, be good for us. People even equate *natural* with *good* when they're not talking about biology; this is why stamping the phrase *natural flavors* on a food product can lead to a jump in sales.

The fallacy comes from the fact that much of what's natural is not actually good — when by *good*, we mean *moral*, or *prosocial*, or even something that makes us happy. Our genes' only goal is to reproduce themselves, and while this often generates outcomes that do make us happier and healthier humans, it just as often generates outcomes that help our genes at the expense of our happiness or the health of our society. As a consequence, there are human behaviors that may well be natural — in the sense that they result from evolutionary processes and are effective in promulgating genes — but far from good, in the sense of building or maintaining the kind of society we'd like to live in. Most evolutionary scientists know this, so it's at best inappropriate and at worst offensive to assume that a scientist who discusses the evolutionary origins of some horrible human behavior like rape or child abuse in fact believes that this strategy is *good*. However, so long as we acknowledge this distinction — that *evolved* does not mean *good* — it can be useful to pose the question: To what extent *are* certain naturally endowed behaviors good for us or for our social groups?

More specifically for the present purposes, is dominance good? There's a strong case to be made that it's natural — an evolved strategy for attaining social rank, which effectively boosts status and, as a result, increases the likelihood that the dominant individual's genes will survive and reproduce. But is this a good thing? Sure, dominants acquire power, but should they? Group members defer to these people because they're afraid not to, not because they want to, and that can't possibly be good for society. Won't this result in unhappy or chronically fearful group members? And won't groups led by dominants eventually falter, given that they're ruled by people who lack the skills or competence needed to ensure success? Perhaps dominance hierarchies are constantly burdened by within-group conflicts, as lower-status members form coalitions and try to overpower a despised and incompetent leader.

As it turns out, the small body of evidence accumulated thus far suggests both pros and cons for groups ruled by dominant leaders. In one example, my colleagues and I conducted another study examining hierarchy formation again by bringing small groups of undergraduates into our lab to work together in teams. This time, these students completed several different group tasks. Most involved problem-solving and analytic skills — using logic to identify a pattern in a puzzle with a missing piece or figuring out how best to organize a shopping trip. But these groups also completed a task that required more outside-the-box creative thinking: the brick test.

The other difference from our prior group study — the one where groups worked together only to rank a list of items that would serve them well if they were lost on the moon — was that this time, we assigned one person in the group to be the leader instead of letting a hierarchy emerge naturally. We wanted each group to have a clearly defined person in charge so we could determine whether it mattered — in terms of how the group performed on the various tasks — if the leader wielded dominance or prestige. Would groups do better if the people we assigned to lead them gravitated toward a prestigious style, making themselves respected and well liked and becoming valued contributors to the groups? Would groups led by dominants — people who used the power we had given them to intimidate and manipulate others — suffer?

What we found surprised us. The groups that were led by prestigious people — based on ratings made by all the other group members — did well, *but only on one task.* These groups came up with more creative uses for the brick. In contrast, groups led by dominants did better *on every other task we gave them.* These tasks required analytic thinking and logical deduction. Each was a puzzle that needed to be solved in a limited amount of time and that had a correct answer. Dominant leaders steered their groups toward that answer far more successfully than their prestigious counterparts. It's not that dominant leaders were any smarter; they were simply more effective at getting the groups to reach the correct answer or at making decisions about what that answer was without worrying whether the whole group agreed.

Interestingly, the ability of dominant people to lead groups to problem-solving success has been given a name by Apple employees who saw it all too frequently in their former leader Steve Jobs. They call it the reality-distortion field. Apparently, Jobs was so effective at convincing his subordinates they could complete a seemingly impossible task that they ended up feeling like they had no choice, and they somehow got the job done — despite its implausibility.

There are times when it pays to put a dominant person in charge — but not always. Our data suggest that being led by a dominant is not so useful when the goal is to demonstrate divergent thinking — to be creative and come up with as many answers as possible. In our study, groups did better on the brick test when their leaders were supportive, helpful, and encouraging. If you feel like the boss is ready to jump on you for any wrong answer, and you're even a bit afraid of her as a result, you're probably going to shy away from volunteering answers that fall somewhere outside the box — exactly the kind of answers that lead to a strong brick-test score. In contrast, if your group is led by someone who seems friendly and wise and eager to hear from his subordinates, you'll probably feel more comfortable spitballing even the most bizarre ideas — and will be more likely to land on the one, or many, that work.

There are also other disadvantages to belonging to a dominant-led group. In our study, group members in this situation reported greater fear and anxiety; they were scared of the boss, and they enjoyed their time in the study less. Meanwhile, those in prestige-led groups were happy with the experience. They didn't perform as well overall, but they liked their group and their leader. They were satisfied with the job and felt a greater sense of belongingness and loyalty to their group. They also reported a stronger sense of confidence in their own performance and higher levels of authentic pride, suggesting that prestigious leaders somehow foster their own adaptive emotions in their subordinates.

The message from this study is clear. If a company hopes to promote creativity and diverse thinking among happy, confident, and psychologically healthy workers, then hiring prestigious leaders should be a paramount goal. But if the aim is to quickly solve a problem, there may be reason to let a dominant take over. Group members will probably enjoy themselves less and dislike working for these individuals, but they may be more likely to get the job done — though potentially at the cost of lowered employee satisfaction, higher turnover, and reduced creativity.

There are other situations too in which groups benefit from the leadership of a dominant dictator at least as much as a prestigious consensus-builder. One study found that dominant undergraduates become particularly good leaders when their groups are forced to compete with others. Dominants thrive on competition. Unlike prestigious individuals, who seek cooperation both within and between groups, dominants are always on the lookout for a fight. This can be problematic when the conflict they're creating is among those within their own groups, but it's a boon for groups seeking to best each other. In these circumstances, dominant leaders step up their game and will even strategically place the most skilled and competent group members in positions of power, despite the fact that doing so can threaten their own control.

This finding, that dominant leaders do well in the presence of intergroup strife, may be one reason that developing nations and tribal societies frequently at war tend to be governed by despotic rulers. While these leaders make daily life difficult, costly, and even painful for their citizens, they may ensure their groups' survival.

And regardless of what's good for the group, there are certain people in any society who clearly benefit, at an individual level, from adopting a dominant leadership style. These may be individuals who lack socially valued skills and competencies, aren't particularly smart, or don't have the genetically endowed personality disposition to work hard or be a nice person. In a prestige-only world, these individuals would stay far at the bottom of the social ladder. The viability of dominance provides them with another route to the top. If you don't have the wisdom or skills to benefit your group or you're a generally grumpy and hostile person, you can still get power — as long as you're bigger, stronger, or wealthier than others.

Of course, these dominant people pay for their less kindly road to status by incurring the dislike, and even hatred, of their fellow group members, and for many of us this price is simply too high; we'd rather be low on the totem pole than be perceived as arrogant and domineering. In fact, researchers have found that people who place a high value on social harmony are unwilling to use dominance-based tactics to get ahead. According to these social scientists, it is partly for this reason that people of low socioeconomic status often stay that way. Individuals belonging to the more disadvantaged classes tend to place particular importance on their social relationships and connections with others, yet, like many in contemporary North American society, they believe (incorrectly) that coercion and manipulation is the only way to get to the top. Rather than violate some of their most important social norms and the ideals of their *me* self, these individuals often bow out of the status game altogether. Meanwhile, for others, the sacrifice of warm and supportive interpersonal relationships is well worth the status gain that can be won through dominance. After all, a powerful enough leader can buy a group of friends, or at least temporary alliances.

The conclusion to be drawn, based on the research evidence collected thus far, is that both dominance and prestige come with advantages and disadvantages and are likely to be helpful in some situations but harmful in others. Perhaps more important, we can also conclude that both dominance and prestige are equally viable routes to power, so hubristic and authentic pride are therefore equally adaptive emotions. Although the two prides motivate completely different patterns of behaviors and cognitions, they both provide precisely the ammunition needed to reach the highest rungs of society.

These findings help clarify not only our evolutionary questions about pride (questions like why humans have evolved to feel arrogant), but also our moral associations with it. The accumulated research explains why pride has, throughout history, been deemed both a sin and a virtue and also reminds us that, from an evolutionary perspective, neither form of pride is sinful or virtuous. As an evolved emotion, pride motivates adaptive behavior, and the two prides motivate different sets of adaptive behaviors — achievement, conscientiousness, and empathy on the one hand; arrogance, aggression, and selfishness on the other.

The critical question, from a scientific perspective, is not whether authentic and hubristic pride are good or bad but whether and how they increase fitness — meaning an individual's chances of surviving long enough to reproduce. Based on what we now know, both forms of pride are functional in this way. By facilitating the attainment of power and influence, both prides increase the likelihood that the humans who experience them will do well in the everlasting inter-individual competition for life-sustaining resources and mates.

We've now seen how pride makes people who they are: how it motivates them to achieve and be moral, or aggressive and demanding, and to seek power, status, and climb the social ladder. In the next chapter, we'll turn to the question of what this means for human societies and culture more broadly. Because of what pride does for us — the way it motivates us to be the best or highest-ranking group members we can be — it also influences the things we do for our groups and the ways in which our cultures progress.

Pride is not just a part of human nature; this two-sided emotion has also *shaped* that nature. We humans are by far the most cultural species in existence; we are better than any other animal at learning from those around us and making what we learn our own. This ability to share, copy, and spread cultural knowledge is largely responsible for the kind of species we have become. And as we will see, we would not have gotten here without pride. Indeed, many of the most important human successes and inventions throughout history can be traced back to this vital but long-misunderstood emotion.

6

The Highest Form

Most people have, at one point or another, experienced something like the following fortuitous event: You're walking down the street with a friend, chatting casually, when you notice something greenish and a bit familiar out of the corner of your eye. You bend down to take a closer look, and, sure enough — it's a twenty-dollar bill! Or maybe, when this happened to you, you weren't quite *so* lucky; perhaps it was a five-dollar bill, or just a single, but chances are, at least once in your life, you've found yourself face to face with an unexpected city-street windfall for no reason other than your good luck and keen eyesight.

But what if, as you reach down to claim your earnings, you notice that your companion is also bending down and also reaching. She thinks *your* twenty dollars is *hers!* You quickly snatch it up, but now you're staring at an empty-handed friend. What do you do?

Chances are that the twenty-dollar bill no longer feels like yours alone. Dumb luck put it in your hand first, but keeping it and letting your friend leave the scene with nothing doesn't feel right. Instead, perhaps you propose that the two of you take the twenty dollars out for a spin at the local café, treating yourselves to a couple of fancy beverages and croissants. Or maybe you tell your friend that the movie you were en route to will be your treat.

But now I'd like you to imagine this permutation of the situation: Instead of a friend, your co-discoverer is a complete stranger walking on the street next to you (think Manhattan, not Mayberry). You both see the cash, but you're the one who happens to grab it first. You probably wouldn't offer to take the less lucky stranger out for coffee or to a movie, but maybe you'd think about digging into your wallet to offer up that ten-dollar bill — or at least the five — that you know is in there. Or maybe you would shrug, smile (or smirk), and walk away, knowing that you'll never see this stranger again, and enjoy being twenty dollars richer than you were two minutes ago.

As it turns out, social scientists have been putting pairs of total strangers in exactly this situation for years, and their results tell us something about how you — or at least most people — would respond.

In the experimental version, two research participants are randomly assigned to play one of two roles, proposer or responder, in what they are told is a game. The proposer is given twenty one-dollar bills and instructed to do with them whatever she pleases. She can keep the money and walk out of the room, knowing that she'll never see that responder guy again. Or she can share some of her windfall with the responder — an unlucky soul who signed up to participate in the very same study but somehow ended up with no cash — and divvy it up between the two of them however she sees fit.

If you were the proposer in this study — the metaphorical first person to pick up that twenty-dollar bill on the ground — what would you do? It would be entirely within your rights to keep the twenty dollars for yourself and leave the stranger with nothing. And, clearly, this would be the best way to maximize your own financial gain. That's what everyone in this situation *should* do, right?

It's what everyone should do if the only thing humans cared about was maximizing their own financial gain. But as you probably suspected if you thought about what you *actually* would do, keeping all the cash is *not* what most people do. In fact, most adults in the Western world split this free money fairly close to fifty-fifty, or maybe sixty-forty, perhaps with the justification that they deserve a finder's fee. And let's be real: almost no one gives more than ten dollars, half the pot. There is the odd participant — typically under the age of twenty-three — who does play for profit, giving her partner nothing. But the large majority of adults beyond college age who've played this game — and it's been played many, many times in many North American and European psychology labs — give their partners just under half of whatever the researcher gave them.

Why? Because it's the fair thing to do. Just because a flip of the coin left you holding the twenty doesn't mean it's legitimately your money to keep. Could you live with yourself if you took the twenty dollars and ran, knowing that your partner got nothing?

This well-replicated finding, emerging from studies using what's known in social science circles as the Dictator Game (for fairly obvious reasons), is one of the key pieces of evidence cited by psychologists and economists to make the point that humans do not behave purely on the basis of self-interest. We don't always do what's best for our own immediate financial good. We do what feels fair.*

But there's another interesting point to be made from this research. What's fair, it turns out, is not the same everywhere. In Western societies, splitting the unexpected windfall close to fifty-fifty feels right. But in non-Western, pre-industrialized societies, that's not the case. For the Fijians on Yasawa Island, the average Dictator Game offer is seven dollars if the pot starts with twenty. Among the Tsimane of Bolivia, it's five dollars.

These massive cultural differences — and, yes, the difference between believing that *fair* means sharing 25 percent of your unexpected windfall rather than a full 50 percent is about as massive as things get in human behavioral research — tell us that people's beliefs

---

* As economists are quick to point out, behaving fairly in this situation can still serve a person's financial interests in an ultimate sense, because fairness norms ensure that he will be protected in the future when he's the unlucky one, the one not holding the twenty dollars. Nonetheless, this kind of long-term calculation is not the proximate explanation for why people behave fairly. We do so because it feels right, even though we simultaneously believe it's not the best way to maximize our own profit.

about what's fair are something that they've learned. Fairness is a social norm.* We learn this norm from others in our culture, and once we internalize the knowledge, it becomes part of who we are. North Americans give about half the money we randomly and undeservedly receive to a stranger we'll probably never see again, because our culture has indoctrinated us to believe that this is the right thing to do. And the *me* self—that set of self-representations and identity concerns we're always trying to live up to — wants us to behave in ways that our culture tells us are right.

Fairness is just one of many social norms that vary drastically by culture (for another example, watch how your *garçon* responds when you douse your French fries — aka *pommes frites* — with ketchup while dining at that adorable Parisian bistro). These are the norms we learn through socialization, and they eventually become part of our identity. What it means to be a good person in any society is to follow the norms of that society, and as I have argued, part of the reason we have an identity is to remind us what those norms are and to make us care whether we successfully follow them. We feel pride when we see ourselves meeting or — even better — exceeding our society's norms, and the desire to feel pride is what makes us want to do everything we can to ensure that the *me* self is an exemplary societal member.

Pride, it turns out, is essential not only to making us want to be the best cultural beings we can be, but also to helping us figure out what that means. Pride allows us to learn and fully encode what our cultural norms are. As a result, pride is one of the emotions most directly responsible for a phenomenon known as *cumulative cultural evolution,* a force that's led to the majority of advances that humans have made since the beginning of our species' existence.

Cumulative cultural evolution is the process through which all of a society's cultural knowledge — art, science, technology, religious belief

---

* According to evolutionary anthropologist Joe Henrich, this kind of fairness — which regulates the way we treat strangers but not necessarily people we actually know — is best understood as impersonal fairness and should be distinguished from the fairness norms that tell us how to treat people we know well.

systems, institutions, and values — build on each other and progress. The result is a set of cultural systems that include advances far beyond what would be possible from any one person alone or any one community of people alone. The importance of these cultural systems is so great — and they have become so fundamentally linked to the survival and ultimate success of our species — that many evolutionary scientists agree: to understand why humans are the way they are now, we need to look beyond genes to examine how human cultures evolve and change over time, shaping human psychology in the process. According to these thinkers, it is the evolution of cultures, *more than the evolution of genes alone,* that has made us the unique species we are.

Perhaps the most remarkable thing about cultural evolution is not how ubiquitous it is but how unaware we are of its ubiquity. We give so much credit to our genes for making us who we are — and our genes *do* deserve a lot of credit — that we tend to forget or fail to realize that genes without cultural learning would not get us far. I'm not even talking about the complex parts of our culture that obviously require learning — it's a no-brainer that we need more than genes to figure out how to use a computer, let alone build one — but the fact is, we need more than genes to survive on a desert island with no computers anywhere in sight. Without a fairly sophisticated knowledge base about which of the local plants are edible and which are poisonous or an ability to build some sort of spear for catching and killing fish, you wouldn't make it more than a few days on that island. Even considering the non-desert-island world most of us actually live in, how would you go about feeding yourself if your culture hadn't developed a system of agriculture that provides you with plentiful nourishment, along with a market system that allows you to trade supplies or services for food (and do so via rectangles made of a green-and-white cotton-linen blend that have been imbued with deep cultural meaning and value)?

The necessity of cultural learning becomes readily apparent when we think about the many nineteenth-century European explorers who found themselves stranded in faraway lands that had long been successfully inhabited by other humans and nonetheless failed to survive unless they joined forces with the locals. These explorers lacked the skills needed to forage, gather, or hunt for food, not to mention the knowledge required to convert plants into forms digestible by the delicate human stomach.*

To take one poignant example, two British explorers lost in the Australian wilderness, Robert Burke and William Wills, thought they were going to make it when they figured out how to harvest the local diet's major staple: a fern plant known as *nardoo,* which the aboriginals made into cakes. Burke and Wills filled themselves with four to five pounds of *nardoo* bread a day, only to slowly but surely die of "*nardoo* starvation": an inability to properly digest the bread, combined with poisoning from thiaminase, a mild toxin present in the plant. Going at it on their own — without the help of a local cultural knowledge base — the explorers failed to realize that when the aboriginals made their *nardoo* cakes, they first completed a number of well-honed cultural practices that may have appeared ritualistic but in fact were essential to making the plant edible. These included grinding and leaching the flour with excessive water, exposing it to ash, and eating the cake meal with spoons made of mussel shell. Each of these practices, seemingly trivial, contributed in some critical way to breaking down or destroying the toxic effects of thiaminase.

The knowledge that's required to properly process *nardoo* is one of many skill sets that is far too complex for any human to figure out on his or her own. Instead, these skills are developed by groups of people over time and passed from one generation to the next. And within each new generation, improvements are made. Small-scale societies that exist today survive off skills that have been honed to perfection over many millennia.

This is a critical difference between humans and every other ani-

---

* Joe Henrich compellingly uses stories such as these to make a strong argument for the necessity of cultural learning in his book *The Secret of Our Success,* but Henrich's principal argument is that the majority of human advances resulting from cumulative cultural evolution are due not only to genes or only to culture but to a combination of the two — culture-driven genetic evolution, also known as gene-culture coevolution. Describing how this process works is beyond the scope of this book, but I encourage interested readers to seek out Henrich's very accessible explanation.

mal species, including many now-extinct species that shared most of our genes. Cumulative culture most likely began with *Homo erectus,* a forerunner of *Homo sapiens* that lived in Africa for about one and a half million years. These prehumans made and used fairly sophisticated stone tools and cooked with fire — two indications of a body of knowledge that could not be attained by any one individual, or any single group of individuals at one time. But the kind of cultural advances that even these prehumans made cannot be compared with the kind we see in our own species. *Homo erectus* lived for over a million years and during that time came up with several variations of hand axes and cleavers. That's a far cry from we *Homo sapiens,* who are forced to deal with a new iPhone upgrade every few months.

Neanderthals, the prehuman ape that followed *Homo erectus,* shared 99.5 percent of our modern human genes and produced a number of substantial advances in tool technology, but they still had nothing like modern human culture or cultural evolution. And, like *Homo erectus* before them, Neanderthals eventually became extinct. The critical difference between *Homo sapiens* and all of the prehumans who came before us is *not* that modern humans are smarter — Neanderthals, in fact, had the larger brains — but, rather, that *we are more social.* As a result, our species has progressed beyond all others in mastering the art of taking other people's good ideas, copying them, and making them better. We acquire knowledge from others in our society, and it is this accumulated knowledge — *more than our genes alone* — that makes us unique.

The reason that we can do this — take others' inventions and make them better — is that we are social learners. Again, it's not that humans are smarter than other apes; in fact, if we go head-to-head with chimpanzees on many cognitive tasks, we tie, or, in some embarrassing cases, the chimps win. But there's one cognitive arena where chimps can't touch us: the human ability to copy and learn from others.

To be sure, chimps copy one another, but they do so mindlessly rather than purposefully. This is an important distinction. Copying without intention or understanding results in pointless behaviors, like that of the new student from Israel assigned to sit next to me in second grade. Not having learned English yet, he copied my work, but he did it so perfectly that he wrote *my* name at the top of his worksheet instead of his own. Knowing *why* we copy — what the goal is — can make us particularly proficient learners, and it allows us to innovate, to build on others' successes and push them forward.

Humans are great learners because we copy with the intent of getting a particular job done well, which means we can choose when to add our own stylistic flair or make a major advance that improves on the technique. Think of when you first learned to ride a bike. You probably began by watching what the older human teaching you did and trying your best to faithfully mimic her behaviors: where she stood next to the bike before she got on, where on the pedal she placed her foot, and when she started pedaling. Eventually, as you began to ride and got a feel for what it was like, you probably stopped doing *exactly* what your teacher did and found your own way, starting with the foot that felt most comfortable to *you* and with the pedal in the position that gave *you* the most leverage. But the thing that made all this possible was that other person who had been willing to spend time teaching you through direct instruction, allowing you to copy her behaviors, and, most heroically, running alongside your bike whilst bending down in that lumbar-destroying position in order to hold tight to your saddle while you got comfortable balancing yourself on two wheels.

Studies have shown that social learning — that is, learning from those kind and generous others who are willing to teach us or allow us to copy them — is by far the best way to master any difficult skill, be it riding a bike or building a computer. To demonstrate this point, a group of evolutionary biologists used a well-known means for getting people to solve a problem: make it a contest.

These researchers designed a game that they called a multi-armed bandit, after the all-too-appropriate moniker for a slot machine (one-armed bandit). The game was essentially a very complicated slot machine, one with a hundred different arms, or game moves. To perform well, contestants had to quickly learn which moves resulted in the highest payoffs. Their assignment was to design a computer program that would accomplish this goal using three different available strategies for learning and making moves. Each program could use all three strategies as many times and in any order as the programmers liked.

The three available strategies were (1) trial-and-error learning, (2) observational learning, and (3) something the researchers called exploiting. Trial-and-error learning meant acquiring accurate information about the utility of a particular move by trying it out. Observational learning referred to learning from others: watching what happened when other players pulled particular arms. This strategy could result in useful information if the other player was observed pulling a fruitful arm that the observing player didn't already know about, but it could also result in useless information and a wasted move if the observer happened to catch the other player making a move he already knew about. The final strategy was exploiting — this meant pulling an arm that the player believed would pay off. Exploiting was the only move that would actually result in a payoff, so all programs had to exploit fairly often in order to play out the moves they'd learned about through the other two strategies.

The 104 programmers who entered the contest developed programs that combined these three strategies in a wide diversity of ways. Some relied largely on trial-and-error learning combined with exploitation; others used trial-and-error and observational learning equally frequently; and others mostly observed. There were also differences in how often programmers exploited — some did so often, giving themselves plenty of opportunities to hit the jackpot, whereas others allowed for numerous rounds of learning between each exploit, maximizing their chances that every exploit would bring a large payoff.

What the researchers found was that all of the top-performing programs had one clear-cut pattern in common. All the programs that did best — that is, that received the highest payouts in the shortest amount of time — relied heavily on observational learning combined with plenty of exploiting, using what they'd learned to make a profitable move. The overall winner, a program that its creators called Discountmachine, observed more than 95 percent of the time it was learning, with only 5 percent of its efforts going to trial and error. This result emerged even though the researchers had thrown a number of wrenches into their bandit to make social learning *less* profitable; in many cases, they made sure that the information acquired this way wasn't particularly useful. But it didn't matter. Programs that relied on social learning still outperformed those that relied more on trial and error.

The research evidence is clear: Allowing yourself to benefit from what others have already learned is a far more expedient way to develop skills and an understanding of one's world than going at it on your own. Social learning is the single best way to acquire knowledge and to make advances on the basis of that knowledge. As a result, social learning is the process that underpins humans' cumulative cultural evolution; without it, we would have gotten no further than our ape cousins. And the emotion that enables social learning — and therefore makes cultural evolution possible — is *pride*. Pride is the emotional reason for our species' success.

We humans have a set of cognitive capacities that every other species lacks. These capacities of the human brain are what allow for cumulative culture, and they have gotten us where we are.

Cumulative cultural evolution depends on three distinct cognitive accomplishments. First, there needs to be an ability to develop skills and acquire useful knowledge. Second, there needs to be an ability to share this knowledge with others. And third, there needs to be an ability to effectively learn shared cultural knowledge so that the process can start all over again, with newly acquired skills becoming the starting point for advances and innovations.

Another, perhaps more deeply psychological way to think of these three abilities that enable cultural learning is in terms of the three motivations that underpin them: (1) a motivation to create and build, (2) a motivation, or at least willingness, to share and teach one's creations to others, and (3) a motivation to learn from others who are experts in certain domains. Each of these three motivations benefits — in some cases enormously — from the human capacity for pride.

As we now know, pride is what motivates us to do so many of the things we do to become the kind of person our society wants us to be. As a result, pride's role in pushing us to create and build (the first of those three abilities that enable cumulative cultural evolution) should not be surprising. Pride gets us to engage in our most moral behaviors, like helping people who need it, giving away our possessions to those who need them more, and being good citizens who vote. But pride also drives us to put in the hard work that helps us get ahead; it makes us persist at boring tasks, come up with creative ideas and engage in innovative thinking, solve difficult problems, and change our ineffective work habits so we become more productive. Many of these behaviors are the result of authentic pride, but, as we've seen, hubristic pride can also promote hard work and creativity — albeit in the service of attaining power and dominance or impressing others, rather than out of a pure desire for mastery or accomplishment.

Whether authentic or hubristic, pride is the central emotional force that motivates us to create, build, and achieve — to take what we know and make it better. Without pride, humans would have little impetus to improve on the cultural knowledge we already possess. We'd use tools as needed to get by, but we would not be particularly interested in pushing beyond what we already have or doing much more than getting by.

This is a point I made in the very first pages of this book: one of the most important reasons that people do many of the things we care most about — the things that get us beyond simple survival — is that we want to feel pride. It's why Dean Karnazes runs all night, why Steve Jobs revolutionized the personal computer (and the cell phone), and why Paul Gauguin abandoned his family and comfortable Parisian life to produce groundbreaking works of art. But if you still doubt that inventors, artists, creators of any kind, do what they do because of pride — if you think, perhaps, that these innovators are driven more by a pure search for beauty, or truth, or knowledge, that their passion for their work has little to do with wanting to feel good about themselves — let me give one more example.

Several decades ago, a philosopher of science named David Hull used a methodology known as ethnography — an approach regularly used by anthropologists to understand remote foreign cultures — to study a population that couldn't be more different from anthropologists' standard samples of hunter-gatherer tribes or small-scale farmers. Hull's population of choice was a group of lab-coat-wearing, scientific-problem-solving biologists, and the goal of his research was to figure out what makes science progress; that is, what forces drive the development of new scientific ideas as well as their eventual acceptance or rejection by the field at large. What is it that motivates successful scientists to work all hours, often day and night, for not particularly impressive academic salaries, conducting research that has the potential to improve human life?

This may seem like a question with a foregone conclusion. Scientists seek the truth. They conduct experiment after experiment to better understand the nature of things — the world, the universe, the mind, and the body. And they do it because they want to learn and use their knowledge to make the world better. They want to make discoveries that advance our species and, ultimately, help people. It is this goal that makes science progress. Right?

Wrong.

Contrary to the popular view of scientists as disinterested seekers of truth, Hull's ethnography portrayed a society of individuals who worked very hard to find the evidence they were looking for — as long as it was evidence that supported *their own theoretical beliefs.*

This research failed to support the myth of the archetypal scientist, that scrupulous individual who selflessly slaves away in a lab all day and night with the sole aim of helping humanity through the accumulation of scientific wisdom. Instead, Hull observed, "During the hundreds of hours of interviews that I conducted . . . numerous motivations were offered for why [the individuals he studied] became scientists and continued to pursue their labors. Not once did anyone mention the good of humanity. When I raised the issue, they tended to respond, 'Oh, yes, yes, I certainly want to help humanity.' . . . To be sure, scientists are willing to take credit for applications of basic research which people take to be good, [but] good intentions are not adequate to explain the peculiar success of science."

As Hull noted, the practice of crediting scientists only if they are the first to *publish* a new finding was originally instituted as a way of incentivizing these individuals to share their work with people outside their own field who might implement it in a practical way as soon as possible. Over time, however, this practice came to serve a secondary motivational function. Scientists seek out the most difficult problems to solve, work all hours to solve them, and then come up with new problems in need of solving each time a particular question has been answered, *because of their desire to be the solver on record.*

Solving a scientific problem or making a scientific discovery is the ultimate achievement and the ultimate source of pride within this field. It's what underpins the entire scientific enterprise. Scientists strive to prove their own theories right and others' wrong. That is what drives science — much more than a desire to acquire new knowledge or understanding for the simple sake of knowledge and understanding.

And according to Hull, *this is a good thing.* Scientists' self-interested motivation ensures that science progresses. The desire to feel pride in one's endeavors and discoveries is what allows major advances to occur. Pride promotes innovation, because pride is the reason that people — all people, from scientists and inventors to artists, architects, and carpenters — work hard to create.

Of course, self-interested scientific pursuit doesn't always result in genius-level discoveries. Hubristic pride in one's work can prompt an unwillingness, or even an outright refusal, to admit when one is wrong. The mathematical physicist Lord Kelvin provides just one example among hundreds, perhaps thousands, of historical and contemporary scientists who refused to modify their theories in the face of contradictory evidence. In Kelvin's case, rather than backing down when his estimates of Earth's age were soundly challenged, he conducted new experiment after new experiment, trying, unsuccessfully, to prove that he was right. While this is more evidence for the irrepressible impact of pride on science and against the idea that science is a dispassionate search for truth, it's also a reminder of the dark side of the human desire for pride.

None of this means that scientists are bad people, striving to work hard and produce acts of genius only for the selfish reason of want-ing to feel good about themselves. The fact is, scientists work hard and *care deeply* about their pursuits precisely because they want to be good people, the kind of people their society rewards with high status. But the *knowledge* that one's work might eventually garner a promo-tion or even the opportunity to name a newly discovered theorem is not what keeps these scientists going all those late nights in the lab. It's the emotion that accompanies this knowledge that does it, and that's what gives all human achievers, discoverers, creators, and innovators the constant and repeated kick in the pants to become the people they want to be.

So pride is crucial to the first psychological process that drives cu-mulative cultural evolution: the human devotion to building and creat-ing. But what about the second of the three processes? How does pride contribute to the human willingness — even eagerness — to teach what we know to others?

The answer is that pride pushes us to share our knowledge with fel-low humans because doing so fosters prestige. Teaching others what you know is what the prestige route to rank attainment is all about. Prestige evolved in humans as a way of making sure that society's wis-est and most skilled experts reach a place of power, where they can in-fluence the rest of the group.

Because humans are social learners, those who have the most to teach are rewarded. Learners defer to them in exchange for access to their skills and knowledge. And to retain their power, prestigious in-dividuals must be generous and helpful teachers. Their high rank is directly predicated on their willingness to share the boons of their ex-pertise with the rest of their group. If they are unwilling to do so, they lose their power; after all, why defer to a cultural expert who won't let you learn from her? A prestigious person can't intimidate or manip-ulate you into following her without getting a reputation for being a dominant bully.

So prestigious individuals have a natural incentive to make them-selves available to those who wish to learn from them. The result is a system where the people in a society who have most proficiently acquired the society's cultural norms, values, beliefs, and knowledge *want* to teach what they know to others, and they are rewarded for doing so.

This system is effective because when each individual member of a society tends toward copying the most prestigious of the group, the society as a whole benefits. Even if the large majority of learners fail to master a given skill at the same level as their teacher, if just a few do reach that level, then a few of *those* will move beyond mastery; they'll innovate. They'll find a way to perform the skill better than their teacher did, and *they* are the ones who will teach the next generation. After twenty generations, *everyone* in the society will have acquired a set of skills that are twice as good as the original teacher's. As long as most learners take care to learn from the experts, the entire group will progress.

Pride is critical to this societal-level progression, because, as we have seen, authentic pride is the emotion that drives the attainment of prestige. The desire to feel authentic pride motivates people to seek out achievements and learn new knowledge, and these acquisitions, in turn, make these people ideal social models — the people most likely to become their group's prestigious leaders. Authentic pride also makes people care for others — recall that momentary experiences of authentic pride can promote empathic concern — and these feelings of empathy are part of why prestigious people are motivated to make sure those others learn. In fact, demonstrating kindness and generosity is an important part of developing a prestigious reputation. The most prestigious members of a group are the ones who not only have a great deal to contribute but who do so generously and supportively. They are also the group members who report high levels of authentic pride.

So pride is the emotional force that drives the first two psychological processes behind cumulative cultural evolution. What about the third — our desire to learn from experts?

This third and final component of cumulative cultural evolution is all about learning; figuring out who the wisest, smartest, and most skilled cultural group members are and then treating those people like prestigious social models who deserve our respect. This means copying their behavior and deferring to their wishes and desires so that they allow themselves to be copied.

An important clue to the role of pride in this process comes from the fact that adaptive social learning — that is, social learning that results in the transmission of valuable cultural knowledge — requires that copying be discriminatory. Learners need to choose *which* models to copy; ideally, those with the cleverest ideas, most useful skills, or largest body of knowledge. Pride, it turns out, is what tells learners who those models are likely to be.

Thanks to cumulative cultural evolution, scientists don't always need to be right, ideas don't always need to be good, and Lord Kelvin can get away with a mistake or two in an otherwise illustrious career. Over time, the best ideas and most accurate results are the ones that get copied, learned, and improved upon. The weaker ideas or results that turn out to be nonreplicable eventually fade away.

Bad ideas get weeded out because cultural evolution works in a similar way to genetic evolution. Genes that get copied and passed on to the next generation are the ones that encode for traits or behaviors that, in some way, make the genes' replication more likely. Genes that do nothing to ensure their own replication will, quite simply, not be reproduced. This means that if certain genes encode for a trait that stops being useful, those genes will eventually die out. It's why modern humans who mastered the art of tenderizing meat with fire lost the large and extra-sharp incisors of their ancestors.

In the same way, ideas that aren't worth learning die out, even when they originate from a highly reputable thinker. Have you ever heard of Einstein's repulsive gravitational force? It was eventually proved wrong — in Einstein's words, his "biggest blunder" — and, as a result, you won't find it on nearly as many T-shirts as $E = mc^2$. The beauty of cumulative culture is that progress never rests on any single person. Advances are made by combining the wisdom of many people, and many generations of people. Over time, the process manages to sort out the good ideas from the bad. Like a gene that codes for behaviors that weaken its own chances of being reproduced, an idea that weakens its own likelihood of spreading simply won't spread.

Of course, what determines the reproducibility of ideas is very different from what determines the reproducibility of genes. Suicide bombing is very bad from a gene's point of view, and if there were a gene for suicide bombing it wouldn't be replicated, because it promotes a behavior that would spell its own demise. As an idea, however, all suicide bombing needs to do is be perceived by social learners as something valuable, something that promotes power, or fame, or wealth, or any other resource that's widely desired by society. And this is why suicide bombing is an idea that gets repeatedly transmitted. In some cultures, bombers are seen as martyrs after their deaths, and because these individuals live in societies where life after death is highly valued (another replicable idea), the reward of martyrdom is considered by some very small proportion of the population well worth the massive genetic price.

In many cultures, however, suicide bombing is considered an act of insanity — clearly *not* a good idea that should be copied. This is because these societies hold different ideas about martyrdom, suicide, life after death, and even mental health than the extremist religious terrorist organizations that foster suicide bombing. But how can social learners know this? Members of these societies must somehow figure out that the best move is *not* to treat a suicide bomber as a social model — to learn, in other words, *whom* to learn from.

There are many different ways that humans determine whom we should follow and whom we shouldn't. Studies of early childhood learning show that young kids prefer to learn from people who are like them, rather than people who are different. So you might decide to avoid copying the suicide bomber because he belongs to a different ethnic group than you or holds a different set of beliefs than you or simply because his behavior makes him an obvious social deviant, based on all the other social norms you've already learned.

This approach to social-model discrimination works well for ruling out models who are different from us in some clear-cut way, but it doesn't solve the problem of figuring out whom to copy within our own social group. It's not advantageous to copy everyone who looks or thinks like us, and, in fact, we don't; individuals who are seeking knowledge (i.e., learners) show a strong preference toward copying those in their social group who have *prestige* — the most knowledge-able experts. But how do we figure out who those people are?

One good way to identify people with prestige is to look for those who know things. This might seem like an overly simplistic recom-mendation, but it's actually a complex standard that's reliably observed in human behavior from early on in development. By two years of age, toddlers choose to learn from social models who know what they're talking about: those who label a toy car with the word *car*, for example, instead of the word *duck*.

But of course there are many situations in which we don't have ac-cess to the kind of information that would allow us to know whether a potential model has a history of being right. There are also situa-tions in which it might be adaptive to learn from someone who's been wrong in the past but nonetheless has something of value to offer in the present. Can learners look beyond evidence of past accuracy to benefit from potentially knowledgeable experts in these cases?

In fact, two-year-olds don't rely *only* on concrete evidence of prior knowledge. When kids lack access to information about actual exper-tise, they seek out *cues* of expertise in the form of displays of *certainty*. If it's not completely clear that an adult knows what he's talking about, young children will still trust him as long as he *seems* to know what he's talking about. Kids will decide to use an object like a hairbrush or a light switch in the same way they saw an adult use it if the adult used it confidently: speaking with conviction, smiling, and saying "Aha!" while raising an index finger. Kids are more likely to copy the behav-iors of social models who display these signs of confidence than mod-els who demonstrate uncertainty: shrugging, scratching their chins, saying "Hmmm," and generally appearing confused.

In fact, even when five-year-olds learn that their local expert may not possess the expertise she claims to have — when they find out later that the model's certainty was misplaced, and she actually had no idea what she was talking about — they still trust her over a model who seems appropriately unsure about what she doesn't know. Adults don't usually make this mistake; we take into account whether a certain-seeming model has a history of accuracy and, especially, whether her certainty is linked to her accuracy such that she's more confident about things she knows and less confident about things she doesn't know. But this involves complicated mental processing; it requires one to distrust easily observed but imperfect signals of accuracy (that is, the appearance of certainty) and pay attention to more reliable indications of accuracy that may or may not be linked to the signals. As a result, adults, too, default to the appearance of certainty when things get tricky. When adults are distracted — asked to count backward aloud, preventing them from devoting their full set of cognitive resources to the task at hand — they respond just like five-year-olds. They trust whatever the confident model says, even though they've learned that this model's confidence might be misplaced.

So, displays of confidence and certainty — statements like "I know" and nonverbal behaviors like index-finger-raising, smiling, and standing upright — trigger social learning. And by this point in the book, you might find these kinds of displays more than a little familiar.

When I read about this research, my first thought was that displaying certainty is, in essence, another way of conveying one's pride. Social models who communicate a sense of confidence in what they know are telling observers that they are proud of themselves. As a result of showing these displays, they are treated as prestigious experts and used as a source of cultural learning.

If this account is right — that social models' pride displays are the reason these individuals effectively earn learners' respect — then the pride expression itself might be a cue to expertise. In addition to signaling high status, pride displays might trigger social learning. The same displays that, we now know, instantaneously tell onlookers that the proud individual merits a boost in social rank might also prompt these onlookers to want to learn from the displayer.

Studies from developmental psychology show that two-year-olds will copy adults who seem sure of themselves, but it's not entirely clear whether these toddlers' behaviors are driven by perceptions of pride.

In these studies, young kids were more likely to copy confident models than confused models. While this might be because kids came to trust the confident model, it might also be that they *dis*trusted the clueless model. Furthermore, knowing something about how kids learn doesn't necessarily tell us anything about how adults learn. Kids are naturally prone to copy an adult's behavior, but adults are not. Yet if pride displays communicate expertise and prestige and thereby bias social learning so that members of a culture can most effectively figure out whom to learn from, then pride should trigger copying behaviors in adults too. Adults are the people most likely to learn advanced skills and build on them — that is, to innovate — so if the pride expression is what prompts this component of cumulative cultural evolution, then adults' social learning, and not just kids', should be guided by others' pride displays.

Supporting the idea that adults, too, choose to learn from social models who display pride, my colleagues and I found that adult research participants behave exactly the same way kids do when placed in a situation where they need to obtain new knowledge. We told a sample of undergraduates (the "adults" in many of our studies) that they would be entered into a drawing for a cash prize of fifty dollars if they could correctly answer a very difficult trivia question. The question was one that we knew they wouldn't immediately be able to answer — *What is the smallest bird in the world?* or *What is the value of pi (π) to the 9th decimal place?* — so this was a situation that required some learning for them to perform well. And we gave these participants the opportunity to learn; we let them watch as another participant answered the same question right before them. What we didn't tell them was that this "other participant" was actually one of our research assistants who'd been told to answer the trivia question incorrectly while displaying an expression of pride, shame, happiness, or neutrality.

According to the results of this study, participants who did not know the correct answer to the trivia question (i.e., all of them) copied the research assistant's wrong answer about 80 percent of the time — *but only if the assistant displayed pride.* As can be seen in figure 6.1,

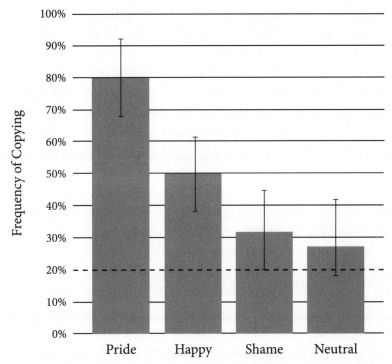

Figure 6.1. Frequency of participants who copied the (incorrect) answer to a trivia question first provided by another participant (actually one of our research assistants) depending on the other participant's displayed expression. The dotted line indicates chance responding (that is, the frequency that would be expected if participants were simply guessing among the response options provided). Pride displays led to greater copying than any other emotion expression; participants were no more likely to copy individuals who displayed neutral or shame expressions than they were to guess randomly.

when our assistants displayed happiness, participants copied their answer 50 percent of the time. Shame- and neutral-expression displayers were copied between 20 to 30 percent of the time, which is the same as what we'd see if participants were guessing randomly among the options we gave them.

Our participants selectively chose to learn from the person they saw displaying pride, suggesting that they inferred, on the basis of his or her pride expression, that this individual knew what he or she was talking about. This result tells us that the pride expression — an evolved status signal — is also a cue to expertise, and one that shapes one of the most important human behaviors: social learning. Pride displays communicate not only that the displayer deserves high status but also that she possesses valuable cultural knowledge that's worthy of being copied.

In fact, the impetus to learn from pride displayers goes beyond the moment when the display is observed. In another study, we found that participants also chose to copy individuals whom they'd seen display pride previously, even if those individuals were not displaying pride while answering the critical to-be-copied question. When we see a person display pride, we assume not only that he knows what he's talking about in that moment but also that he has a broader expertise. When we're later given the opportunity to learn from this person, we choose to do so even if he's no longer showing pride.

This research tells us that the pride expression provides a critical missing link to our understanding of cumulative cultural evolution. Pride displays tell people who the best social models in a group are; whom they should copy and learn from. And because these displays tend to be shown by people who actually do have something to be proud of, heeding this message is adaptive for the rest of us. When we copy pride displayers, we help to ensure that, on average, the ideas and behaviors of society's smartest, wisest, and most competent individuals will endure and spread.

But wait — you might have noticed that there is a critical flaw in this logic. In our research, participants were *not* copying the smartest or wisest social models. They were copying people who displayed pride *even though they got the answer wrong.* Of course, this was because we had told these models to answer incorrectly, but in real life, proud people get answers wrong all the time; sometimes because of an innocent mistake (for example, forgetfulness), but other times because they in fact lack competence or expertise.

Just because pride displays are systematically linked to success, status, and competence doesn't mean that these are the only situations in which pride is shown. It's not difficult, after all, to fake a pride expression. And the benefits of faking could be enormous; as we've seen, pride displays bring power, status, and an ability to spread one's own beliefs to others. But a systematic tendency to copy the behaviors exhibited by those who fake pride would not be good for cumulative culture. Cumulative cultural evolution requires that the best and brightest models get copied — not just any old model who can convincingly pose pride.

Fortunately, faking pride doesn't work in the long run. When observers figure out that a seemingly confident model actually knows nothing, *they stop copying him.* As we've seen, adults do this easily, as long as they're not distracted by a simultaneous cognitive task. But research shows that kids do it too. In one study, four- and five-year-olds chose to trust and learn from a social model who lacked confidence but had a clear history of being right over a model who demonstrated signs of confidence — including pride displays — but had been known to show these displays even when she was wrong. In this study, children watched as adults made four fairly egregious mistakes (for instance, saying that whales lived in the ground). When presented with this kind of clear-cut indication that the adults should *not* be trusted as solid social models, kids stopped treating them that way — even when the adults showed pride.

While this finding seems to contradict the prior research discussed above in which children weighted confidence displays over accuracy, the critical difference is that, here, kids could plainly see that the adult was an idiot. In the prior studies, kids learned only later that some certain-seeming, confidence-displaying adults had been wrong. Taking these studies together, what this means is that when kids (and distracted adults) see clear signs of confidence alongside subtle hints of inaccuracy, they go with the confidence and bias their learning in that direction. But when kids and adults *know,* without a doubt, that a model's pride display is unmerited — that his pride is meaningless, because it's obviously not tied to accurate knowledge — they ignore the pride.

Applying all of these research findings to the real world might explain why people are willing to trust, and even seek to learn from, hubristic cultural leaders like Donald Trump and Steve Jobs. We see their displays of confidence, and we know that in the past, at least some of the time, they have been right. Learning from them is, on average, good for us. But if these people keep displaying pride long after they've stopped achieving, we will stop looking up to them and find someone else to learn from.

In fact, pride displays are clearly not the only information we use to determine whom we should learn from. The fact that few human relationships exist without some prior familiarity — we rarely have the opportunity to learn from people with whom we have absolutely no history — means that historical information about a social model's accuracy or body of knowledge can be incorporated into most decisions we make about learning. This historical knowledge is the basis for determining who deserves prestige. Displaying pride is just a shortcut. It provides a quick and dirty way for prestigious people to inform others that they should be copied and used as a source of learning, but if these displays aren't eventually backed up with demonstrations of actual expertise, they will lose their effectiveness. And, as we will see in the next chapter, there are real costs to abusing the power of pride by faking it.

In sum, because it contributes critically to each of the three components of cumulative cultural evolution — creation and innovation, sharing the fruits of one's creations with others, and figuring out whom to learn from — pride lies at the heart of the evolutionary process that got humans where we are today. By motivating us to find out what our society's norms are and how best to follow them, pride is partly responsible for human culture and, therefore, human nature. The question, then, is what this means for individual members of our species who want to get the most out of their pride. Should you seek out pride, with the aim of becoming a prestigious leader of your group, or does seeking pride risk finding hubris, making the emotion a self-indulgence that's best avoided? What does the science of pride mean for the pride we humans feel — and want to feel — in our lives?

7

Take Pride

A T THE AGE of thirteen, while all of the other Texas kids were
playing football in the sun or swimming at the local country club,
Lance Armstrong was riding his bike. As he later wrote, "I had started
with nothing . . . but on my bike, I had become something . . . I was
biking for miles after school, because it was my chance." Young Lance
rode roughly twenty miles every day and soon began entering junior
triathlons. By the age of sixteen, he was earning twenty thousand dollars a year in prize money, contributing significantly to his family's income.

What happened next is well-trod history. Armstrong eventually became the second American ever to win cycling's most grueling race: the
2,200-mile-plus, twenty-day-long Tour de France. And he didn't win
it just once or twice; he won it seven times. In 2005 — the year Armstrong achieved his final Tour de France victory — he was widely considered the fastest long-distance cyclist in the world. But Armstrong
was much more than an enormously talented athlete. He had become a
major philanthropist, beloved and respected for the money and awareness he'd raised for millions suffering from cancer through Livestrong,
the multimillion-dollar charitable organization he founded. Lance

Figure 7.1. Lance Armstrong displaying pride while crossing the finish line to win the seventeenth stage of the 2004 Tour de France (a win that was subsequently revoked by the International Cycling Union)

was, in every way, a real hero, and people all over the world publicly conveyed their admiration and downright worship of him by wearing the ubiquitous Livestrong yellow bracelets.

Armstrong worked as hard as he did to become the strongest cyclist in the world for many reasons, but one key emotional motivator stands out. He says that biking was his way out, a way of getting beyond life as a poor kid in Plano, Texas, with a hard-working mom, a dad who'd abandoned him, and a stepdad he butted heads with. And all those factors certainly contributed to Armstrong's unsurpassed determination and drive. But it took more than *knowledge* that cycling might eventually earn him a better life to motivate Lance to put in those uncountable hours of tedium and pain on his bike. Armstrong cycled —

at least in part — because he wanted to feel pride, the kind of pride that comes from being the best.

But as we all now know, this is not where Lance's story ends. Somewhere along that road to becoming the best, something changed. Armstrong stopped caring about becoming the fastest cyclist he could be — a goal that had to matter tremendously to the *me* self he'd built up over the years — and started caring about how fast other people *believed he was.* He went from being intrinsically motivated to become the best to focusing instead on extrinsic rewards: the glory of each big win. And he found another way to attain that glory. Lance found a way to win that wasn't dependent on working as hard as he possibly could and that, in fact, *separated the act of winning from doing his best.* By using illegal EPOs to boost his blood oxygen levels — doping — Lance managed to win races *without* simultaneously proving that he was the best.

That is what's ironic about cheating: When people get away with it — whether it's athletes doping to win races, students copying answers on an exam, or scientists fabricating data to get published in a top-tier journal — these cheaters are accomplishing a seemingly impossible feat. They are succeeding *and* failing at the very same time. They succeed in the eyes of the public; they're applauded for winning the race, getting the A, or producing a groundbreaking scientific result. But they're also failing, and at the very thing that made them care about succeeding in the first place: *actually becoming* the fastest cyclist, a strong student, or a scientist who acquires new knowledge. The old adage is right: when you cheat, you're cheating yourself — although, as Armstrong's former teammates, sponsors, and opponents would be the first to point out, not *only* yourself.

What made Lance Armstrong shift from wanting to be the best cyclist he could possibly be to wanting to win races any way he possibly could? What caused this change in motivation? We see it all the time; a star athlete who's been indoctrinated to feel good about himself every time he hits a home run decides to do something to his body that makes his home runs meaningless — or, at least, no longer meaning something that he can feel genuinely proud of. A scientist who devotes years of education and training toward the goal of making major discoveries and advancing human knowledge decides that she'd rather create fictions to get the credit and admiration without the understanding. How can we explain this shift?

The obvious answer, of course, is the money. The fame. The fortune. But there must be something else too — something in the cheater's psychology — that makes her decide to prioritize these tangible external outcomes over building and maintaining the best *me* self possible. As I've argued throughout this book, we work harder than we need to because we want to feel good about ourselves — we want to feel pride. The promise or potential of an effortless payday, or even fame and fortune, doesn't easily overpower that goal. Or, when it does — when we choose to seek rewards that are external to our sense of who we are and that, often, require us to give up a piece of who we are — we regret it. Like twenty-nine-year-old Dean Karnazes mindlessly climbing the corporate ladder or bourgeois suburban dad Paul Gauguin keeping it together as a salesman while longing to make art, we feel a loss, or a deep dissatisfaction. We know that something is missing, and all those concrete rewards are not a sufficient replacement.

Karnazes and Gauguin each made a switch, from focusing on the attainment of external tangibles to focusing on the attainment of authentic goals that shaped their ideal *me* selves. Lance Armstrong, by contrast, moved in the opposite direction. He knew what he had to do to feel good about himself, and he gave it up for larger but falser glories. Chances are, Armstrong didn't even realize he was losing something, because *he still felt a great deal of pride* in his successes. External rewards — wealth, power, and notoriety — can bring pride. But the pride is different. Armstrong couldn't feel authentic pride in a hard-earned victory when his victories were at least partially earned by performance-enhancing drugs, but he *could* feel hubristic pride based on an inflated and aggrandized sense of himself instead of on reality. This is the pride that narcissists depend on to avoid succumbing to deep-seated feelings of shame. It's the pride that can lead to frequent demonstrations of arrogance, defensiveness, and outright aggression — all displayed regularly by Armstrong during his cheating years.

Like Lance Armstrong, many people begin their careers, or their adult lives in general, wanting to feel authentic pride. They work hard or try to do the right thing because the authentic pride they experience as a result feels good. They attain prestige in the eyes of those around them, and that feels good too. But then, something changes. They start experiencing success, and with it, the thrill of others' admiration. Their focus shifts from the hard work and effort that got them where they are to the self-satisfied glow that comes from observing the way others look at them. They forget that they had to work hard to make themselves into people who were worthy of all that admiration. They see only the outcomes, or ends of their achievements, and not the means; they focus on the tangible external rewards but not the effort, drive, and desire to achieve a certain kind of *me* self that initially brought those rewards. Eventually, they no longer want to do whatever it takes to be the best selves they can be, and instead — as Armstrong told Oprah Winfrey — they do whatever it takes to win, to make sure everyone else sees them as the best, regardless of whether those perceptions are valid.

Armstrong told Oprah that he got lost in the "momentum" — the adoration from his fans, the media, and the cycling world — and that, in the end, he "couldn't handle it." Winning became all that mattered, and, as he admitted, Lance allowed himself to become a lying, arrogant bully in order to get the wins he desperately needed. He knew that his victories weren't meaningful anymore. He got caught up in the "process," to use his word, of biking, doping, and bullying others into doping, and winning became a given, something that, he said, was "phoned in."

The switch from authentic to hubristic pride is deeply problematic and even hurtful, not just for others, but also for the cheater himself. Hubristic pride can turn people into jerks and, as a result, cost them their closest friendships and relationships and make them anxious, unhappy, and even clinically depressed. Armstrong suffered many of these costs. It's not just that he lied about doping. It's that he fiercely, aggressively, and frighteningly attacked every person who challenged him, from his team's longtime massage therapist, to Greg LeMond, the only other American ever to win the Tour de France, to the overly honest wife of one of his most valued teammates, to his former teammates themselves, people who'd supported him and lied for him for years.

Hubristic pride turned Lance into someone he probably didn't recognize. Armstrong told Oprah that he was a better human being — "better and smarter" — now that the truth was out than he was during all those years of cheating and winning. There is no true glory in a false win, and the thrill of hubristic pride is, ultimately, an empty thrill.

Although hubristic pride is adaptive in the evolutionary sense — increasing one's chances of surviving long enough to reproduce by virtue of boosting social rank — it is unquestionably maladaptive from a mental-health standpoint. It hurts one's sense of self and, as a result, one's psychological well-being. But hubristic pride *happens;* it's experienced by all of us to some degree at some point, and it can happen as a natural outcome of the successes that come from authentic pride.

In his early years on the bike, Lance Armstrong was almost certainly motivated by authentic pride. There had to be a time when he wanted not only to show others that he was the best but to actually *be* the best. And there are countless examples of people whose early successes — the ones that propelled them to fame — were driven by authentic pride, but then something changed. At some point along the road to stardom, their strategy shifted, and they began to work hard not for the sake of achievement itself or to become the kind of person they wanted to be, but to show off, defend their egos against hidden insecurities, or maintain a falsely inflated impression held by others.

The question, then, is how to cope with this two-sided emotion in the most psychologically effective way possible. Pride is part of human nature. We evolved to experience it and to display it in our nonverbal expressions. Authentic pride motivates us to do what's needed to become the best we can be — to achieve, create, innovate, and behave morally. Hubristic pride is also motivating, but it fosters a completely different set of behaviors. It makes us aggressive, manipulative, and domineering; we become primed to do whatever it takes to get power and influence over others.

Both prides are the result of our uniquely human *me* selves — selves that we will do anything and everything to feel good about. We evolved to care so much about our *me* selves, we find it exceedingly difficult to pass up any opportunity to feel a sense of grandiosity in those selves — especially since grandiosity can serve as an antidote to insecurity. When we feel bad about ourselves, our instinct is to reverse that feeling in as extreme a way as possible.

There is a solution to this problem. We don't have to succumb to the darker side of pride just because human nature makes us desperate to feel good about ourselves. We can regulate our feelings and behaviors to maximize experiences of authentic pride while simultaneously minimizing our chances of falling into the hubris trap.

For religious scholars through the ages, the only viable solution to hubris was to avoid pride altogether — to deem it a sin deserving of punishment. But as we now know, sacrificing authentic pride for the sake of preventing its flip side would be a massive loss; authentic pride is the emotion that brings out the best we have to offer. Without it, we would have little motivation to achieve, create, or lead. Tamping down this powerful emotion is not the answer. As Dean Karnazes or Paul Gauguin might attest, when we lack a clear path for seeking authentic pride in our lives, we feel a void.

The answer, instead, lies in knowing the difference between authentic and hubristic pride and maintaining — during every pride experience — an awareness of this distinction. As we seek out experiences of authentic pride — by working hard toward what's most important to us and striving to figure out what that is — we must also bear in mind the dangers of hubris. We must remember that the *getting there* — the hard work or perseverant effort toward something that feels meaningful — is what earns us the pride we seek, much more than reflecting back on the successes we've already attained. This understanding will help us stay true to our authentic *me* selves and mitigate the darker side of pride by reminding us to focus closely on who we are and what we want.

It's not easy, but it is straightforward: Figure out who you are and who you would like to become. Put in the necessary work to attain and maintain that ideal *me* self—to feel good about the part of yourself that is hard earned and *real*. Even when you think you might be there, don't stop. Don't bask in the glory. Instead, find that next hurdle to jump. To maintain authentic pride, the work is never really done, because it is the process of working toward some meaningful goal that makes us the kind of person we want to be. But the reward—for our sense of self, our relationships, and our societies—makes it worth the price.

West Point—one of the top military training academies in the United States—is also one of the most selective universities in the country. A competitive applicant must come bearing not only the same stellar record of grades and extracurricular activities as someone applying to Harvard, but also a letter of recommendation from a U.S. congressperson or the Department of the Army. Students are evaluated on their academic abilities, but also on their physical and leadership potential. Even once they get in, sticking it out for four years is a serious challenge. It's not uncommon for cadets to drop out during the first grueling summer—and, yes, I said grueling *summer;* at West Point, there is no rest for the weary.

Unsurprisingly, the psychological factors that determine which cadets make it and which don't are of great interest to military leaders and outside researchers alike. To figure out what attributes promote success at the academy, a team of social scientists asked 10,239 West Point cadets to report their reasons for choosing the university. And as it turned out, those cadets who cited reasons intrinsic to their identity—factors like wanting to become an officer in the U.S. Army or a strong leader in any domain—ended up with more successful careers ten years later than cadets who chose to attend West Point for reasons external to the *me* self, like earning money or because they liked the school's prestigious reputation. The cadets who were motivated by internal factors were more likely to graduate, be promoted early on in their careers, and become commissioned as officers.

Broadly speaking, this is a well-replicated finding: when people engage in behaviors for the sake of their *me* selves — because they are intrinsically motivated to accomplish a particular goal that has some significant personal meaning to them — they work harder, do better, and end up happier. What's more surprising, though, is the other finding that came from this study. Cadets who reported external motivations for attending West Point were less likely to graduate or become officers even if they *also*, simultaneously, reported internal, self-relevant motivations. In other words, not all of the cadets who said they were there to become officers or strong leaders did well. Cadets who said these things but added that they were also there to make money or for the school's reputation did *less* well.

The implications of this finding, if it can be generalized beyond West Point, are profound. It's not enough to work hard for the sake of feeling authentic pride in one's *me* self. To attain the best possible career outcomes, individuals need to work hard *only* for the sake of becoming their best selves and feeling authentic pride in those selves. If your job makes you feel good about yourself and also pays well, you'll have a more successful career if you don't care about the pay.

Of course, if the money you earn is an integral part of becoming your best self — if, for example, your ideal *me* is someone who provides the income her family needs to live on — then thinking about the money you're earning and, more important, the person that money will allow you to become is exactly the right way to get ahead. The critical point, from this study, is that you need to take the time to figure out *who* you want to be and then work hard to become *that person,* not for any other external reasons or rewards. Do it for authentic pride, but not for the hubris that comes with wealth, praise, and admiration from others.

One positive message we can take from this research is that our human desire to experience pride and show it to others is not a bad thing. Sages throughout history have tried to shame people for their pride, calling it the "queen of all sin" and declaring that "pride doth go before the fall," but we need not — and, in fact, cannot — shun pride. It is only by caring about one's sense of self and wanting to feel pride in that self that we take the time and make the effort to seek out what's most important to us, be it a long career in the military, a new discovery, or a brilliant invention. In fact, because authentic pride is what motivates achievement, innovation, and empathy toward others, this kind of pride *should* be sought and nurtured. People who regularly experience authentic pride are happy, healthy, popular, and successful, and they often attain prestige. By physically displaying the pride expression after a success, they signal their expertise to others and become trusted leaders and teachers.

More broadly, the search for authentic pride can fill the void that many people feel when they reach a point in their lives when their work is no longer challenging or fulfilling or their relationships are no longer engaging. Many of us instinctively know the solution to that feeling that something is missing; we seek to regain pride by going to the gym, volunteering at the local soup kitchen, learning the art of photography, or coaching our children's soccer teams. In each case, it is the evolved desire to feel good about the self that motivates change and that ultimately guides us toward becoming the kind of person we most want to be.

Those successful cadets — the ones who attended West Point because they wanted to become the best military officers they could possibly be and *not* because they wanted to make money or put themselves in a solid position for future career opportunities — had what psychologist Angela Duckworth calls *grit*. According to Duckworth, grit is "perseverance and passion for long-term goals," and it involves "working strenuously toward challenges, maintaining effort and interest over years despite failure, adversity, and plateaus in progress." Grit is about more than being able to stick with a task or getting one's work done. It's about holding on to a goal that might take years, or even decades, to accomplish and working hard toward it, no matter what.

Duckworth also studied West Point cadets, and she found that the grittiest among them — those who reported high levels of this kind of long-term perseverance and goal orientation — were more likely to make it through that first torturous summer. In fact, a cadet's level of grit was a better predictor of whether he or she would make it through that summer than the overall applicant score given to each cadet upon applying, a score based on a composite of his or her academic, physical, and leadership abilities.

Grit is all about being motivated to accomplish a singular goal that will result in the attainment of a particular kind of identity. People who have grit aren't working hard because they want to make a lot of money or impress others. They work hard because they want to become a particular kind of person. In study after study, Duckworth and her colleagues have shown that people who report high levels of grit — endorsing questionnaire items like "I have overcome setbacks to conquer an important challenge" and "I have achieved a goal that took years of work" — succeed in all kinds of domains. Gritty teenagers are more likely to attend college and to get good grades once they're there. Gritty spelling-bee champions are more likely to become National Spelling Bee finalists.

What is it that makes people gritty? What allows an individual to figure out who he wants to be — not just today or tomorrow, but in the long-term future — and then put in days, months, and even years of hard work to become that person? The answer is authentic pride, a desire to develop a certain kind of *me* self and feel genuinely good about it. The grittiest people among us are those who are able to harness their desire for authentic pride and use it as a continual source of motivation to move themselves closer and closer to the ideal *me* self they want to reach. To have grit, you need to know who you are and who you want to be. And those who have it are the ones who make it.

Gritty individuals consistently manage to outperform their less gritty peers, but not because of a superior raw intelligence or academic talent. In their study of spelling-bee champs, Duckworth and her colleagues found that gritty kids aren't any smarter than their less gritty peers; in fact, in all of Duckworth's studies, grit tends to be unrelated to measures of intelligence like IQ or SAT scores. Gritty spellers also don't spend any more time reading or engaging in other at least moderately fun activities that might promote a strong vocabulary and spelling skills than less gritty ones. Instead, the critical difference that matters for ultimate spelling-bee success is the number of hours kids spend *deliberately practicing spelling words.*

The most tedious, boring, downright painful part of becoming a spelling champ — that's what the gritty kids are best at. And that's what gets them to the final round of the competition. Grit makes kids spend more time performing the most mind-numbing part of learning to spell, and it's this — not reading, and not even being quizzed on tough words — that turns these kids into champions.

Does this remind you of anything? Recall the psychology experiment in which some participants were manipulated to feel pride after completing a boring mental-rotation task. These participants responded by volunteering to spend *extra* time in the lab to work away at another, equally boring task. The many hours that Duckworth's spelling champs put in memorizing words are much the same as the extra minutes those pride-induced participants stuck around to complete a task that they believed would stand them in good stead for their academic futures. The critical motivating force is pride — feeling it, and wanting to keep that feeling going strong.

Pride is the juice that gets people to work the long and tiring hours needed to achieve and to choose to do this work over many other much more fun and engaging activities. Another study demonstrated this point by following a sample of German adults for seven days to examine how emotions influenced these individuals' ability to resist temptations — those desires we face every day that run directly counter to our larger, *me*-self goals. There's the desire to go out with friends rather than stay at home studying, or to eat delicious, greasy, and decidedly unhealthy French fries instead of an apple. The only way to avoid succumbing to every temptation is to keep in mind the larger goal: that what you really want is not a fun night out but to become a strong student, or a lean and mean body instead of a belly full of fries. Remembering this, we somehow manage to make our behaviors conform to the larger goals instead of giving in to the immediate, compelling, and often intensely aromatic temptation.

Pride is the reason we are able to — sometimes — prioritize those less fun but more constructive goals over the more pleasurable ones. The desire to succumb to temptation is shaped by emotion — feelings of pleasure — so the best way to fight it is with another, potentially more powerful emotion. In the study of Germans' daily temptations, those participants who reported feelings of pride each time they successfully resisted a temptation — each time they chose the apple over the fries — demonstrated a stronger resistance to temptation the next time they faced it. Pride made these people decide that their larger goal was more important than the immediate, pleasure-motivated goal — that passing up the French fries was worth it.

What this means is that pride can trump pleasure. This is a point I made in the first chapter of this book. Pride is the reason we do many of the things we do that are about more than pleasure and that, quite often, require us to forgo pleasure. If you're looking for a way to convince yourself to finally commit to that diet, start going to the gym, give up smoking or drinking, or even just clean your basement, pleasure seeking will not get you there. But pride might. If, like those German research participants, you can focus on the pride you've felt in the past from committing to a goal and sticking to it — showing your grit — those feelings will guide you where you need to go to do it again and again and again.

Duckworth's research on grit also addresses a longstanding question that emerges from even a quick perusal of the literature on achievement and prominence: Why is it that raw intelligence doesn't predict success as powerfully as it should? Over a century ago, intelligence researcher (and, more unfortunately, eugenics proponent) Sir Francis Galton studied high-achieving individuals who had earned fame in a variety of ways, some through science or art, others through politics, and still others through athletics. What Galton found was that across these diverse disciplines, raw talent — even genius — could not account for the difference between those who reached the highest tiers of success and those who did well but not nearly as well as they could have. More recent studies tracking the lives of the world's most famous creators and leaders confirm this result. IQ scores are only weakly related to eminence in one's field.

This point — the surprising disjunction between intelligence and success — is one that journalist and popular science writer Malcolm Gladwell made famous with his rule of the ten thousand hours. In his book *Outliers,* Gladwell tells the story of Bill Gates, who came to acquire, early in life, an incomparable amount of experience programming computers; more than ten thousand hours, according to Gladwell. These many hours made Gates one of the most proficient programmers in the world and the person perhaps best suited to drop out of Harvard in 1975 to start his own computer company. Gladwell carefully tallied the many hours Gates spent programming, beginning when he was a Seattle eighth grader fortunate enough to find a well-funded computer club to join through all four years of high school when he and his friends would regularly steal shared computer time from the University of Washington. As Gladwell tells it, Gates was obsessed with the newfangled technology. At one point he found a computer in the UW medical center that went unused for a brief period between three and six each morning. Gates left his house in the middle of the night, every night, to spend these hours programming.

Gladwell's argument is that these thousands and thousands of hours in front of a computer made Gates who he is today — one of the richest people on the planet and the founder of the world's largest and most successful computer company, a business that's responsible for not one, or even several, but many distinct inventions that changed history. To become that person, Gates worked tirelessly, endlessly, and obsessively.

Gates is probably too busy to fill out Duckworth's grit questionnaire, but it's undeniable that he's one of the grittiest guys around — yet neither Gates's tremendous success nor Gladwell's theory of the ten thousand hours that got him there resolves the fundamental question of what made Gates so gritty, what made him *want* to work so tirelessly. What pushed him to get up in the middle of the night and sit in front of a computer screen? What drives anyone to put in the ten thousand hours that, according to Gladwell, are necessary to become an outlier — someone who succeeds in ways far beyond what we expect of even the most accomplished people we know? What makes spelling-bee champions willing to sit alone in a room, hour after hour, memorizing words like *serrefine* and *vivisepulture* — words they must know they'll never use again once the bee is done?

This kind of enduring, difficult, and typically tedious hard work needs to be motivated, and the simple knowledge that all that effort will get us somewhere does not have motivational force. Emotions are what motivate us, and, in the case of the grittiest high achievers, the emotion we're talking about is authentic pride. Quite clearly, this is not an emotion that we should avoid; on the contrary, to become the best selves we can be, we must seek it out and relish the push it gives us — the nudge to keep on working and become better and better.

In 1968, ecologist Garrett Hardin wanted to warn the world of the dangers of overpopulation. To do so, he made an argument that's become widely known across the social sciences as the tragedy of the commons. The idea behind this tragedy is that, because we humans live in social groups, we are regularly faced with tough decisions about whether to behave according to our own self-interests (for example, to eat a juicy, sloppy burger dripping with ketchup and mayonnaise and using the fifteen paper napkins required to survive this meal) or what's best for our group's future interests (for example, using a cloth napkin so as to avoid planetary deforestation or eating a veggie burger so as to avoid the massive negative environmental impact of the meat industry).

The tragedy comes from the fact that, at the level of the individual making the decision, the optimal choice is clear: your forgoing the fifteen napkins and one meat burger will have a negligible effect on the forests and the cows but a massive effect on your ability to enjoy a meal without covering your face, hands, and lap in a ketchupy, grain-filled, mushroom-and-barley mess. At the level of the individual, the decision is a no-brainer. But if everyone made that same calculation, the environmental effects would be massive instead of negligible. And the large majority of the world's burger-eating population would agree that their personal enjoyment of that burger is not worth the cost of their grandchildren never climbing a tree.

As you might imagine, the tragedy of the commons arises with almost every decision any of us make that has some impact on the environment. This is why it's so difficult, even for someone like former vice president Al Gore, to get people to change their behaviors to help save the forests or the world's limited fossil-fuel resources. We humans are bad at sacrificing a present self-interest for the sake of a future group interest, even if the group interest is hundreds of times more valuable than the self's.

The tragedy of the commons might seem inescapable, but what if one's present self is reminded that doing the right thing—the thing that's best for her social group—could make her proud? Might the desire to feel pride motivate individuals to behave in the way that an unselfish and prosocial *me* self would want them to? After all, pride makes people want to achieve, but only because achievements are what earn us acceptance and high status. And achievements are not the only way to build a *me* self that we can feel good about; our society wants much more of us than just success. Being a good social-group member means being generous, empathic, and helpful. It means sharing with others and voting in local elections. The *me* self is not only accomplished, but also moral; someone who behaves in the ways society sees as right and good. As a result, the desire for pride motivates people not only to work hard to achieve, but also to work hard to be *good*—to do the right thing, however that thing is defined by their society. For this reason, pride might be exactly what's needed to avert the tragedy of the commons.

Several psychologists tested this proposition by asking research participants to play a computer game that evoked a miniature version of the tragedy. The goal of the game was to catch as many computerized fish as possible from a shared computerized pond—the commons. Each round, participants learned how many fish they'd caught and decided how many to throw back into the sea.

Participants had a clear incentive — a self-interest — to keep as many fish as possible. But there was also a group interest at stake. The pond, they were told, was in grave danger of being overharvested, and if that happened, all fish profits obtained by all players so far would be confiscated. Participants were thus faced with two directly competing goals. On the one hand, they wanted to keep as many fish for themselves as possible. But on the other hand, they knew that if any player took too many fish, everyone would end up with nothing. The best strategy at the level of the individual was, of course, to take the maximum number of fish available and let other players worry about overharvesting. But that strategy came with the same problem as using fifteen napkins and eating meat: if everyone follows it, it backfires. So, instead, players had to find some middle ground between self-interest and self-sacrifice for the sake of the group.

How does the human desire to feel good about the *me* self — to feel pride in a moral *me* — influence this decision-making process? What the researchers found was that reminding participants of events that made them feel pride, and of how good those events feel, prompted these individuals to throw more fish back into the shared pond. Thinking about pride they wanted to feel made these people willing to sacrifice their own self-interests for the sake of their group. In the same way, thinking about the pride you'll feel from doing what your society wants you to do increases the likelihood that you'll do that thing.

Of course, not everyone would feel pride about sacrificing his or her own self-interests for the sake of the group. Some people — maybe many people — would feel just as much pride from catching the most fish. Perhaps this study happened to capture a particularly prosocial and cooperative group of participants, and that's why thoughts of pride made them behave better. Surely we could find some participants somewhere who'd be just as motivated by thoughts of pride to catch as many fish as possible for themselves.

In fact, another social-dilemma study demonstrates exactly this. In this study, participants were asked to play what's known as the Ultimatum Game. It's a game much like the Dictator Game, in which one

participant must divide a sum of money between himself and his partner. The difference is, in the Ultimatum Game, the other player — the
responder — doesn't just sit quietly and do nothing. Instead, she gets to
decide whether to accept the proposer's offer. And if she doesn't accept
it — if she decides to reject it — neither player gets anything. While this
might sound like a silly addition — why would a responder *ever* reject an offer, knowing that this means she gets nothing? — in fact, responders reject on a regular basis. Yes, these rejections hurt responders as well as proposers. But by rejecting offers that feel unfair — which
is how most offers falling substantially below 50 percent feel to those
of us from a Western industrialized society — responders ensure a fair
system of wealth distribution. Refusing to accept offers that are unfair prevents inequalities from emerging between the two players, but,
more important, the very existence of responders who have the power
to reject prompts proposers to make fairer offers.

Proposers in the Ultimatum Game — in contrast to those in the Dictator Game — thus have a built-in incentive to think about responders
when making their offers. And, like all humans, these proposers also
have a built-in, pride-driven incentive to make offers that will allow
them to feel good about themselves. Knowing the results from the fish-
overharvesting study, you might expect that Ultimatum Game proposers who are reminded of how proud they'll feel from doing the right
thing for their group — in this case, making a generous offer to ensure
a fair system of resource distribution — would offer more. And that is
exactly what happened among participants who were first instructed to
think about the pride they'd feel from making a generous offer. These
people responded by making more generous offers. But this study also
produced another interesting result. Some participants were asked to
think not about how proud they'd feel from making a generous offer
but, instead, of how proud they'd feel from keeping most of the stash
for themselves. Somewhat disturbingly, these participants who were
reminded that they might feel pride from going home with more cash
in their pockets than their partners *offered less.*

Unfair distributions ultimately hurt both responders and proposers, because responders will reject the offers, sending everyone home

empty-handed.* The self- and other-destructiveness brought out in these proposers highlights a fundamental truth about pride: it can make people good, but it can also make people bad. The critical question — the thing that determines which of these two outcomes we experience — is what we're proud of and *which kind of pride* we're feeling. Although pride is essential to attaining a fulfilling, productive, creative, and moral life, these benefits are derived from the authentic variety, not the hubristic one.

Authentic pride may be exactly what we need to reap the rewards of ten thousand hours of effort and years of grit, but opening ourselves up to experiencing one form of pride can bring on the other. When we start to receive the external benefits of our authentic pride — be they increased status, fame, or fortune — it becomes exceedingly easy to forget that these outcomes are indirect consequences of striving to be a certain kind of person. They are the rewards of achieving a certain *me* self and should not be directly sought for their own sake. But the temptation to forget about meeting the goals of one's *me* self and instead do whatever it takes to get those rewards — even if this means cheating, lying, or faking — is strong.

Faking the pride expression seems like one easy shortcut to higher status, so why not do it? It's not difficult to enact this pose — most people can push out their chests and hold their heads up high — and, as we now know, displaying this expression comes with major benefits. It sends an automatic message to all who see it, telling them that the displayer deserves high status. If you pose pride, people will treat you differently. Even if you ran out of the house unshowered and wearing sweatpants and an old T-shirt, your pride display would still tell onlookers that you deserve high rank. After all, if it works for a homeless person draped in a dirty blanket, it's going to work for you, even on the most casual of Fridays.

But that's not all that posing pride does. A team of psychologists

---

* In the case of this study, the proposers' unfair offers did not end up hurting them, because, unbeknownst to them, they were making offers to fictional responders.

found that holding a pride expression — or other powerful postural positions — can boost testosterone, the high-status hormone, and temporarily change the way individuals see themselves. Regardless of whether people start out feeling pride, once they pose the expression they experience a sense of power and start to behave more powerfully; they're more likely to make a risky move in a card game and more willing to speak first in a debate. These poses can even increase their tolerance for pain and boost physical strength. In the face of this evidence, it's not surprising that psychologist Amy Cuddy — one of the authors behind this research — told an audience of over twenty million people who watched her immensely popular TED talk that posing pride was a viable solution to their anxieties and insecurities. According to Cuddy, pride posing — or power posing, as it's often called — is valuable not only because of what the expression tells others, but because of what it does for the poser. As Cuddy says, "When you pretend to be powerful, you are more likely to feel powerful." The implication of this statement is a well-worn piece of advice we've all heard at some point in our lives: fake it till you make it.

And Cuddy is right; numerous studies show that posing pride boosts feelings of power. But recall that there is more than one way to become powerful and more than one kind of power. In subsequent work, these researchers found that after just one minute of posing these high-power displays, participants became more likely to steal cash from an unsuspecting experimenter, cheat on a test, and commit a traffic violation. To state the obvious, these are not the behaviors of people experiencing a sense of prestige. Stealing, cheating, and lawbreaking are all examples of acts not infrequently reported by individuals who feel a strong sense of hubristic pride and whose peers call them dominant.

Posing pride, the research evidence shows, makes us feel strong. The question we need to ask ourselves is whether it's the kind of strength we want to feel. If we know that our display is not genuine — that is, if we know we are faking it — but nonetheless come to feel powerful as a result, what does that mean? If your feelings are based not on actual accomplishments but instead on an easy-to-perform nonverbal display, which kind of pride do you think you'll be feeling?

Given what we know about the effects of power posing, we can make a strong prediction about the answer to this question. It's very likely that the kind of pride people feel from falsely posing in a powerful stance is the hubristic variety.

Perhaps for this reason, Cuddy was adamant in her TED talk that faking it until you make it is not the way to go. She does not want people to feel like impostors. Instead, she suggests that faking it will get you where you want to go, telling viewers: "Don't fake it till you make it. Fake it till you become it." This recommendation, to become the person you're pretending to be, is great advice. The problem, as Cuddy would surely agree, is that you can't become that person simply by displaying an emotion expression. Instead, you need to do what Cuddy did in order to make it through college and earn a PhD from Princeton University after suffering a massive brain injury in a horrific car accident. As Cuddy told her TED talk audience, she managed to accomplish things that doctors told her she'd never be capable of, but she didn't get there by posing a powerful emotion expression. Instead, she explained, "I worked and worked and worked. And I got lucky. And worked. And worked." Cuddy, it seems, had grit.

This is not to say that following Cuddy's advice to take a few minutes before a big job interview to hide away in a restroom and pose pride is a bad idea. Doing so probably will give you that extra bit of confidence, or at least, arrogance, that could be exactly what you need to get the job. Recall, too, that displaying pride also has other benefits — including increasing your likelihood of getting hired. And if you can pose in a genuine way — reminding yourself, à la Stuart Smalley, that, doggone it, you are good enough! — that pose just might become the real deal: a genuine expression of authentic pride linked to a true sense of self-confidence and feelings of self-worth.

In the short term, posing pride (even when we don't feel it) can have noticeable effects, both positive and negative — but we know less about the long-term effects of power posing, in the sense of displaying the expression intentionally and not as a spontaneous result of genuine or warranted feelings of pride. The research hasn't been done. But we do know this: showing too much pride can be costly.

This point was demonstrated by a team of psychologists who examined how people evaluate those who display blatant pride expressions. Rather than measure people's responses to unwarranted pride displays, these researchers decided to examine reactions to pride displays shown by people who completely deserved to be showing them: winners. They found video footage of tennis stars, game-show champions, and Oscar winners, some celebrating their success with full-on, arms-to-the-sky, over-the-top expressions of pride, and others with much more subtle expressions. They asked observers what they thought of these people; that is, how much they liked them.

Even though the participants knew that all the people in the videos had just won a major event, making their pride entirely deserved, these observers still didn't like the winners as much when they showed intense versions of pride. Call it the James Cameron Oscar-acceptance-speech effect: participants rated these overtly proud winners as less likable and less concerned about the losers' feelings. They also reported a reduced interest in becoming friends with these people.

This study further found that the reason participants disliked the blatantly prideful winners so much was that they believed these individuals were expressing *hubristic* pride. Winners who displayed intense pride expressions were perceived as more arrogant, conceited, and egotistical than winners who did not display pride, and these perceptions made participants like the obviously prideful winners less.

In contrast, winners who were less expressive were judged to be much more likable, even though the observers believed these individuals were suppressing their emotions. This is an important point: It's not that observers thought that unexpressive winners weren't feeling pride. These winners showed just enough pride to let people know they *were* feeling it, but also made it clear that they were holding back a bit, perhaps out of respect for their opponents. This made them likable, much more so than winners who conveyed their pride with no regard for anyone else around.

Other studies show that displaying pride when it's *not* warranted — when observers didn't just see you experience a major win — can have worse consequences than making you disliked; it can lead to actual punishment. Or at least, it can result in the deprivation of much-needed help.

In a series of studies, my graduate students and I measured the pride displays shown by needy individuals requesting financial aid through the online micro-lending charity website Kiva.org. These individuals post photos of themselves along with information about why they need the funds they're asking for (which come in the form of loans), and potential altruists browse these profiles and decide where to direct their charitable donations. Kiva lenders are people who want to give — they are choosing to invest in Kiva's loan requesters not because they expect to make money off their loans (in fact, the individuals requesting the loans pay no interest on them), but because they want to help people in developing nations generate investment capital for their small-business ventures.

We might expect Kiva lenders to *seek out* signs of high status, like pride displays shown in requesters' profile photos, and direct their loans accordingly. After all, a nonverbal signal of high rank is a good indicator of future business success; those who show pride should be particularly likely to make good on the loan. But, in fact, we found exactly the opposite. Nonverbal displays of pride — more specifically, pride's signature behavior of expansive posture — substantially *reduced* the amount of money loan requesters received. Lenders direct their donations away from pride displayers, presumably because they perceive these displays as inappropriate when shown by people who are asking for help. When requesting financial aid, displaying expressions of pride makes individuals appear arrogant, and they are punished for it.

These findings have important implications for individuals seeking help, but these implications run directly counter to the conclusions of research studies demonstrating that pride displays tell observers that the expresser deserves a status bump. It would appear that pride displays simultaneously let others know that the displayer deserves higher status *and* that the displayer is unlikable and deserving of punishment. This raises some thought-provoking questions for would-be pride displayers. Is it worth posing pride for the sake of increasing your social rank and feeling powerful if that pose will also make others decide that you're arrogant and choose not to help you?

The problem here is, again, hubristic pride. When we see people showing pride in a completely uninhibited, excessive way or in a situation where it's clearly not warranted, this is what we assume they're feeling. It's not a fair assumption; authentic pride is associated with the same nonverbal expression, and those who feel authentic pride (for example, the congenitally blind judo champions in my research on Olympic and Paralympic athletes) show that same display. But, somehow, our society expects more of us.

We know that pride displays can indicate either authentic or hubristic pride, but we expect those who feel it authentically to be kind, empathic, and humble — and therefore to suppress their expression, at least to some extent, even when we know they're feeling it. If Obama had pumped his fist wildly in the air when announcing bin Laden's assassination, it might have given him an even greater status boost, but it would also have made many of us like him just a little bit less.

All of this helps to explain why it doesn't pay (and, in fact, can cost) to go around faking pride displays. Even though humans evolved to automatically perceive these displays as status signals, human cultures everywhere have developed social norms to prohibit the most overt versions of these expressions, even when they're warranted. We saw this in Fiji; our research participants there explicitly denied any association between pride expressions and high status, even though when we probed their unconscious, automatic associations, we found a similar pattern to what we'd seen among Western college students. The aforementioned study demonstrating participants' negative responses to overt pride displays shown by actual winners was conducted in Australia, an industrialized Western society with cultural norms very similar to those in North America.

These norms — telling us when, where, and how much we should show our pride — are ubiquitous, but they do vary from culture to culture. Americans are certainly more accepting of pride displays than Fijians and perhaps more than Australians — yet even among the most individualistic, status-oriented segments of American culture, there's a limit to how much excessive pride is acceptable. Business leaders and a number of Republican voters might grant Donald Trump power, but many of them also scoff at his extreme narcissism, even if they're afraid to do so to his face. And they accept Trump's grandiosity at all only because he can back it up. He is one of the world's most successful (or at least most successfully marketed) businessmen, so as much as we might despise his arrogance, and force him to suffer certain social penalties as a result, our society's cultural emphasis on financial achievement leaves us no choice but to grant him power — albeit the kind of power that's derived from dominance.

At the other end of the spectrum, Kalahari bushmen, much like Fijians, go out of their way to derogate and punish those who display any pride at all. A tribe member explained this social process with a hypothetical example: "Say a man has been hunting. He must not come home and announce like a braggart, 'I have killed a big one in the bush!' He must first sit down in silence until I or someone else comes up to his fire and asks, 'What did you see today?' He replies quietly, 'Ah, I'm no good for hunting. I saw nothing at all . . . maybe just a tiny one.' Then I smile to myself because I know now he has killed something big."

This story provides a telling example of the kinds of social sanctions members of traditional small-scale societies regularly use to ensure that their groups remain largely egalitarian. Punishing overt pride prevents power claims and extreme status stratification. Without pride displays, it becomes much more difficult to make sharp status-based distinctions among people on the basis of either prestige or dominance. Another tribe member explained how this works: "When a young man kills much meat, he comes to think of himself as a chief or a big man, and he thinks of the rest of us as his servants or inferiors. We can't accept this. We refuse one who boasts, for someday his pride will make him kill somebody. So we always speak of his meat as worthless. In this way we cool his heart and make him gentle."

From an evolutionary perspective, this makes sense. Once pride became a reliably recognized, automatic status signal in humans, cultural groups everywhere needed to develop social-control mechanisms that would penalize those who displayed too much pride or unwarranted pride. By invoking norms that punish individuals who appear overly arrogant, cultures can effectively reduce the rivalries over status that would occur constantly if individuals felt no constraint about displaying an emotion that communicates, at a minimum, their own belief that they deserve a status boost.

In the highly individualistic, status-stratified society I come from, faking pride is tolerated, at least to some extent. In much of the Western world, and certainly in the United States, we accept grandiosity and even arrogance in many of our leaders, and, in some cases, we admire them for possessing these qualities. Trump's former television show — which for ten seasons was little more than a public display of the tycoon's own self-satisfaction — was for several years ranked among the fifteen most-watched American television programs. Trump's political following has proved remarkably robust as well, despite — or because of — his repeated assertions of his superior intelligence, strength, toughness, and even hand size. According to a *USA Today*/Gallup poll in December of 2011, Trump was among the top six of the ten most admired men and women alive, and as this book goes to press, in the spring of 2016, Trump is the leading Republican candidate for U.S. president. Overt or exaggerated displays of hubristic pride are obviously not a deal breaker.

Americans might be willing to tolerate hubristic pride up to a point — but they do expect those who convey hubris to back up their grandiosity with something more than the mere induction of fear. Like most Westerners (and most people everywhere), we don't like bullies. Steve Jobs would never have gotten away with treating his employees the way he did — calling their work "shit" on a regular basis — if he hadn't first proven his technological and marketing genius and then continued to prove it again and again. In fact, for those who lead through dominance, power doesn't last beyond their ability to wield control, and in the case of technological innovator Steve Jobs, his power disappeared when he was no longer able to create products that sold. Nine years after founding Apple, Jobs was ousted by his own board of trustees. The official reason was his failure to build quality products. The second-generation Mac, the Apple 3, and the Lisa (your recognition — or lack thereof — of this name probably tells you something about how well it did) were all considered major failures. But Jobs wasn't fired only because of these poor products. He was fired because he didn't acknowledge his failures. Instead, he battled fiercely over them with Apple's CEO John Sculley.

This is what happens when arrogant and aggressive people — that is, dominants — fail. They don't go down easily. And because they've never bothered to secure others' admiration or love and have always made themselves difficult to work with, their associates are constantly on the lookout for ways to get rid of them. When a dominant makes that first critical mistake (or, in Jobs's case, the third), he's out.

Keeping dominant people — those who tend to follow their hubristic pride — in check is good business policy and good for human cultures. A society whose only form of hierarchical stratification is dominance cannot promote innovation or the kinds of progressive advances that are necessary for cumulative cultural evolution to occur. That's why we need prestige. And because prestigious leaders are generous, kind, and widely admired, they don't have to constantly contribute new value to retain their place in the group. They will not always hold the same influence as they do when they're at their most successful or creative, but as long as they don't veer toward dominance, the group will find a place for them.

Hubristic pride is, quite clearly, different from the invigorating, achievement-motivating pride that made Paul Gauguin, Dean Karnazes, and Bill Gates work day and night to perfect their craft. The more arrogant, gloating form of pride is part of what makes us human, but it's also what triggers the darker human behaviors, like aggression and deception, instead of creativity and innovation. If any part of pride is sinful, it's this.

Fortunately, we have a choice between these two prides. We have the ability to choose which one we let into our lives; we decide which kind of pride will shape us and our relationships. Ultimately, both authentic pride and hubristic pride hold only as much power as we grant them.

Feeling pride for something that's hard earned and showing that pride — in moderation — is a wise strategy. Authentic pride will, eventually, earn you prestige. And until then, it can guide you toward what you need to do to become the kind of person you want to be. It might even help you figure out who that person is.

The fact that authentic pride is part of human nature is something to be celebrated; it brings out the best of what we have to offer. But there is a catch. Our pride must be linked to actual successes or to morally good, empathic, generous, and compassionate behaviors. Our pride must be used to help each of us become the kind of person our societies want us to become *and* the kind of person that feels like an authentic part of who we are. If we can find a way to do that — to feel authentic pride in the person we most want to be — we will have the power to achieve, innovate, and create, and to use our prestige to help others do the same.

My advice, based on the accumulated research evidence, is this: Seek out authentic pride. Find a way to feel good about your best *me* self. Display the nonverbal expression of pride when you feel the emotion but don't exaggerate it, and suppress it when it's not warranted. Perhaps most important: Pay attention to your group's norms. The situations in which pride displays become culturally inappropriate vary dramatically by society; from Donald Trump to a Kalahari bushman, there is, quite clearly, no one-size-fits-all answer to the question of when to show your pride. Is it acceptable to pump your fist when you score a goal in a friendly game of soccer? What about when you beat a child at a game of Connect Four? Do your friends cheer for themselves after every victory, or do they attempt to maintain the appearance of humility? Do the people you respect the most — or the ones who seem most respected by others — publicly brag about their conquests on Facebook, or do they find more subtle ways to get the message across, perhaps allowing others to brag for them? The decisions that people make in contexts such as these determine how their pride is interpreted and how useful — or harmful — it is.

The fact is, almost all of us know how to regulate our pride displays — or at least how to acquire the information we need to do so effectively. Most of us manage to figure out the rules of modesty and self-promotion within our social groups. Our failure to follow these rules is not a failure of understanding. Resisting that impulse to tell a roomful of people about the elite university you attended, the big promotion you just received, the model you dated, or the book you wrote (says this tired but prideful author) can be a strenuous exercise in self-control. But suppressing our most self-aggrandizing expressions of pride is critical to avoiding hubris.

The other thing that's critical is staying true to yourself. Put best by Shakespeare, this advice has always served as a necessary counterpart to "fake it till you make it" — which, as we've seen, may have a totality of effects more negative than positive for you and society at large. In the words of the Bard, "This above all: To thine own self be true, and it must follow, as the night the day, thou canst not then be false to any man."

These words still carry wisdom centuries after they were written, and even after being subjected to the test of science. Figure out who you *really* are and who you *really* want to be and never stop working to become that person. Allow yourself to feel the pride you have earned. Most important: Don't suppress your desire to experience this emotion. Wanting, seeking, and struggling for pride is part of our human nature, and it may be the part that most makes us — as individuals, and as a species — who we are.

Acknowledgments

Ever since I read James Watson's *The Double Helix*, I've wanted to try to write a book that turned science into a story. This book is no *Double Helix* (and it goes without saying that I'm no Watson), but I'm supremely grateful for this opportunity to tell the story of the science I know best in a way that, I hope, will engage — and maybe even excite — at least some readers. Many people in my life made this possible, and I am so appreciative of all of them.

I need to begin by offering my most profuse thanks to two people who read early (and later) drafts of every single page of this book and made themselves available at a moment's notice to give me feedback on any random passage that needed an outside eye: Kristin Laurin and Aaron Tracy. Thank you both so much — Kristin for telling me, honestly, what just didn't make sense, and AT for telling me what non-psychologists would find most (and least) interesting and for making me (occasionally) funny.

Kristin, you also get extra special thanks for, well, everything else. I don't know what this project would have been without you in my life, but I am so happy and grateful that I didn't have to find out.

Two of my closest colleagues and collaborators over the past seven years were kind enough to read several chapters of the book to make sure I got everything right: Joey Cheng and Joe Henrich. I also am extremely grateful to Joey and Joe as well as to Azim Shariff for being such smart and inspirational collaborators; all three of you have forced me to think much harder and deeper about all things hierarchy, status, and evolution.

Very big thanks also go to Josh Hart, who provided a deeply psychological voice of reason in every chapter and whose enthusiasm for the project gave me hope early on.

I'm also grateful for the captive audience of amazing graduate students in my lab who took the time to read every page of an early draft and then to spend several hours dissecting it over mediocre snack food: Alec (aka Virtuous Sin) Beall, Marlise Hofer, Dan Randles, Conor Steckler, and Aaron Weidman. Thanks, also, to all of you, along with Zak Witkower and Jason Martens, for making our collaborative research endeavors over the past bunch of years so fun and, on occasion, *almost* DNA-discovery-level exciting. Working with grad students is one of the best parts of my day job, and I've been extremely lucky to get such a fantastic bunch. Massive thanks, too, to the person who makes the lab run smoothly and can be counted on to help out with uncountable things, many of which I'm not even aware of: six-time winner of the World's Best Lab Manager Award, Jeff Markusoff.

Moving backward in time, tremendous thanks go to Rick Robins, without whose training, mentorship, and friendship none of this would be possible. So much of what I've learned, I learned from you. The research described in this book that was conducted while I was in grad school would have been impossible without Rick, but it also would have been much harder and much less fun without Kali Trzesniewski, Robin Edelstein, Anna Song, and Kate Isaacson. I'm also grateful to Phil Shaver and Paul Ekman, who served as secondary research advisers and mentors and taught me much.

My research on pride really took off with the trip that Rick and I took to Burkina Faso, which turned into what will probably always be the most amazing research experience of my life. I'm deeply thankful to all the people who made this voyage and experience possible, most notably our travel partners Simona Ghetti and Jill Tracy and our wonderfully gracious, hospitable, and enthusiastic African collaborators Maggie and Jean Traore.

For the past ten years I have been extremely fortunate to be part of a vibrant community of scholars and researchers who work, think, write, and ski hard. These people push me constantly, and I feel extremely indebted to them for their encouragement, support, and simple presence: Liz Dunn, Toni Schmader, Ara Norenzayan, Steve Heine, Mark Schaller, Del Paulhus, Kiley Hamlin, and Greg Miller. The Psychology Department at the University of British Columbia has been a truly idyllic research home for me, and I'm especially grateful to all the people who made me feel so welcome when I arrived in 2006 and who continue to go well above and beyond what's necessary to remind me how much of a home I have here, especially Darrin Lehman, Eric Eich, Alan Kingstone, and Geoff Hall.

One of the many ways in which British Columbia and, more broadly, Canada has been a wonderful place to do research is the many funding opportunities that have been available to me here. I am very grateful to the Michael Smith Foundation for Health Research of B.C., the Social Sciences and Humanities Research Council of Canada, and the Canadian Institute for Health Research for funding almost all of the research I have conducted over the past ten years and also for providing additional major funds that have allowed me to focus the large majority of my time on research. The generosity of these granting agencies is what makes all of this work possible.

I am deeply grateful to the people who helped me realize that this book might be a possibility: my agents John Brockman, Katinka Matson, and Max Brockman. And many thanks to Steve Pinker for reading my proposal early on and seeing it as something that might, eventually, be worth publishing. I also want to thank Steve for *The Blank Slate,* the other book that, some years ago, made me want to try to write something like this.

Perhaps most important, the two people who turned this book from something that I'm glad no one will ever read into something I actually hope many people will: my editors at Houghton Mifflin Harcourt,

Courtney Young and Alex Littlefield. Courtney, your early input gave the book its basic shape, and your enthusiasm and encouragement made me believe I could get it there. Alex, thank you so much for taking on this project and really, truly, making it your own. Your extensive notes and feedback have taught me how to write for a broader audience, and I will always be grateful for that and for what you have done for this book. I eagerly await our next collaboration. Thanks also to Bruce Nichols, Naomi Gibbs, Lisa Glover, Tracy Roe (who has helped cure me of a serious comma addiction), and the rest of the wonderfully supportive HMH team.

Many thanks to my four parents: Bob Tracy, Laura Tracy, Marty Gross, and Doug LaBier. Each of you contributed to the making of this book, each in different ways, and I am grateful for everything.

I'm also eternally appreciative for the support and friendship of Mason Weintraub, Ari Makridakis, Les Schroeder, Jim Winslow, Patty McKenny, and Gina Daggett. I can't thank you six enough for being there for me these past four years. Also thanks to Cor Naylor for sticking it out to photograph a person who might literally be the world's least comfortable in front of a camera.

And, finally, thanks to Jill Tracy. I would not have become the person who wrote this book without you.

Notes

Preface: The Most Human Emotion

page

ix *eventually having four more children:* D. Sweetman, *Paul Gauguin: A Life* (New York: Simon and Schuster, 1995), 61–118.

x *bohemian corners of the city:* Ibid.

xii *"long march we call life":* Lena Dunham, *Not That Kind of Girl* (New York: Random House, 2014), 185.

1. The Nature of Pride

2 *"missing in my life":* Dean Karnazes, *Ultramarathon Man* (New York: Penguin, 2005), 48.
"my life was being wasted": Ibid., 51.
"and really fat. And bitter": Ibid.
"precisely where I belonged": Ibid., 62.

3 *"harder to answer, is . . . 'Why?'":* Ibid., 13.

7 *learned from other members of one's culture:* Steven Pinker, *The Blank Slate* (New York: Viking Penguin, 2002), 5–29.

9 *"plainly observed in this animal":* Charles Darwin, *The Expression of the Emotions in Man and Animals,* 3rd ed. (Oxford: Oxford University Press, 1998), 132.
"'to have his back up'": Ibid., 116.

12 *associated with distinct facial expressions:* Paul Ekman and Wallace V. Friesen, "Constants Across Cultures in the Face and Emotion," *Journal of Personality and Social Psychology* 17 (1971): 124–29.

nothing more than artifacts of our culture: Pinker, *The Blank Slate*, 30–58.

13 *almost always shaped by how we feel:* Jonathan Haidt, "The Emotional Dog and Its Rational Tail: A Social Intuitionist Approach to Moral Judgment," *Psychological Review* 108 (2001): 814–34.

14 *not be considered a real* emotion: Paul Ekman, "An Argument for Basic Emotions," *Cognition and Emotion* 6 (1992): 169–200.

16 *"one thing it is I do best":* Karnazes, *Ultramarathon Man*, 276–77.

17 *well-being, and even longevity:* Patrick L. Hill and Nicholas A. Turiano, "Purpose in Life as a Predictor of Mortality Across Adulthood," *Psychological Science* 25 (2014): 1482–86.

19 *with an average of 83 percent:* Jessica L. Tracy and Richard W. Robins, "Show Your Pride: Evidence for a Discrete Emotion Expression," *Psychological Science* 15 (2004): 194–97.

20 *in-a-business-meeting-style:* Jessica L. Tracy and Richard W. Robins, "The Prototypical Pride Expression: Development of a Nonverbal Behavior Coding System," *Emotion* 7 (2007): 789–801.

22 *expression they know best: happiness:* Jessica L. Tracy, Richard W. Robins, and Kristin H. Lagattuta, "Can Children Recognize Pride?," *Emotion* 5 (2005): 251–57.

23 *recognize pride with ease:* Jessica L. Tracy and Richard W. Robins. "The Nonverbal Expression of Pride: Evidence for Cross-Cultural Recognition," *Journal of Personality and Social Psychology* 94 (2008): 516–30.

25 *understood the questions we were asking:* Ibid.

27 *rather than the other way around:* James A. Russell, "Is There Universal Recognition of Emotion from Facial Expressions? A Review of the Cross-Cultural Studies," *Psychological Bulletin* 115 (1994): 102–41.

29 *"The nail that stands out gets hammered down":* Hazel R. Markus and Shinobu Kitayama, "Culture and the Self: Implications for Cognition, Emotion, and Motivation," *Psychological Review* 98 (1991): 224.

31 *shoulders-back, smiling display:* Jessica L. Tracy and David Matsumoto, "The Spontaneous Expression of Pride and Shame: Evidence for Biologically Innate Nonverbal Displays," *Proceedings of the National Academy of Sciences* 105 (2008): 11655–60.

2. A Virtuous Sin

34 *a hundred different responses:* Jessica L. Tracy and Richard W. Robins, "Show Your Pride: Evidence for a Discrete Emotion Expression," *Psychological Science* 15 (2004): 194–97.

36 *pride as a recipe for failure and death:* Lao Tzu, *Tao Te Ching, Twenty-Fifth Anniversary Edition,* trans. G. F. Feng and J. English (New York: Vintage, 2007).
   to be proud was to be great and unafraid to say so: Aristotle, *Nicomachean Ethics:* Book 4 (350 BC).
   "greater esteem for himself than for anyone else": Jean-Jacques Rousseau, *Discours sur l'origine de l'inégalité,* OC3:219/CW3:91, note O, 222.
   "is the true source of honor": Jean-Jacques Rousseau, *Collected Writings of*

Rousseau, vol. 3, trans. Judith R. Bush et al. (Hanover, NH: University Press of New England, 1992).

37 *"Just to be recognized":* Abe Peck, "Arnold Schwarzenegger: The Hero of Perfected Mass," *Rolling Stone,* June 3, 1976.

38 *seventh-most-narcissistic president in American history:* Ashley L. Watts et al., "The Double-Edged Sword of Grandiose Narcissism: Implications for Successful and Unsuccessful Leadership Among U.S. Presidents," *Psychological Science* 103 (2013): 2379–89.

39 *not so well adjusted after all:* Delroy L. Paulhus, "Interpersonal and Intrapsychic Adaptiveness of Trait Self-Enhancement: A Mixed Blessing?," *Journal of Personality and Social Psychology* 74 (1998): 1197–1208.
    pass more legislation: Watts et al., "The Double-Edged Sword."
    most likely to face impeachment: Ibid.

40 *aggressively punish the challenger:* Brad J. Bushman and Roy J. Baumeister, "Threatened Egotism, Narcissism, Self-Esteem, and Direct and Displaced Aggression: Does Self-Love or Self-Hate Lead to Violence?," *Journal of Personality and Social Psychology* 75 (1998): 219–29.

41 Don't be a jerk: Zlatan Krizan and Omesh Johar, "Narcissistic Rage Revisited," *Journal of Personality and Social Psychology* 108 (2015): 793.

42 *feel about themselves on an explicit level:* Christian H. Jordan et al., "Secure and Defensive High Self-Esteem," *Journal of Personality and Social Psychology* 85 (2003): 969–78.

43 *"I have high self-esteem":* Richard W. Robins et al., "Global Self-Esteem Across the Life Span," *Psychology and Aging* 17 (2002): 423–34.

44 *likely to grow up to lead a life of crime:* Kali H. Trzesniewski et al., "Low Self-Esteem During Adolescence Predicts Poor Health, Criminal Behavior, and Limited Economic Prospects During Adulthood," *Developmental Psychology* 42 (2006): 381–90.
    root words for snow *as English speakers do:* Geoffrey K. Pullum, *The Great Eskimo Hoax and Other Irreverent Essays on the Study of Language* (Chicago: University of Chicago Press, 1991).

46 *semantic interrelatedness of the words we had entered:* Jessica L. Tracy and Richard W. Robins, "The Psychological Structure of Pride: A Tale of Two Facets," *Journal of Personality and Social Psychology* 92 (2007): 506–25.

48 *when writing about an angering event:* Paul Ekman, Robert W. Levenson, and Wallace V. Friesen, "Autonomic Nervous System Activity Distinguishes Among Emotions," *Science* 221 (1983): 1208–10; Robert W. Levenson et al., "Emotion, Physiology, and Expression in Old Age," *Psychology and Aging* 6 (1991): 28–35.
    along with words like conceited, cocky, smug, *and* pretentious: Tracy and Robins, "The Psychological Structure of Pride."

50 *more negative, narcissistic form of the emotion:* Ibid.

51 *an accepted label for this other category:* Ibid.
    in some cases even clinical depression: Jessica L. Tracy et al., "Authentic and Hubristic Pride: The Affective Core of Self-Esteem and Narcissism," *Self and Identity* 8 (2009): 196–213.

52 *somehow fails to produce big results:* Charles S. Carver, Sungchoon Sinclair,

and Sheri L. Johnson, "Authentic and Hubristic Pride: Differential Relations to Aspects of Goal Regulation, Affect, and Self-Control," *Journal of Research in Personality* 44 (2010): 698–703.

"makes me think of writing a book": Charles S. Carver, Michael F. Scheier, and Suzanne C. Segerstrom, "Optimism," *Clinical Psychology Review* 30 (2010): 879–89.

53 *might make people more antisocial:* Claire E. Ashton-James and Jessica L. Tracy, "Pride and Prejudice: How Feelings About the Self Influence Judgments of Others," *Personality and Social Psychology Bulletin* 38 (2012): 466–76.

   it's one that narcissists regularly engage in: Christian H. Jordan, Steven J. Spencer, and Mark P. Zanna, "Types of High Self-Esteem and Prejudice: How Implicit Self-Esteem Relates to Racial Discrimination Among High Explicit Self-Esteem Individuals," *Personality and Social Psychology Bulletin* 31 (2005): 693–702; Steven Fein and Steven J. Spencer, "Prejudice as Self-Image Maintenance: Affirming the Self Through Derogating Others," *Journal of Personality and Social Psychology* 73 (1997): 31–44.

57 *not when someone or something else is:* Bernard Weiner, "Attribution, Emotion, and Action," in *Handbook of Motivation and Cognition: Foundations of Social Behavior,* vol. 1, ed. R. Sorrentino and E. Higgins (New York: Guilford, 1986), 281–312.

58 *or their stable personalities:* Tracy and Robins, "The Psychological Structure of Pride."

59 *one kind of pride or the other:* Ibid.

60 *internal but more controllable:* Frederick Rhodewalt and Carolyn C. Morf, "Self and Interpersonal Correlates of the Narcissistic Personality Inventory: A Review and New Findings," *Journal of Research in Personality* 29 (2005): 1–23; Ellen R. Ladd et al., "Narcissism and Causal Attribution," *Psychological Reports* 80 (1997): 171–78; Jessica L. Tracy et al., "The Emotional Dynamics of Narcissism: Inflated by Pride, Deflated by Shame," in *The Handbook of Narcissism and Narcissistic Personality Disorder: Theoretical Approaches, Empirical Findings, and Treatments,* ed. W. Keith Campbell and Joshua D. Miller (Hoboken, NJ: Wiley, 2011).

   negative attitudes toward pride in general: Steven J. Heine et al., "Is There a Universal Need for Positive Self-Regard?," *Psychological Review* 4 (1999): 766–94; Hazel R. Markus and Shinobu Kitayama, "Culture and the Self: Implications for Cognition, Emotion, and Motivation," *Psychological Review* 98 (2001): 224–53.

   report experiencing both: Yan Shi et al., "Cross-Cultural Evidence for the Two-Factor Structure of Pride," *Journal of Research in Personality* 55 (2015): 61–74.

   about half chose hubristic: Jessica L. Tracy and Richard W. Robins, "The Prototypical Pride Expression: Development of a Nonverbal Behavior Coding System," *Emotion* 7 (2007): 789–801.

61 *which kind of pride was conveyed:* Jessica L. Tracy and Christine Prehn, "Arrogant or Self-Confident? The Use of Contextual Knowledge to Differentiate Hubristic and Authentic Pride from a Single Nonverbal Expression," *Cognition and Emotion* 26 (2012): 14–24.

   "student at the best school in the country": Alexander Mooney, "Trump Says He Has Doubts About Obama's Birth Place," *Politicalticker* (blog), CNN.com, March 17, 2011, http://politicalticker.blogs.cnn.com/2011/03/17/trump-says-he-has-doubts-about-obama%E2%80%99s-birth-place/.

3. Me, Myself, and I

62 *how we'll feel in the future:* Daniel Gilbert, *Stumbling on Happiness* (New York: Knopf, 2006), 4.

figure out alone: Joseph Henrich, *The Secret of Our Success: How Culture Is Driving Human Evolution, Domesticating Our Species, and Making Us Smarter* (Princeton, NJ: Princeton University Press, 2015).

63 *avoiding eating self:* Richard W. Robins, Jessica L. Tracy, and Kali H. Trzesniewski, "The Naturalized Self," in *Handbook of Personality*, 3rd ed., ed. Oliver P. John, Richard Robins, and L. A. Pervin (New York: Guilford, 2010), 421–47.

64 *not some other tiny primate:* Ibid.

"*Self who is Known*": William James, *Psychology: The Briefer Course* (New York: Dover, 2001), 43.

65 "*whose pocket is being picked!*": Jorge L. Borges, "Borges and I," in *The Mind's I*, ed. Daniel C. Dennett and Douglas R. Hofstadter (New York: Bantam, 1982), 20–21.

66 "*reflects the other that doth pass*": Charles Horton Cooley, *Human Nature and the Social Order* (New York: Schocken, 1964), 199. Cooley, knowingly or unknowingly, is paraphrasing Emerson's "Astraea": "Each to each a looking-glass, / Reflects his figure that doth pass."

67 *face in a parent's lap:* Michael Lewis and Jeanne Brooks-Gunn, *Social Cognition and the Acquisition of Self* (New York: Plenum, 1979).

judged according to my society's standards: Suzan Harter, "Emerging Self-Processes During Childhood and Adolescence," in *Handbook of Self and Identity*, 2nd ed., ed. Mark R. Leary and June P. Tangney (New York: Guilford, 2012).

68 *regulations and make them their own:* Richard M. Ryan and Edward L. Deci, "Multiple Identities Within a Single Self: A Self-Determination Theory Perspective on Internalization Within Contexts and Cultures," in ibid.

guilt becomes "I feel stupid": Tamara J. Ferguson, Hedy Stegge, and Ilse Damhuis, "Children's Understanding of Guild and Shame," *Child Development* 62 (1991): 827–39.

69 "*not figuratively but literally*": Ernest Becker, *The Birth and Death of Meaning* (New York: Free Press, 1971), 99.

70 *gave themselves more gold stars:* Sandra Graham, "Children's Developing Understanding of the Motivational Role of Affect: An Attributional Analysis," *Cognitive Development* 3 (1988): 71–88.

71 *changing their ongoing behavior for the better:* For readers who are reminded by this experiment of the distinction made in chapter 2 between attributions to controllable causes, like effort, versus attributions to uncontrollable causes, like ability, it's worth noting that, here, both experimental conditions encouraged kids to attribute their behavior to something controllable (whether they chose to be generous). What varied is how stable these causes were perceived to be — whether a kid chose to be generous just one time or whether he was the kind of person who always chose to be generous. This is an important distinction, because while attributions to uncontrollable causes would be expected to produce hubristic pride — as discussed in chapter 2 — attributions to stable but controllable causes (e.g., "I'm the kind of person who behaves generously") should elicit authentic pride.

73 *in shaping behavior:* Christopher J. Bryan et al., "Motivating Voter Turnout

by Invoking the Self," *Proceedings of the National Academy of Sciences* 108 (2011): 12653–56.

75 *and often by a wide margin:* Editorial Projects in Education Research Center, "Achievement Gap," *Education Week*, updated July 7, 2011, http://www.edweek.org/ew/issues/achievement-gap/.

76 *received a D or worse in the course:* Geoffrey L. Cohen et al., "Reducing the Racial Achievement Gap: A Social-Psychological Intervention," *Science* 313 (2006): 1307–10.

African Americans performing worse in school: Claude M. Steele and Joshua Aronson, "Stereotype Threat and the Intellectual Test Performance of African Americans," *Journal of Personality and Social Psychology* 69 (1995): 797–811; *women performing poorly on a math test:* Steven J. Spencer, Claude M. Steele, and Diane M. Quinn, "Stereotype Threat and Women's Math Performance," *Journal of Experimental Social Psychology* 35 (1999): 4–28; *Christians performing worse on a test of logic:* Kimberly Rios et al., "Negative Steretypes Cause Christians to Underperform in and Dis-Identify with Science," *Social Psychological and Personality Science* 6 (2015): 959–67.

77 *as good, moral, and competent:* Claude M. Steele, "A Threat in the Air: How Stereotypes Shape Intellectual Identity and Performance," *American Psychologist* 52 (1999): 613–29.

sense of belongingness with one's group: Mark R. Leary et al., "Self-Esteem as an Interpersonal Monitor: The Sociometer Hypothesis," *Journal of Personality and Social Psychology* 68 (1995): 518–30.

people who will choose death over it: Liesl M. Heinrich and Elenora Gullone, "The Clinical Significance of Loneliness: A Literature Review," *Clinical Psychology Review* 26 (2006): 695–718.

78 *smart, valuable, confident, and proud:* Leary et al., "Self-Esteem as an Interpersonal Monitor."

using an fMRI scanner: Naomi I. Eisenberger, Matthew D. Lieberman, and Kipling D. Williams, "Does Rejection Hurt? An fMRI Study of Social Exclusion," *Science* 302 (2003): 290–92.

4. Like a Boss

86 *drum performance of mountain gorillas:* George E. Schaller, *The Mountain Gorilla: Ecology and Behavior* (Chicago: University of Chicago Press, 1963).

conveying a "strutting, confident air": Abraham H. Maslow, "The Role of Dominance in the Social and Sexual Behavior of Infra-Human Primates: I. Observations at Vilas Park Zoo," *Pedagogical Seminary and Journal of Genetic Psychology* 48 (1936): 261–77.

in the presence of a subordinate: Jane van Lawick-Goodall, "The Behaviour of Free-Living Chimpanzees in the Gombe Stream Reserve," *Animal Behaviour Monographs* 1 (1968): 161–311; Frans de Waal, *Chimpanzee Politics* (Baltimore: Johns Hopkins University Press, 1989); Glenn E. Weisfeld and Jody M. Beresford, "Erectness of Posture as an Indicator of Dominance or Success in Humans," *Motivation and Emotion* 6 (1982): 113–31.

Primatologists call this a bluff display: Jan A.R.A.M. van Hooff, "A Structural Analysis of the Social Behavior of a Semi-Captive Group of Chimpanzees," in *Social Communication and Movement,* eds. M. von Cranach and I. Vine (New York: Academic Press, 1974), 75–162.

88   *must come at a cost:* Maynard Smith and David Harper, *Animal Signs* (Oxford: Oxford University Press, 2003); Amotz Zahavi and Avishag Zahavi, *The Handicap Principle: A Missing Piece of Darwin's Puzzle* (Oxford: Oxford University Press, 1997).

sending a message about one's wealth: Thorstein Veblen, *The Theory of the Leisure Class* (New York: Macmillan, 1899).

89   *perceptions of high rank in humans:* Judith A. Hall et al., "Nonverbal Communication and the Dimension of Social Relations," in *The Psychology of Social Status,* ed. Joey T. Cheng, Jessica L. Tracy, and Cameron Anderson (New York: Springer, 2014); Jon K. Maner, C. Nathan DeWall, and Matthew T. Gailliot, "Selective Attention to Signs of Success: Social Dominance and Early Stage Interpersonal Perception," *Personality and Social Psychology Bulletin* 34 (2008): 488–501.

will dominate over a smaller one: Lotte Thomsen et al., "Big and Mighty: Preverbal Infants Mentally Represent Social Dominance," *Science* 331 (2011): 477–80.

92   *reproduce again and again:* Jack Hill, "Prestige and Reproductive Success in Man," *Ethology and Sociobiology* 5 (1984): 77–95.

93   *had to be higher in rank:* Larissa Z. Tiedens, Phoebe C. Ellsworth, and Batja Mesquita, "Sentimental Stereotypes: Emotional Expectations for High- and Low-Status Group Members," *Personality and Social Psychology Bulletin* 26 (2000): 560–75.

to be high in dominance: Lisa A. Williams and David DeSteno, "Pride: Adaptive Social Emotion or Seventh Sin?," *Psychological Science* 20 (2009): 284–88.

96   *for pride than for any other emotion:* Azim F. Shariff and Jessica L. Tracy, "Knowing Who's Boss: Implicit Perceptions of Status from the Nonverbal Expression of Pride," *Emotion* 9 (2009): 631–39.

101   *suppress at an explicit level:* Jessica L. Tracy et al., "Cross-Cultural Evidence That the Nonverbal Expression of Pride Is an Automatic Status Signal," *Journal of Experimental Psychology: General* 142 (2013): 163–80.

103   by someone known to be low in status: Azim F. Shariff, Jessica L. Tracy, and Jeffrey L. Markusoff, "(Implicitly) Judging a Book by Its Cover: The Power of Pride and Shame Expressions in Shaping Judgments of Social Status," *Personality and Social Psychology Bulletin* 38 (2012): 1178–93.

106   *when we think about other people:* Lasana T. Harris and Susan T. Fiske, "Dehumanizing the Lowest of the Low: Neuroimaging Responses to Extreme Out-Groups," *Psychological Science* 17 (2006): 847–53.

107   high in rank *as an (ashamed) businessman:* Shariff, Tracy, and Markusoff, "(Implicitly) Judging a Book by Its Cover."

109   *the decision of whom to hire:* Kristin Laurin, Azim. F. Shariff, and Jessica L. Tracy, paper in preparation, University of British Columbia.

111   *may boost their testosterone:* Dana R. Carney, Amy J. C. Cuddy, and Andy J. Yap, "Power Posing: Brief Nonverbal Displays Affect Neuroendocrine Levels and Risk Tolerance," *Psychological Science* 21 (2010): 1363–68; Li Huang et al., "Power-

ful Postures Versus Powerful Roles: Which Is the Proximate Correlate of Thought and Behavior?," *Psychological Science* 22 (2010): 95–102. Also see Eva Ranehill et al., "Assessing the Robustness of Power Posing: No Effect on Hormones and Risk Tolerance in a Large Sample of Men and Women," *Psychological Science* 26 (2015): 653–56.

a hormone associated with social rank: Allan Mazur, "Hormones, Aggression, and Dominance in Humans," in *Hormones and Aggressive Behavior,* ed. B. B. Svare (New York: Plenum Press, 1983), 563–76; Robert M. Rose, Thomas P. Gordon, and Irwin S. Bernstein, "Plasma Testosterone Levels in the Male Rhesus: Influences of Sexual and Social Stimuli," *Science* 178 (1972): 643–45; Allan Mazur and Theodore A. Lamb, "Testosterone, Status, and Mood in Human Males," *Hormones and Behavior* 14 (1980): 236–46.

5. The Carrot and the Stick

114 *think they don't deserve it:* Azim F. Shariff and Jessica L. Tracy, "Knowing Who's Boss: Implicit Perceptions of Status from the Nonverbal Expression of Pride," *Emotion* 9 (2009): 631–39.

that she merits high status: Larissa Z. Tiedens, Phoebe C. Ellsworth, and Batja Mesquita, "Sentimental Stereotypes: Emotional Expectations for High- and Low-Status Group Members," *Personality and Social Psychology Bulletin* 26 (2000): 560–75.

116 *and fragrance his own name:* Jeffrey Kluger, *The Narcissist Next Door: Understanding the Monster in Your Family, in Your Office, in Your Bed — in Your World* (New York: Penguin, 2014).

118 *inducing within them a sense of threat:* David M. Buss and J. D. Duntley, "The Evolution of Aggression," in *Evolution and Social Psychology,* ed. Mark Schaller, Jeffry A. Simpson, and Douglas T. Kenrick (New York: Psychology Press, 2006), 263–85; Napoleon Chagnon, *Yanomamö: The Fierce People* (New York: Holt, Rinehart and Winston, 1983); Vlad Griskevicius et al., "Aggress to Impress: Hostility as an Evolved Context-Dependent Strategy," *Journal of Personality and Social Psychology* 82 (2009): 980–94; Kim Hill and A. Magdalena Hurtado, *Aché Life History: The Ecology and Demography of a Foraging People* (New York: Aldine de Gruyter, 1996); Liisa M. Kyl-Heku and David M. Buss, "Tactics as Units of Analysis in Personality Psychology: An Illustration Using Tactics of Hierarchy Negotiation," *Personality and Individual Differences* 21 (1996): 497–517; Margaret T. Lee and Richard Ofshe, "The Impact of Behavioral Style and Status Characteristics on Social Influence: A Test of Two Competing Theories," *Social Psychology Quarterly* 44 (1981): 73–82; Allan Mazur, "A Cross-Species Comparison of Status in Small Established Groups," *American Sociological Review* 38 (1973): 513–30.

many American high schools: Elizabeth Cashdan, "Smiles, Speech and Body Posture: How Women and Men Display Sociometric Status and Power," *Journal of Nonverbal Behavior* 22 (1998): 209–28; Patricia H. Hawley, "Social Dominance and Prosocial and Coercive Strategies of Resource Control in Preschoolers," *International Journal of Behavioral Development* 26 (2002): 167–76; Robert G. Lord, Christy L. de Vander, and George M. Alliger, "A Meta-Analysis of the Relation Between Personality Traits and Leadership Perceptions: An Application of Validity Generalization Procedures," *Journal of Applied Psychology* 71 (1986): 402–10; Ritch C. Savin-Williams, "Dominance Hierarchies in Groups of Early Adolescents," *Child Development* 50 (1979): 923–35.

and we all know it: David M. Buss et al., "Tactics of Manipulation," *Journal of Personality and Social Psychology* 52 (1987): 1219–29; Kyl-Heku and Buss, "Tactics as Units of Analysis."

119 *"high levels of competence, generosity, and commitment":* Cameron Anderson and Gavin J. Kilduff, "The Pursuit of Status in Social Groups," *Current Directions in Psychological Science* 18 (2009): 295–98.

by being nice and competent: Joseph Berger, Bernard P. Cohen, and Morris Zelditch, "Status Characteristics and Social Interaction," *American Sociological Review* 37 (1972): 241–55; Peter M. Blau, *Exchange and Power in Social Life* (London: Transaction Publishers, 1964); Edwin P. Hollander and James W. Julian, "Contemporary Trends in the Analysis of Leadership Processes," *Psychological Bulletin* 71 (1969): 387–97; John W. Thibaut and Harold H. Kelley, *The Social Psychology of Groups* (Oxford: John Wiley, 1959).

have the greatest social influence: Robert F. Báles et al., "Channels of Communication in Small Groups," *American Sociological Review* 15 (1951): 461–68; John D. Coie, Kenneth A. Dodge, and Heide Coppotelli, "Dimensions of Types of Social Status: A Cross-Age Perspective," *Developmental Psychology* 18 (1982): 557–70; James E. Driskell, Beckett Olmstead, and Eduardo Salas, "Task Cues, Dominance Cues, and Influence in Task Groups," *Journal of Applied Psychology* 78 (1993): 51–60; Lord et al., "A Meta-Analysis"; Fred L. Strodtbeck, "Husband-Wife Interaction over Related Differences," *American Sociological Review* 16 (1951): 468–73; Robb Willer, "Groups Reward Individual Sacrifice: The Status Solution to the Collective Action Problem," *American Sociological Review* 74 (2009): 23–43. For a review, see Anderson and Kilduff, "The Pursuit of Status."

threat of force are simply untenable: Anderson and Kilduff, "The Pursuit of Status"; Jerome H. Barkow, "Strategies for Self-Esteem and Prestige in Maradi, Niger Republic," in *World Anthropology,* ed. Thomas R. Williams (Chicago: Mouton, 1975).

120 *think of selfish, cruel, and* bad: Joseph Henrich and Francisco J. Gil-White, "The Evolution of Prestige: Freely Conferred Deference as a Mechanism for Enhancing the Benefits of Cultural Transmission," *Evolution and Human Behavior* 22 (2001): 165–96.

meat earned from their kills: Christopher von Rueden, Michael Gurven, and Hillard Kaplan, "The Multiple Dimensions of Male Social Status in an Amazonian Society," *Evolution and Human Behavior* 29 (2009): 402–15.

121 *"If we fail, it will be because of you":* Fred Vogelstein, *Dogfight: How Apple and Google Went to War and Started a Revolution* (New York: Farrar, Straus and Giroux, 2013), 17.

knowledge about how to survive: Peter J. Richerson and Robert Boyd, *Not by Genes Alone* (Chicago: University of Chicago Press, 2004); Kevin N. Laland and Bennett G. Galef, *The Question of Animal Culture* (Cambridge, MA: Harvard University Press, 2009).

127 *working together in groups:* Joey T. Cheng et al., "Two Ways to the Top: Evidence

That Dominance and Prestige Are Distinct Yet Viable Avenues to Social Rank and Influence," *Journal of Personality and Social Psychology* 104 (2013): 103–25.

129 *"donors are afraid of him":* Alexander Burns and Maggie Haberman, "To Fight Critics, Donald Trump Aims to Instill Fear in 140-Character Doses," *New York Times*, February 26, 2016.

130 *others who are easy targets:* Jessica L. Tracy et al., "Authentic and Hubristic Pride: The Affective Core of Self-Esteem and Narcissism," *Self and Identity* 8 (2009): 196–213; Jessica L. Tracy and Richard W. Robins, "Emerging Insights into the Nature and Function of Pride," *Current Directions in Psychological Science* 16 (2007): 147–50.

131 *study hard for their exams:* Aaron C. Weidman, Jessica L. Tracy, and Andrew J. Elliot, "The Benefits of Following Your Pride: Authentic Pride Promotes Achievement," *Journal of Personality*. Published electronically June 25, 2015. doi: 10.1111/jopy.12184.

132 *to feel good about themselves:* Rodica Ioana Damian and Richard W. Robins, "Aristotle's Virtue or Dante's Deadliest Sin? The Influence of Authentic and Hubristic Pride on Creative Achievement," *Learning and Individual Differences* 26 (2013): 156–60.

134 *and want to show others up:* Rodica Ioana Damian and Richard W. Robins, "The Link Between Dispositional Pride and Creative Thinking Depends on Current Mood," *Journal of Research in Personality* 46 (2012): 765–69.
that he or she could think of: Joy P. Guilford, *The Nature of Human Intelligence* (New York: McGraw-Hill, 1967).

135 *the rare very special monkey:* Allan Mazur, "Hormones, Aggression, and Dominance in Humans," in *Hormones and Aggressive Behavior,* ed. B. B. Svare (New York: Plenum Press, 1983), 563–76; Robert M. Rose, Thomas P. Gordon, and Irwin S. Bernstein, "Plasma Testosterone Levels in the Male Rhesus: Influences of Sexual and Social Stimuli," *Science* 178 (1972): 643–45; Allan Mazur and Theodore A. Lamb, "Testosterone, Status, and Mood in Human Males," *Hormones and Behavior* 14 (1980): 236–46.
and are often unemployed: James M. Dabbs, "Testosterone and Occupational Achievement," *Journal of Consumer Research* 70 (1992): 813–24.

136 *assertive, confrontational, and violent:* James M. Dabbs et al., "Testosterone, Crime, and Misbehavior Among 692 Male Prison Inmates," *Personality and Individual Differences* 18 (1995): 627–33; Elena M. Kouri et al., "Increased Aggressive Responding in Male Volunteers Following the Administration of Gradually Increasing Doses of Testosterone Cypionate," *Drug and Alcohol Dependence* 40 (1995): 73–79.
relatively lower levels of testosterone: Ryan T. Johnson, Joshua A. Burk, and Lee A. Kirkpatrick, "Dominance and Prestige as Differential Predictors of Aggression and Testosterone Levels in Men," *Evolution and Human Behavior* 28 (2007): 345–51.
as it did among the men: Cheng et al., "Two Ways to the Top."
peers judge them as lower *status:* Elizabeth Cashdan, "Hormones, Sex, and Status in Women," *Hormones and Behavior* 29 (1995): 354–66.

137 *violence committed in self-defense:* James M. Dabbs et al., "Saliva Testosterone and Criminal Violence Among Women," *Personality and Individual Differences* 9 (1988): 269–75.

chronically elevated serotonin levels: Michael J. Raleigh and Michael T. McGuire, "Serotonin, Aggression, and Violence in Vervet Monkeys," in *The Neurotransmitter Revolution,* ed. Roger D. Masters and Michael T. McGuire (Carbondale: Southern Illinois University Press, 1994), 129–45.

the attainment of higher rank: David M. Taub and James Vickers, "Correlation of CSF 5-HIAA Concentration with Sociality and the Timing of Emigration in Free-Ranging Primates," *American Journal of Psychiatry* 152 (1995): 907–13; Michael J. Raleigh et al., "Dominant Social Status Facilitates the Behavioral Effects of Serotonergic Agonists," *Brain Research* 348 (1985): 274–82.

tend to climb in social rank: D. S. Moskowitz et al., "The Effect of Tryptophan on Social Interaction in Everyday Life: A Placebo-Controlled Study," *Neuropsychopharmacology* 25 (2001): 277–89.

while also making them nicer: Wai S. Tse and Alyson J. Bond, "Serotonergic Intervention Affects Both Social Dominance and Affiliative Behavior," *Psychopharmacology* 161 (2002): 324–30.

138 *like rape or child abuse:* Randy Thornhill and Craig T. Palmer, *A History of Rape: Biological Basis of Sexual Coercion* (Cambridge, MA: MIT Press, 2000); Martin Daly and Margo Wilson, *Homicide* (New Brunswick, NJ: Transaction Publishers, 1988).

believes that this strategy is good: See Alice Dreger, *Galileo's Middle Finger: Heretics, Activists, and the Search for Justice in Science* (New York: Penguin, 2015), for a fascinating discussion of multiple instances in which scientists' careers suffered substantial damage largely as a result of the naturalistic fallacy.

139 *to work together in teams:* Joey T. Cheng, Jessica L. Tracy, and Joseph Henrich, paper in preparation, University of British Columbia.

140 *got the job done—despite its implausibility:* Walter Isaacson, "The Real Leadership Lessons of Steve Jobs," *Harvard Business Review* 90 (2012): 92–102.

141 *can threaten their own control:* Jon K. Maner and Nicole L. Mead, "The Essential Tension Between Leadership and Power: When Leaders Sacrifice Group Goals for the Sake of Self-Interest," *Journal of Personality and Social Psychology* 99 (2010): 482–97.

142 *dominance-based tactics to get ahead:* Peter Belmi and Kristin Laurin, manuscript submitted for publication (under review).

bow out of the status game altogether: Ibid.

6. The Highest Form

147 *Tsimane of Bolivia, it's five dollars:* Joseph Henrich et al., "Markets, Religion, Community Size, and the Evolution of Fairness and Punishment," *Science* 327 (2010): 1480–84.

149 *the unique species we are:* Joseph Henrich, *The Secret of Our Success: How Culture Is Driving Human Evolution, Domesticating Our Species, and Making Us Smarter* (Princeton, NJ: Princeton University Press, 2015).

joined forces with the locals: Ibid., 22–33.

150 *the toxic effects of thiaminase:* Ibid., 27–30.

151 *group of individuals at one time:* Ibid.

variations of hand axes and cleavers: Mark Pagel, "Infinite Stupidity," *Edge Conversation,* https://edge.org/conversation/mark_pagel-infinite-stupidity.

substantial advances in tool technology: Talia Lazuen, "European Neanderthal Stone Hunting Weapons Reveal Complex Behaviour Long Before the Appearance of Modern Humans," *Journal of Archaeological Science* 39 (2012): 2304–11; Jayne Wilkins et al., "Evidence for Early Hafted Hunting Technology," *Science* 338 (2012): 942–46.

that we are more social: Henrich, *The Secret of Our Success,* 8–21.

that makes us unique: Mark Pagel, *Wired for Culture: Origins of the Human Social Mind* (New York: W. W. Norton, 2012).

we are social learners: Lewis G. Dean et al., "Identification of the Social and Cognitive Processes Underlying Human Cumulative Culture," *Science* 335 (2012): 1114–18.

copy and learn from others: Henrich, *The Secret of Our Success,* 8–21.

152 *make it a contest:* Robert Axelrod and William D. Hamilton, "The Evolution of Cooperation," *Science* 211 (1981): 1390–96.

one-armed bandit: Luke Rendell et al., "Why Copy Others? Insights from the Social Learning Strategies Tournament," *Science* 328 (2010): 208–13.

156 *the accumulation of scientific wisdom:* Alex Mesoudi, *Cultural Evolution: How Darwinian Theory Can Explain Human Culture and Synthesize the Social Sciences.* (Chicago: University of Chicago Press, 2011).

"explain the peculiar success of science": David L. Hull, *Science as a Process: An Evolutionary Account of the Social and Conceptual Development of Science* (Chicago: University of Chicago Press, 1988), 350.

157 *to prove that he was right:* Mario Livio, *Brilliant Blunders: From Darwin to Einstein — Colossal Mistakes by Great Scientists That Changed Our Understanding of Life and the Universe* (New York: Simon and Schuster, 2013).

159 *as good as the original teacher's:* Henrich, *The Secret of Our Success,* 219–20.

160 *his "biggest blunder":* In fact, some uncertainty exists as to whether Einstein ever used this particular phrasing to describe his mistake; see Livio, *Brilliant Blunders,* 231–43.

the good ideas from the bad: Pagel, "Infinite Stupidity."

161 *rather than people who are different:* Katherine D. Kinzler, Kathleen H. Corriveau, and Paul L. Harris, "Children's Selective Trust in Native-Accented Speakers," *Developmental Science* 14 (2011): 106–11.

162 *instead of the word* duck: Melissa A. Koenig and Amanda L. Woodward, "Sensitivity of 24-Month-Olds to the Prior Inaccuracy of the Source: Possible Mechanisms," *Developmental Psychology* 46 (2010): 815.

appearing confused: Susan A. J. Birch, Nazanin Akmal, and Kristen L. Frampton, "Two-Year-Olds Are Vigilant of Others' Non-Verbal Cues to Credibility," *Developmental Science* 13 (2010): 363–69; Patricia E. Brosseau-Liard and Diane Poulin-Dubois, "Sensitivity to Confidence Cues Increases During the Second Year of Life" *Infancy* 19 (2014): 461–75; Chris Moore, Dana Bryant, and David Furrow, "Mental Terms and the Development of Certainty," *Child Development* (1989): 167–71; Mark A. Sabbagh and Dare A. Baldwin, "Learning Words from Knowledgeable Versus Ignorant Speakers: Links Between Preschoolers' Theory of Mind and Semantic Development," *Child Development* (2001): 1054–70.

163 *unsure about what she doesn't know:* Elizabeth R. Tenney et al., "Accuracy, Confidence, and Calibration: How Young Children and Adults Assess Credibility," *Developmental Psychology* 47 (2011): 1065–77.
model's confidence might be misplaced: Ibid.

165 *randomly among the options we gave them:* Jason P. Martens and Jessica L. Tracy, "The Emotional Origins of a Social Learning Bias: Does the Pride Expression Cue Copying?," *Social Psychological and Personality Science* 4 (2013): 492–99.

166 *answering the critical to-be-copied question:* Jason P. Martens, "The Pride Learning Bias" (PhD dissertation, University of British Columbia, 2014).

167 *distracted by a simultaneous cognitive task:* Tenney et al., "Accuracy, Confidence, and Calibration."
even when the adults showed pride: Patricia Brosseau-Liard, Tracy Cassels, and Susan Birch, "You Seem Certain but You Were Wrong Before: Developmental Change in Preschoolers' Relative Trust in Accurate Versus Confident Speakers," *PLoS ONE* 9 (2014): e108308.

7. Take Pride

169 *"because it was my chance":* Lance Armstrong with Sally Jenkins, *It's Not About the Bike: My Journey Back to Life* (New York: Berkeley, 2000), 14.

172 *by Armstrong during his cheating years:* Joseph Burgo, "How Aggressive Narcissism Explains Lance Armstrong," *Atlantic,* January 28, 2013.

173 *he "couldn't handle it":* Oprah Winfrey Show, January 18, 2013.
was "phoned in": Ibid.

174 *years of cheating and winning:* Ibid.

176 *no rest for the weary:* Angela Duckworth et al., "Grit: Perseverance and Passion for Long-Term Goals," *Journal of Personality and Social Psychology* 92 (2007): 1087–1101.
and become commissioned as officers: Amy Wrzesniewski et al., "Multiple Types of Motives Don't Multiply the Motivation of West Point Cadets," *Proceedings of the National Academy of Sciences* 111 (2014): 10990–95.

177 *do better, and end up happier:* Edward L. Deci and Richard M. Ryan, "The 'What' and 'Why' of Goal Pursuits: Human Needs and the Self-Determination of Behavior," *Psychological Inquiry* 11 (2000): 227–68.
did less well: Wrzesniewski et al., "Multiple Types of Motives."

179 *academic, physical, and leadership abilities:* Duckworth et al., "Grit."
intelligence like IQ or SAT scores: Ibid.

180 *that turns these kids into champions:* Angela L. Duckworth et al., "Deliberate Practice Spells Success: Why Grittier Competitors Triumph at the National Spelling Bee," *Social Psychological and Personality Science* 2 (2011): 174–81.

181 *French fries was worth it:* Wilhelm Hofmann and Rachel R. Fisher, "How Guilt and Pride Shape Subsequent Self-Control," *Social Psychological and Personality Science* 3 (2012): 682–90.
not nearly as well as they could have: Francis Galton, *Hereditary Genius: An Inquiry into Its Laws and Consequences* (London: Macmillan, 1892).
weakly related to eminence in one's field: Catherine Morris Cox and Lewis

Madison Terman, *Genetic Studies of Genius,* vol. 2, *The Early Mental Traits of Three Hundred Geniuses* (Stanford, CA: Stanford University Press, 1926).

182 *more than ten thousand hours, according to Gladwell:* Malcom Gladwell, *Outliers: The Story of Success* (Boston: Little, Brown, 2008).

183 *memorizing words like* serrefine *and* vivisepulture: These are just two examples of winning words in the National Spelling Bee used during the past few decades.

184 *throw back into the sea:* Anna Dorfman, Tal Eyal, and Yoella Bereby-Meyer, "Proud to Cooperate: The Consideration of Pride Promotes Cooperation in a Social Dilemma," *Journal of Experimental Social Psychology* 55 (2014): 105–9.

185 *more fish back into the shared pond:* Ibid.

186 *by making more generous offers:* Job Van Der Schalk, Martin Bruder, and Antony Manstead, "Regulating Emotion in the Context of Interpersonal Decisions: The Role of Anticipated Pride and Regret," *Frontiers in Psychology* 3 (2012): 513.

188 *change the way individuals see themselves:* Dana R. Carney, Amy J. C. Cuddy, and Andy J. Yap, "Power Posing: Brief Nonverbal Displays Affect Neuroendocrine Levels and Risk Tolerance," *Psychological Science* 21 (2010): 1363–68; but also see Eva Ranehill et al., "Assessing the Robustness of Power Posing: No Effect on Hormones and Risk Tolerance in a Large Sample of Men and Women," *Psychological Science* 26 (2015): 653–56.

to speak first in a debate: Li Huang et al., "Powerful Postures Versus Powerful Roles: Which Is the Proximate Correlate of Thought and Behavior?," *Psychological Science* 22 (2010): 95–102.

boost physical strength: Vanessa K. Bohns and Scott S. Wiltermuth, "It Hurts When I Do This (or You Do That): Posture and Pain Tolerance," *Journal of Experimental Social Psychology* 48 (2012): 341–45.

posing pride boosts feelings of power: Carney, Cuddy, and Yap, "Power Posing"; Ranehill et al., "Assessing the Robustness of Power Posing."

commit a traffic violation: Andy J. Yap et al., "The Ergonomics of Dishonesty: The Effect of Incidental Posture on Stealing, Cheating, and Traffic Violations," *Psychological Science* 24 (2013): 2281–89.

whose peers call them dominant: Jessica L. Tracy et al., "Authentic and Hubristic Pride: The Affective Core of Self-Esteem and Narcissism," *Self and Identity* 8 (2009): 196–213.

189 *what you need to get the job:* Amy J. C. Cuddy et al., "Preparatory Power Posing Affects Nonverbal Presence and Job Interview Performance," *Journal of Applied Psychology* 100 (2015): 1286–95.

increasing your likelihood of getting hired: Laurin, Shariff, and Tracy (in preparation), University of British Columbia.

190 *no regard for anyone else around:* Elise K. Kalokerinos et al., "Don't Grin When You Win: The Social Costs of Positive Emotion Expression in Performance Situations," *Emotion* 14 (2014): 180–86.

191 *they are punished for it:* Conor Steckler, Daniel Randles, and Jessica L. Tracy, manuscript submitted for publication (under review).

193 *"he has killed something big":* Richard B. Lee, *The !Kung San: Men, Women, and Work in a Foraging Society* (Cambridge: Cambridge University Press, 1979), 244–46.

groups remain largely egalitarian: Christopher H. Boehm, *Hierarchy in the Forest: The Evolution of Egalitarian Behavior* (Cambridge, MA: Harvard University Press, 1999).

"cool his heart and make him gentle": Ibid., 45.

194 *among the top six of the ten most admired men and women alive:* "Donald Trump Places Sixth on Gallup's 'Most Admired' List," *Huffington Post*, December 28, 2011, updated February 27, 2012, http://www.huffingtonpost.com/2011/12/28/donald-trump-sixth-gallup-most-admired-list_n_1172416.html.

195 *with Apple's CEO John Sculley:* Daniel Terdiman, "John Sculley Spills the Beans on Firing Steve Jobs," CNET.com, September 9, 2013, http://www.cnet.com/news/john-sculley-spills-the-beans-on-firing-steve-jobs/.

Illustration Credits

Figures 1.1, 1.2, and 1.3 Photographs courtesy of the author. **Figure 1.4** Photos reprinted by permission from Bob Willingham, Studio Southwest. Photos previously published in Jessica L. Tracy and David Matsumoto, "The Spontaneous Expression of Pride and Shame: Evidence for Biologically Innate Nonverbal Displays," *Proceedings of the National Academy of Sciences* 105 (2008): 11655–60. **Figure 2.1** Original version of this figure previously published in Jessica L. Tracy and Richard W. Robins, "The Psychological Structure of Pride: A Tale of Two Facets," *Journal of Personality and Social Psychology* 92 (2007): 506–25. **Figure 3.1** Illustration reproduced by permission from Kip Williams. **Figure 4.1** Photograph reproduced by permission from Stephen Jaffe/Getty Images. **Figure 4.2** Photograph reproduced by permission from Frans de Waal. **Figure 4.3** Graph originally created by Azim Shariff; re-created in part by Danielle Laurin. Photo credit: Jessica L. Tracy. Based on a figure previously published in Azim F. Shariff, Jessica L. Tracy, and Jeffrey L. Markusoff, "(Implicitly) Judging a Book by Its Cover: The Power of Pride and Shame Expressions in Shaping Judgments of Social Status," *Personality and Social Psychology Bulletin* 38 (2012): 1178–93. **Figure 4.4** Graph originally created by Azim Shariff. Photo credit: Jessica L. Tracy. Based on a figure previously published in Azim F. Shariff, Jessica L. Tracy, and Jeffrey L. Markusoff, "(Implicitly) Judging a Book by Its Cover: The Power of Pride and Shame Expressions in Shaping Judgments of Social Status," *Personality and Social Psychology Bulletin* 38 (2012): 1178–93. **Figure 5.1** Reprinted by permission from Thomas Foulsham. Previously published in Thomas Foulsham, Joey T. Cheng, Jessica L. Tracy, Joseph Henrich, and Alan Kingstone, "Gaze Allocation in a Dynamic Situation: Effects of Social Status and Speaking," *Cognition* 117 (2010): 319–31. **Figure 6.1** Previously published in Jason P. Martens and Jessica L. Tracy. "The Emotional Origins of a Social Learning Bias: Does the Pride Expression Cue Copying?," *Social Psychological and Personality Science* 4 (2013): 492–99. **Figure 7.1** Photograph reproduced with permission from Jasper Juinen/epa/Corbis.

Index

Page references in italics refer to illustrations.

accumulated knowledge, 151
achievement-oriented pride. *See*
    authentic pride
adaptive behaviors, 16–17, 85, 143
adaptive emotions
    anxiety, 51
        in dominant-led groups, 141
        hubristic pride and, 54, 112
        motivation from, 3–4
        in narcissists, 39
    defining, 7
    fear, 3–4, 7, 57
        emotional experience of, 5–6
        social status and, 118–20, 129
    feelings of pride, 111–12, 124, 138,
        141–43
    rejection, 69, 77–80, 82–83
    shame
        displays of, 29, 102–10, 165
        for feeling pride, 177
        hubristic pride and, 51, 54
        motivations of, 18n
        narcissism and, 41, 43, 172
        as self-conscious emotion, 68, 69
        self-relevance of, 17–18
adaptive social learning, 160–62
adaptivity of pride, 18, 32, 138, 143, 174
affective science, 13, 37
aggression
    and hubristic pride, 112, 130, 138, 172,
        195
    narcissistic, 40–41, 44
    and social rank, 125
    testosterone and, 135–36
anxiety
    in dominant-led groups, 141
    hubristic pride and, 51, 54, 112

motivation from, 3–4
    in narcissists, 39
appraisals of events, 57
Aristotelian pride, 50–51
Aristotle, 36
Armstrong, Lance, xiii, xiv, 169–74, *170*
arrogance, 33–35, 38–39. *See also*
        grandiosity; hubristic pride;
        narcissism
attributions, internal, 57–58
authenticity, xv–xvi, 49–50
authentic pride. *See also* prestige
    adaptivity of, 138, 143
    benefits of, 177–78, 187, 196
    consequences of, 117
    grit and, 178–180
    vs. hubristic pride
        in athletics, 130–31
        choosing between, xv–xvi
        Obama and Trump, 115–17, 124
        personality characteristics and,
            51–61
        prejudicial attitudes and, 54–56
        semantic representations, 47–49
        in student achievement, 131–33
    internal attributions and, 57–60
    maintaining, 175–77
    motivational effects of, 131–33, 155, 159
    recognition of in others, 60–61
    serotonin and, 137–38
    shift to hubristic pride, 171–74

Becker, Ernest, 69
belongingness, sense of, 77
bluff displays, 86–90, *87*
Bolt, Usain, xiii
Borges, Jorge Luis, 65

brick test, 134, 139–40
Buffett, Warren, xiii
Burke, Robert, 150

certainty displays, 162–67
cheating, xii, xiv–xv, 171–74, 187, 188
Clinton, Bill, 38
confidence displays, 162–67
conspicuous consumption, 88–89, 89n
Cooley, Charles, 66
copying behaviors. *See also* social
     learning
  discriminatory, 160–62
  effects of displayed expressions of
        models, 162–66
  effects of faked pride expressions on,
        166–67
  innovation in, 159
  intention in, 151–52
Cuddy, Amy, 188–89
cultural evolution. *See* cumulative
     cultural evolution
cultural learning, 121–22
cultural norms, 148
culture-driven genetic evolution, 150n
cumulative cultural evolution, 148–68
  components of, 154–55
  create and build motivation, 154–58
  share and teach motivation, 154,
        158–59
  social learning, 151–54, 160–67
    adaptive, 160–62
    copying behaviors, 151–52, 159–68
    exploiting, 153
    observational, 153
    trial-and-error, 153–54
  social-model discrimination, 161–66
  ubiquity of, 149
  whom to learn from, 154, 159–68

Dante, 35
Darwin, Charles, 8–10
Dictator Game, 147, 185–86
displays of pride. *See* pride displays
Divine Comedy (Dante), 35
dominance hierarchies, 139–43. *See also*
     rank attainment
dominance-prestige model of rank
     attainment
  in hierarchically structured groups,
        130–32

model derivation, 120–24
  in non-hierarchically structured
        groups, 125–29
dominant leaders or leadership. *See also*
     hubristic pride
  advantages and disadvantages of,
        139–42
  failure and, 195
  hormones and, 135–36
  rank attainment via, 123–24, 128–30
doping, 171–72
Duckworth, Angela, 178–80
Dunham, Lena, xii

Edwards, John, 84, 102
Einstein, Albert, 160
Ekman, Paul
  emotion research with the Fore, 10–14,
        21–22, 25–26
  on six universal emotions, 14, 15–18
embarrassment, 67
emotions
  adaptive. *See* adaptive emotions
  biological vs. social construction of,
        9–14
  evolution of, 5–10
  and motivation, 3–4, 15–16
  physical expressions of. *See also* pride
        displays
    Ekman's research with the Fore,
          10–14, 21–22, 25–26
    inheritance of, from animals, 8–10
  relived emotion research, 47–49, 53–60
  self-conscious, 69–70. *See also* guilt;
        pride; shame
  six universal, 14, 15–18
empathy, 54, 56
environmental consciousness,
     183–84
ethnography, 156–57
evolutionary science
  naturalist fallacy, 138–39
  and social status perception of pride
        displays, 91–101
  and survival of pride, 139–43
*The Expression of the Emotions in Man
     and Animals* (Darwin), 8–9, 19
expressions
  vs. gestures, 21
  physical, of emotion, 8–14
eye-tracking device, 127–28, *128*

factor analysis, 48
failure, 52, 171, 195
fairness, 145–48, 148n, 186–87
faking pride. *See* posing pride displays
fear. *See also* anxiety
  emotional experience of, 5–7
  from event appraisals, 57
  as motivation, 3–4
  social status and, 118–20, 129
Fore (tribe), 10–14, 21–22, 23, 25–26
Franken, Al, 43
Freud, Sigmund, 41

Galton, Francis, 181
Gates, Bill, xiii, 182, 195
Gauguin, Paul
  driving force of pride within, ix–x, xvi,
    32, 155, 195
  pride's effect on choices of, xii, xiii
  sacrifices in order to feel pride, 17, 73,
    172
gene-culture coevolution, 150n
genetic replication, 160–61
gestures, vs. expressions, 21
Gil-White, Francisco, 120–24
Gladwell, Malcolm, 182
Gore, Al, 184
grandiosity. *See also* arrogance; hubristic
    pride
  acceptance of, 194
  of Donald Trump, 116, 193, 194
  insecurity and, 175
  low self-esteem and, 42
  shame and, 43
grit, 178–80
guilt, 68–70. *See also* shame

Hardin, Garrett, 183
Henrich, Joseph, 120–24, 150n
hierarchies. *See* rank attainment
high-status words, 95–96, 104
hiring practices, 109–10
Homo erectus, 151
Homo sapiens, 151
hubris, 36
hubristic pride. *See also* narcissism
  adaptivity of, 138, 143, 174
  vs. authentic pride
    in athletics, 130–31
    choosing between, xv–xvi
    Obama and Trump, 115–17, 124

  personality characteristics of, 51–61
  semantic representations, 47–49
  in student achievement, 131–33
  consequences of, 117, 174
  controlling, xvi, 175–77
  grandiosity and, 42, 43, 116, 175, 193, 194
  internal attributions and, 57–60
  motivational effects of, 133–34, 155, 174
  narcissism vs. high self-esteem, 49–50
  power posing and, 188–89
  recognition of in others, 60–61
  shift from authentic pride to,
    171–74
  testosterone and, 135–37
Hull, David, 155–57

Icarus, 50
identity. *See also me* self
  children's development of, 67–72
    behavior driven by self-conscious
      emotions, 69–70
    effects of identity-based praise,
      70–72
    internalizing social norms,
      68–69
    self-consciousness, 67
  distortion of, from inferences of others'
    perceptions, 66–67
  grit and, 178–80
  human desire for, xvi, 16–17, 32
  reminders of, 70–74, 148
  and value affirmation, 74–77
implicit-association test (IAT)
  basis of, and uses, 94–95
  and pride displays of low-status
    individuals, 103–8
  results in use with North American
    undergraduates, 95–96
  results in use with Yasawa Islanders,
    97–102
insecurity
  grandiosity and, 175
  narcissism and, 41–43
  posing pride and, 187–88
  self-defense against, 174
intelligence, role in success, 181–82
internal attributions, 57–60
Inuit (Eskimo), 45–46

James, William, 64
job interviews, 109–10

Jobs, Steve
  driving force of pride within, 155
  loss of power, 194–95
  motivational style of, 121, 123–24, 124n,
    135, 140
  reasons for public trust in, 167
Johnson, Lyndon B., 38

Kalahari bushmen, 193, 196
Karnazes, Dean
  driving force of pride within, 1–4, 14,
    16, 32, 61, 133, 155, 195
  sacrifices in order to feel pride, 172, 175
Kelvin, Lord, 157
Kerry, John, 84–85, 85, 101–2
Kiva, micro-lending charity, 191
knowledge, accumulated, 151

Lao-tzu, 36
leadership. *See also* rank attainment
  athletics and, 130–31
  dominance hierarchies, 139–43
  dominant vs. prestigious, 123–25
    in athletics, 130–31
    and pride displays, 167–68, 193–95
  grit and, 178–80
  hormones and, 135–37
learning
  adaptive social, 160
  by copying. *See* copying behaviors
  cultural, 121–22. *See also* cumulative
    cultural evolution
  from experts, 159–60
  exploiting, 153
  observational, 153–54
  through sharing or teaching, 158–59
  social. *See* social learning
  trial-and-error, 153–54
Leary, Mark, 77–78, 82
Lehrer, Jonah, xiv
LeMond, Greg, 173
looking-glass self, 66–67
Lowery, Richard, 129
low-status words, 95–96, 104

manspreading, 96
Matsumoto, David, 28, 31
me self. *See also* identity
  authentic pride and, 176, 177, 179, 187,
    196
  distinction from *I* self, 64

effects on behavior, 82, 148
grit and, 179
internalizing social norms, 68–69
motivational power of, 72
motivation of pride and, 184–85
and social value, 90
motivation, xvi
  to create and build, 154–58
  cultural motivators of pride, 155–60
  effects on authentic pride, 131–33, 155,
    159
  effects on hubristic pride, 133–34, 155,
    174
  emotions and, 3–4, 15–16
  grit, 178–80
  and identity of self, 69–75
  intrinsic vs. extrinsic, 4–5, 133, 171, 176
  pride as, 80–82, 131–35, 143
  for prosocial reasons, 184–86
  to share or teach, 154, 158–59
  and tragedy of the commons, 183–84

narcissism, 37–44
  acceptance of, 193
  and aggression, 40–41, 44
  anxiety and, 39
  characteristics of, 37–39
  insecurity and, 42–43
  internal attributions in, 59–60
  and negative feedback, 41–42
  and prejudice, 53–54
  relationship to self-esteem, 42–44, 47,
    49–50, 61
  research on, 39–41
  semantics of, 47
  shame and, 172
  testosterone and, 136–37
naturalist fallacy, 138
Neanderthals, 151
nonverbal pride expression. *See* pride
    displays
Not That Kind of Girl (Dunham), xii

Obama, Barack, 113–16, 124
Outliers (Gladwell), 182

peacocks, tail display of, 88–89
performance-enhancing drugs, 171–72
perseverance, 80–81
personality effects of pride, 51–58. *See also*
    authentic pride; hubristic pride

posing pride displays, 166–67
  behavioral changes from, 111, 187–89
  benefits of, 188–89
  costs of, 191–92
power. *See* leadership; rank attainment
power posing. *See* posing pride displays
prejudice, 53–56
prestige. *See also* authentic pride
  advantages and disadvantages of,
      140–43, 195, 196
  defining, 122, 137n
  dominance-prestige model of rank
      attainment
    in hierarchically structured groups,
        130–32
    model derivation, 120–24
    in non-hierarchically structured
        groups, 125–29
  identification of, 162
  through sharing or teaching, 158–59
pride. *See also* authentic pride; hubristic
      pride
  adaptivity of, 18, 32, 138, 143, 174
  cultural motivators of, 155–60
  defining, 33–37
  in job interview process, 109–10
  physical expressions of. *See* pride
      displays
  purpose of, xv
  in search for identity. *See* identity
  semantics of, 34–36, 44–50, *46*
pride displays, 60–61, 85, *85*, 114
  bluff displays, 86–90, *87*
  effects of competing status
      information, 102–5
  effects on likability, 189–91
  faking. *See* posing pride displays
  overt, 192–94. *See also* hubristic pride
  recognition of in others, 18–27,
      60–61
    body posture, 19–21
    in Burkinabé people, 23–26
    by children, 22
    facial expressions, 18–19
  regulating, 196–97
  and social learning. *See* social learning
  and social status perception, 91–111,
      104, 107
    evolutionary basis, 91–101
    in hiring decisions, 109–11
    identical twins research, 102–8

    in presidential candidates, 102
    in Yasawa Islanders, 97–102
  pride expression, as evolved status
      symbol, 111
  proximate causes, 56–57
  psychoanalytic theory, 41–42

  race-based achievement gap, 75–77
  rank attainment, 117–132
    and aggression, 125
    cultural learning and, 121–22
    dominance and, 118–19
    dominance hierarchies, 139–43
    dominance-prestige model of
      in hierarchically structured groups,
          130–32
      model derivation, 120–24
      in non-hierarchically structured
          groups, 125–29
    evolutionary psychology vs. social
        psychology perspective, 118–20
    hierarchy formation, 125–36, 139–43
    hormones and, 111, 135–38, 188
    serotonin and, 137–38
    sports teams and, 130–31
    testosterone and, 111, 135–37, 188
    through sharing or teaching, 158–59
  reaction formation, 41–42
  reality-distortion field, 140
  rejection, 69
    avoiding, 82–83
    self-esteem and, 77–80
  relived emotion research, 47–49, 53–60
  repulsive gravitational force, 160
  Robins, Rick, 19, 45, 58
  Rolling Stone (magazine), 37
  Romney, Mitt, 114
  Rousseau, Jean-Jacques, 36

  Saturday Night Live (TV show), 43
  Schwarzenegger, Arnold, 37
  science
    affective, 13, 37
    evolutionary, 138–43
      naturalist fallacy, 138–39
      and social status perception of pride
          displays, 91–101
      and survival of pride, 139–43
    scientists and motivation, 155–58
  Sculley, John, 195
  self-conscious emotions, 68

self-consciousness, 65, 67–68
self-esteem
    defined, 17
    in defining pride, 35
    and rejection, 77–79
    relationship to narcissism, 42–44, 47,
        49–50, 61
semantics of pride, 34–36, 44–50, 46
sense of self, 62–65. *See also* identity; *me*
    self
serotonin, 137–38
shame
    displays of, 29, 102–10, 165
    for feeling pride, 177
    hubristic pride and, 51, 54
    motivations of, 18n
    narcissism and, 41, 43, 172
    as self-conscious emotion, 68, 69
    self-relevance of, 17–18
sharing of knowledge, 158–59
sinful nature of pride, 143, 175, 177, 195
social constructivism, 7–8
socialization, 121
social learning, 151–54, 159–68
    adaptive, 160–62
    copying behaviors
        discriminatory, 160–62
        effects of displayed expressions of
            models, 162–66
        effects of faked pride expressions on,
            166–67
        innovation in, 159
        intention in, 151–52
    exploiting, 153
    historical knowledge and, 168
    observational, 153
    trial-and-error, 153–54
social-model discrimination,
    161–63
social norms, internalizing, 68–75
    in children, 68–69
    identity reminders and, 70–74, 148

negative effects on behavior, 73–74
positive effects on behavior, 70–73
social pain, 77–80
social rank. *See* rank attainment
social status, xv, 118–19. *See also* rank
    attainment
societal norms, 148. *See also* cumulative
    cultural evolution
sociometer, 77–80, 82
Stapel, Diederik, xiv
status signaling, 96–101
stereotypes, overcoming, 76–77
student achievement, and authentic
    pride, 131–33
success, role of intelligence in,
    181–82

Tao Te Ching (Lao-tzu), 36
temptation, 180–81
ten-thousand-hours theory, 182
testosterone, 111, 135–37, 188
tragedy of the commons, 183–84
Trump, Donald
    dominant characteristics of, 129–30,
        135, 136
    grandiosity of, 116, 193, 194
    hubristic pride of, xiii, 61, 115–17, 124,
        129–30, 167, 194, 196

ultimate causes, 56–57
the Ultimatum Game, 185–86
Ultramarathon Man (Karnazes), 2
universal expression of emotions, 8–14

value affirmation, 74–77

West Point, 176–79
Wills, William, 150
Winfrey, Oprah, 173, 174
Wozniak, Steve, 124n

Yasawa Islanders, 97–101